People and Work Organizations

iversity
Information Serv

·NISI·

People and Work Organizations

J. G. CAPEY

Vice Principal
Wakefield District College

N. R. CARR

Head of the Faculty of Applied Studies
Crewe and Alsager College of Higher Education

HOLT, RINEHART AND WINSTON
London · New York · Sydney · Toronto

Holt, Rinehart and Winston Ltd: 1 St Anne's Road,
Eastbourne, East Sussex BN21 3UN

British Library Cataloguing in Publication Data
Capey, J. G.
  People and work organizations.
  1. Business enterprises
  I. Title   II. Carr, N. R.
  338.7'024658   HDZ731

ISBN 0–03–910365–X

Photoset by Paston Press, Norwich.
Printed in Great Britain by The Thetford Press Ltd, Thetford, Norfolk.

Cartoon illustrations by Alan Leese and Sheila Leese.
Front cover design by Mark Walker.

Last digit is print no: 9 8 7 6 5 4 3 2 1

Contents

Preface

This book has been written primarily to meet some of the needs of students studying for the Higher National level awards of the Business Education Council (BEC). We stress only some of the needs since the book has both restricted coverage and a specific focus. The coverage is limited to an examination of organizational issues relating to work structures and the behaviour of people. This examination is further focused primarily on work organizations rather than organizations generally. The specific focus is the core studies which are a special feature of the BEC courses. These core studies have been developed with the aim of providing business studies students with a balanced perception of what the business activity is all about, particularly in the setting of a free enterprise economy. Therefore, no specific discipline is examined in depth as a separate entity. This is not meant to imply that an in-depth study is not appropriate to BEC courses. On the contrary, the belief is that the students will be better enabled to take their studies further, once a balanced overview has been engendered. Hence the reader will see that the book has been written in an interdisciplinary style in which no chapter is totally free-standing, and where individual experiences are related to many of the issues examined.

The style adopted in the book is one which it is hoped will encourage the reader to become personally excited by the study of business. Academic jargon has been minimized in order to ensure that concepts are truly understood. The further reading given at the end of each chapter is included so that students can obtain a more detailed account of any particular topic raised in the chapter. In addition, most readers will have the benefit of the advice and guidance of tutors. By this means they should obtain both a balanced and an in-depth understanding of the issues raised.

The involvement of the reader has been an important design feature of the book. In most chapters he is required to perform tasks which are then either used to illustrate points or to introduce theories and concepts. This style will be further developed by the teaching approach adopted by most college centres, namely the use of task oriented exercises usually in the form of case studies, simulation exercises, role playing and in-tray exercises.

Although the book has been written with BEC courses particularly in mind, the writers feel that it will also be of value to students taking many undergraduate degree courses; management courses such as the Institute of Personnel Management's, and the DMS; professional courses with a business administrative component, and many similar courses. Indeed, it is hoped that the style and content will encourage many people to read the book who are not taking a course of study at all, but who are just interested in the nature of business activity.

The authors have included several case studies that will be familiar to many readers, and would like to thank those lecturers, colleagues and friends who have given their permission to reproduce them. Many of the case studies have been adapted to illustrate the central theme of the book.

The authors would also like to thank a number of people without whose help and patience the book would not have been possible. First of all our wives, Sue and Denise, who have not only put up with the many hours it has taken to prepare the script, but have proof-read much of the material and have helped with the indexing. Secondly, particular thanks are due to Richard Latham who has read most of the material, and given very valuable advice and comment. Finally, there are the three ladies who have typed the manuscript: Margaret Gater, Janet Graham and Nancy Woodward who have all done a marvellous job. Particular thanks are also due to Ron Fisher who has allowed much of his personal material to be used in Chapter 6. His experience in the personnel and training field, particularly on the Industrial Training Boards, has been most valuable.

J. G. CAPEY
N. R. CARR

1

Organizations: Individual to Corporate Goals

GENERAL OBJECTIVES

After reading this chapter the student should have a sufficient framework of knowledge to examine the processes of goal formulation and be able to contrast goals in different types of organizations within various areas of public and private sector activity.

LEARNING OBJECTIVES

After reading this chapter the student should be able to:

1. critically examine the concept of organizational goals;
2. analyse the processes of goal formulation in public and private organizations. (This learning objective is also related to the content of Chapters 2 and 3.)

1.1 INTRODUCTION: ORGANIZATIONS IN PERSPECTIVE

Business students should not view organization theory as something theoretical and perhaps vaguely concerned with reality – organizations are everywhere. They have either evolved or have been specifically created to fulfil the varied needs of people. From birth to death the individual is affected by the organization phenomenon. We have come to rely on a vast number of different organizations in the process of living in a modern society. This reliance stems basically from the fact that we cannot obtain the same services for ourselves working alone.

It is perhaps not too strong a statement to say that western-style civilization has become totally dependent on formal organizations of one sort or another. Although there are many different organizations with different aims and goals, it is possible to show that there are certain common characteristics which they all possess regardless of their different forms and purposes. To demonstrate this let us consider the following

1

definition: 'Organizations are groups of people who co-ordinate their efforts and activities in the pursuance of some purpose.'

First, organizations are groups of people: they are not buildings, areas of land or space, machinery or equipment. Of course all formal work organization make use of these things and develop their own technology from them. However, all organizations are social structures, that is they are created by man for the purpose of solving a human problem or satisfying a human need. When we refer to an organization by name, we are really referring to groups of people who make up the organization, or in some way influence what occurs in that organization. A private enterprise business organization, for example, consists of shareholders, directors, managers, professional and clerical staff, and skilled and unskilled workers. Business organizations are confronted with technological problems; for example, consider the vast technological problems of extracting oil from the North Sea. Despite these problems, the most intractable issue facing business organizations is that of the nature and behaviour of people. A quick glance at the daily newspapers should be sufficient to illustrate this point. Thus it is through, with and for people that organizations work, and only by a thorough understanding of the nature and behaviour of people in work organizations can we hope to improve their effectiveness. The theme of people in work organizations is the predominant focus of this book.

Second, these groups of people co-ordinate their efforts and activities. Co-ordination of distinct but inter-related activities is an essential feature of organizations. When we use the term 'organize' it is this act of co-ordination which is uppermost in our minds. If the activities of people are not co-ordinated then they are acting alone and perhaps at random, and we do not have an organization at all. In reality organizations co-ordinate activities to varying degrees, and it is frequently on this act of co-ordination that we tend to judge the efficiency and effectiveness of work organizations. Production of a motor-car, for example, requires the availability of thousands of components in the right quantities and qualities, at the right time and in the right place. In achieving this the activities of numerous people have to be co-ordinated; to list a few, production planners, stock controllers, buyers, transport schedulers, drivers, etc. This is necessary just to keep the car assembly-line going and does not include the co-ordination of all the other activities which the organization must engage in. If this co-ordination is not achieved then there will be delays in component deliveries, production and customer deliveries, which will involve the organization in rising costs and lost sales revenue, that is, in being less efficient and less profitable, as well as less effective. Thus for business organizations to be successful at co-ordination it is necessary for them to have clear and identifiable goals, good planning of operations, good organization of the various functions and jobs, good communication of information, and effective control of all activities. These various issues are examined in greater detail later in this book.

Third, organizations exist for some purpose. The co-ordination activity is directed towards some specified purpose, which may be very complex and not always obvious. Most business organizations say that their purpose or goal is to make a profit, but this can be very misleading, because organizations do not usually seek profit at any price, since they are concerned about their reputation, the quality of their products, and their image as employers. Similarly, other work organizations are concerned with standards of service to the general public, for example, the objectives of a hospital are to provide the best medical care possible within the financial limitations within which it has to work.

If we take the example of the motor-car manufacturer again we may agree that the apparent objective is to produce motor-cars to satisfy the public's varying needs for private transport. The organization is also likely to be aiming to maximize its profit potential. In doing this, the different parts of the organization will pursue more limited and specific objectives which will help to achieve the overall objective of the production of cars with the best level of profit possible in the light of the market potential. The production department, for example, will have production level objectives and cost/financial objectives. This does not mean that all individuals belonging to the organization automatically accept or pursue these objectives. Individuals may in fact pursue their own personal objectives, which may or may not coincide with and complement the objectives of the formal work organization. This problem of the possible divergence of goals existing in organizations is repeatedly examined in this book, particularly in this chapter.

It is apparent, therefore, that work organizations are most complex creations, and that a great deal of study is necessary in order to begin to understand them. They are so important that the very fabric of society as we know it rests to a large extent on their efficient operation. Efficiency, rationality, effectiveness, productivity and expertise are the kinds of value by which we judge them. Their complexity has led to a great deal of research concerning the way they are actually structured in order to achieve the objectives or goals for which they were created. How can we structure organizations to achieve the best results? This question has motivated both industrialists and academics for many years, and there has been a considerable attempt to increase the body of knowledge related to the subject.

Most writers agree that the very notion of the need for an organization stems from the fact that individuals working alone cannot fulfil all of their needs and wishes. Because they do not have the skill, knowledge, physical strength or resources to do everything they want, individuals have come to rely on others for help. This can come in the form of informal help, but in the majority of cases it comes in the form of formal organizations designed to accomplish specific purposes. Thus we rely on hospitals for medical help, schools and colleges for education, factories and other such places of work for our income, and all the arms of government bureaucracy for a whole variety of personal services.

This book is concerned with examining the position of individuals in relation to the organization in which they work. It is concerned with examining what organizations are trying to achieve, and how they are structured to achieve it. Are the aims of each individual at work microcosms of the aims of the organization for which they work? This important question links all the chapters in the sense that organizations become complicated and problematical largely because of the influence of the human element. Industrial relations difficulties, communications problems and many other issues all result from human interaction. We do not all hold the same values, have equal powers of influence, or possess the same intellectual capabilities. It is not surprising, therefore, that there exist great differences between the aims of individuals at work and the overall goals of the organization. The question of goals forms the predominant focus of this chapter.

It is often fascinating to talk to people about their work. Questions such as 'Why do you go to work?' or 'What are the main goals or targets of the organization for which you work?' can lead to the most interesting discussions and debates. Admittedly, the spontaneous answers given are generally simple ('To earn my salary or wages', 'To manufacture tyres or motor cars', 'To administer the non-contributory benefits', and so on) but a closer examination reveals that there is rarely a simple answer to either question. Similarly, research has shown that there is equally no clear definition concerning the goals of formal work organizations. (The term 'work organization' in this text implies organizations in both the public and private sectors of industry and commerce.) This creates problems for the student of business, for much that he will study at other times will suggest the existence of clarity of definition in relation to formal organizational goals.

1.2   THE TRADITIONAL VIEW OF WORK ORGANIZATIONS

The traditional view of formal work organizations suggests that they have the following characteristics:

1.   That they consist of groups of people coming together at prescribed times to perform specific tasks.
2.   That people are recruited by the organization to perform specific tasks which match the dominant skills and abilities of each individual.
3.   That the sum total of all the individual tasks equals the corporate task of the organization.
4.   To ensure that the sum total of the efforts of individuals within the organization is in accord with the corporate task, there is a system of control and co-ordination – the managerial component.
5.   This system of control and co-ordination confers status, rights and obligations on individuals within the organization.

These five characteristics are useful in so far as they help to give a model of formal work organizations which will be helpful as a framework for discussion. Further than that, the model is perhaps as over-simplified as the spontaneous answers given by most individuals to questions such as 'Why do you go to work?'. For example, although it is true that men and women are recruited into formal work organizations with a specific contract in relation to a specific task or group of tasks, can it be assumed that when they work within the terms of this contract their energies are uniquely applied to the organizational tasks prescribed for them? To what extent does every individual bring with him personal goals and influences and in what ways are these compatible with the tasks prescribed by the organizational job? These are important questions requiring fuller examination. In particular, the relationship between the concept of clear and stated organizational goals and the existence of unstated individual goals will be developed in order that the business student is able to form his own judgements in relation to activities, decisions and techniques. An analysis of various theoretical approaches to the design and structure of formal work organizations in relation to the achievement of their goals is provided in Chapter 2.

1.3   THE PROBLEM OF LOOKING AT ORGANIZATIONS IN TERMS OF GOALS

Many aspects of study in the field of business and management education start from the premise that formal work organizations have objectives with specific characteristics; that they are, first of all, definable in quantifiable terms suitable for an evaluation of actual against planned activities to take place; secondly, that they are stated and communicated within the organization; and thirdly, that these defined goals form the basis of the structure of the work organization set up to achieve them. This premise can be clearly seen as the underlying framework of such techniques as corporate planning, budgetary control, management by objectives, planning, programming and budgeting systems (PPBS), and so on.

The real problem in attempting to look at organizations in this way is the reality of the existence of corporate objectives. In order to exist at all, organizational goals must be the product of the sum total of the interactions of all the individuals of whom the organization is comprised. In other words, for an organization to have goals which are explicitly defined, it must ensure that the goals of each employee are in accord with the corporate goals. It is difficult to conceive of any organization, whether in the public or private sector, as having any defined goals unless there is an on-going consensus between all the employees in the organization about the role, function and interaction of their various roles. It seems unlikely that such a consensus will exist in reality for the reasons examined later in this chapter.

This does not mean that organizations should not attempt to have goals. On the contrary, the management function must have some method of determining a direction for the organization and a means of evaluating its results. What it does mean is that both managers of organizations and business students should be aware that there could, for example, be a great disparity between the objectives of the policy makers and the objectives of the shop floor workers in any organization.

1.4 INDIVIDUAL GOALS

It would be impossible to provide a formula by which the exact nature of the goals of individuals could be determined. What is possible and legitimate is an attempt to determine the factors which are influential in goal formation at the level of the individual, and an examination of the ways in which these individual goals are influential to the formal work organization.

To understand how an individual determines his own goals we must introduce the concept of an individual *value system*, a code of ethics which forms the yardstick for our beliefs. This book cannot prescribe an ideal value system; it can merely state that many value systems exist, and indicate some of the causal factors which influence their formation. (Since this is not a textbook in sociology, the examination is sufficient merely to illustrate the point.)

Individuals begin to form their own particular value system from birth. They are influenced by the value system of the family, school, culture of the social and geographical environment, and later the place of work, and so on. In addition, factors such as personal wealth, health and the type and level of education are important variables in the process of the development of every value system. Since the nature of the factors will vary between individuals, it is not surprising that there does not exist a single common value system in society, but a multitude of different and often conflicting ones.

Abraham Maslow researched the behaviour of individuals at work and, in particular, the factors which influenced motivation. He came to the conclusion that individuals have needs which they are striving to satisfy. The primary needs are physiological, encompassing the need for food and drink, companionship, continuing the species, warmth, and so on. The secondary needs are psychological, and include the need to be recognized and valued, to achieve, to be creative, and to make a contribution to society. Individuals will often use the work place as a means of satisfying some of these needs, but the actual nature of the needs will vary between people. All employees carry their individual value system with them to their place of employment, and this determines what different employees want from their jobs. They may want monetary reward, since money provides a means for satisfying many of the physiological needs, and perhaps some of the psychological needs as well. They may want status, or an opportunity for achievement. On the other hand, they may want to achieve a different social status, or even some degree of social restructuring through a different distribution of wealth within the economy. An example of these different levels and conflicting goals can be seen in the disparity of apparent goals between the chairman of the National Coal Board and the President of the National Union of Mineworkers. This example illustrates the interaction of goals at a variety of levels. On the one hand we have the stated goals of the formal work organization, the National Coal Board. These include production targets, the selling price of coal, the profit level aimed for, and planned wage rate levels. We also have the goals of a second formal organization, those of the National Union of Mineworkers, which, in this context, is a large pressure group attempting to influence the goals of the National Coal Board. The goals of the trade union will very often challenge the goals of the formal work organization, and in particular such goals as profit levels, wage levels and working conditions. In addition we have the influence of the individuality of the NCB Chairman and the NUM President. In the case of the latter we may also at times see an example of the articulation of beliefs based on a personal value system which may not be in accord with the officially stated goals of the union.

To understand the importance of these individual value systems we must consider the issue of *power of influence*. To what extent can individuals impose their own individual values on others? Has a shop floor worker the same power or influence as a company chairman or head of a government department? At first sight the answer appears obvious, and we might reply – Of course not! But we may be answering for the individual in isolation. Is the answer so apparently obvious when we consider the influence of individuals when they join together in organized groups? We need to consider in much more detail the effects and role of such groups in relation to formal work organizations; this is in large part considered in Group Goals below.

An individual's power of influence is determined by many factors. These include personal wealth and independence, level of education, strength of personality, power of articulation, and perhaps above all, the degree of sympathy between his own value system and that of others. His power of influence will, however, vary according to the nature of the situation to be influenced, and the role being played. Individuals' goals are, therefore, a product of their value systems plus their assessment of their ability to influence others in relation to specific situations or issues. The significant point here is that, as a general rule, individuals attempt to satisfy or realize their own goals rather than the specific purpose of the organization. Thus Max Weber, in describing the characteristics of his ideal form of work organization (ideal form of bureaucracy), talked about defining job roles rather than the characteristics of specific individuals. He saw the need to control the effects of the goals which individuals will always bring to the organization, and he saw job role definition as one method of introducing this control. (The job role was to be so clearly defined and controlled that the influence of the goals of the job holder are minimized.)

1.5 GROUP GOALS

Groups, by definition, consist of two or more individuals. They can be structured or unstructured, formal or informal. Thus social meetings of employees which take place at meal or break times during a normal working day are usually examples of unstructured and informal groupings. On the other hand, a trade union and a business enterprise like Rolls Royce are examples of formal, structured organizations. Both the formal and informal groupings are important to the student of business.

The informal grouping may lack structure and any defined explicit goal, but people usually meet or mix together because of some common factors of attraction. These can be very wide ranging, but will often include matters of interest to the formal work organization. Thus a shop floor worker with strong feelings over an issue concerning payment systems, working methods or working conditions will talk to others with similar feelings over a coffee or lunch break. If the feelings are strong enough, or the individual has strength of personality such that the group respect him as an informal leader, then the values of the group may begin to have an influence on the formal work organization. The informal views may be channelled into a formal system via a trade union or company grievance procedure, or may reveal themselves in informal and unofficial action. Evidence of this facet of informal group influence is given in a variety of forms. Perhaps the most publicized study which illustrates this point is that of Elton Mayo and his research at the Hawthorne plant of the Western Electricity Company in Chicago (see section 2.5). Here the values and beliefs of the working group were shown to dominate those of the formal organization, particularly in relation to payment systems linked to results. The informal group believed that the long-term impact of individual output levels outside certain parameters would have been harmful to the group. Thus too high a level would have meant redundancy because of over-production, and too low a level sacking on the grounds of inefficiency. This was the interpretation determined by the informal group, and nothing that the formal organization did to change the situation was successful, even though there was no objective truth in the assumptions made by the informal group. Other examples are numerous. Many conflicts in modern management labour relations have an element of informal work group activity in them, and students are recommended to read commentaries on recent cases in industrial relations, preferably in such publications as *Industrial Relations Review and Report*, in order to judge the impact of the goals of the informal group on the formal work organization.

The formal group, other than the specific work organization itself, is a most important structure. Pressure groups of a whole variety of types, including trade unions, come into this category. In relation to the work organization the pressure groups articulate goals which attempt to give employees an effective voice in the competition for the allocation of resources. They reduce an individual's anxiety which is often produced by a feeling of personal powerlessness. Pressure groups often evolve from informal groups which have been unable to satisfy their goals without a more formal organization. The historical development of the trade union movement is an example of such an evolution. Examples of other pressure groups which might articulate goals that could well influence the goals of formal work organizations are professional institutions, such as the Institute of Personnel Management, the Institute of Cost and Management Accountants, the professional Engineering Institutes, and the Royal Institute of Public Administration. In addition, social pressure groups made up of local residents, ratepayers, noise abatement societies, anti-pollutionists, and so on often influence the formation and nature of goals in work organizations.

G. K. Roberts shows that pressure groups are only effective if properly organized. They need good leadership in relation to their objectives, a clear, well thought out internal organization, a sound financial base, a clearly defined and limited policy, and strength of membership. One could argue that these are the characteristics required of the successful business organization!

1.6   GOALS AND THE FORMAL WORK ORGANIZATION

E. F. L. Brech defines the management activity in relation to formal work organizations as follows:

It is the responsibility for the effective planning and regulation (or guidance) of the operations of an organization, such responsibility involving:

(i) the installation and maintenance of proper procedures to ensure adherence to plans for the accomplishment of defined objectives

(ii) the guidance, integration and supervision of the personnel comprising the organization and carrying out its operations.

This definition is typical of many to be found in textbooks concerned with management studies. It is not included to indicate a good or bad definition of the management activity, but merely to indicate the over-riding premise on which much of management theory is based, that of defined objectives from which are derived business policies and plans. To a large extent this is an understandable and perfectly legitimate premise as long as it is capable of admitting the presence of other goals at the organizational level.

Even ignoring the existence of individual and group goals which have been discussed so far, organizational goals are far from being easily identified or specified. Goal determination is inextricably intertwined with the need for a planned direction for the organization. This planning process is concerned with forecasting needs, defining objectives, anticipating problems and developing feasible solutions. The first of these, the forecasting stage, is perhaps the most crucial, for it is here that the policy makers set an organization in its environment, and attempt to emphasize the needs and problems that the organization faces in that environment, and the importance of adjusting to those needs and problems. Thus for a manufacturing organization, the forecasting stage is concerned with the ability of the market to buy its products. How many will sell, with what design, and at what price? It is also concerned with identifying changes in demand patterns and assessing the resource implications which are necessary for the organization to be able to accommodate them. In the case of a public organization, say either a department of central or local government, the forecasting stage is concerned with identifying future social needs: health, highways, education, housing, defence, social benefits, etc. In the first instance the primary function is concerned with the identification of targets and methods of achieving them. Thus the primary focus is on the allocation of resources.

In both private and public organizations the primary aims of short- and long-term goal determination are twofold. First, it aims to provide a prescriptive model for the direction of the organization for a given period and thereby a statement concerning the information required by the management function within the organization. Secondly, it is concerned with the provision of a tool of analysis. This is the essential component for organizational control. Comparison of the actual activities of an organization during a specific period of time with those prescribed by the plan provides a basis for appraisal of the performance of the organization. Control is achieved by examining the nature of the differences and action taken where it is felt to be necessary.

1.7 THE FORMULATION OF THE GOALS OF THE FORMAL WORK ORGANIZATION

Formal work organizations vary very considerably in their size, purpose, structure and accountability. The vast range of variations that exists in our economy makes it impossible to talk about the goal formation of specific types of organization, unless particular examples are chosen, and a detailed examination undertaken. On the other hand, a more general examination of the types of factor which are influential in goal formation is a perfectly feasible proposition.

One method of viewing the goal determination process is to take a systems viewpoint. Here we are concerned in identifying groupings of input factors which are most

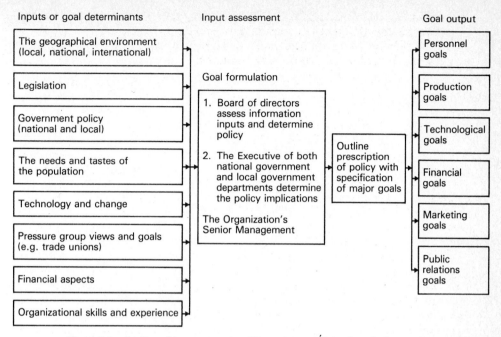

Figure 1.1 *Outline of the process of goal formulation in formal work organizations*

likely to be considered by the policy makers in the formal work organization. Fig. 1.1 shows the types of input groupings which the senior management would need to consider in determining their policy goals. The geographical factor is important for a variety of reasons: it is the market for goods and services; it represents the transportation and distribution problem; it contains regional and national variations in culture and taste; it provides the manpower and physical location of the organization, and so on.

Legislation is of growing influence to formal work organizations. The whole area of statutory law, common law and administrative law needs to be considered in goal formation. Law prescribes minimum standards which must be adhered to. Thus labour law prescribes many employment practices, company law regulates an organization's legal personality, and commercial law its behaviour towards its customers and clients.

Government economic and social policy in particular are most influential factors. Controls on the flow of money, taxation levels, financial support policies, income policies, manpower training policies, education policies, and so on, all impinge on organization goal determination. In the public sector, most particularly, policies such as reductions in public expenditure, decentralization of government services, and changes in government direction through the effects of the ballot box are clearly influential factors in goal formulation.

Goal formulation attempts to set an organization in its environment by assessing the needs and problems that the organization faces in relation to it. Its goods and services must relate to the tastes and needs of the population if it is to succeed. It must be able to attract labour from the environment. Above all, it must be able to adjust to the needs and problems of the environment.

The development and impact of the 'silicon chip' is perhaps the best and most topical example of the impact of technological change on organizational goals. The possibilities for the application of this new technology are so significant for all concerned with formal work organization that the full impact is as yet unknown. One has only to consider the impact on the *Times* in 1978 and 1979 to begin to assess the possible future impact of technological change on organizations in the future.

Technological change is closely related to availability of skilled manpower. In determining its goals, a formal work organization will consider such factors as the sources of trained manpower and the available retraining facilities. It may sound strange to talk of labour as a shortage commodity with the large numbers of unemployed, but what we are talking about is not the simple availability of people, but the availability of people possessing suitable skills, abilities and experience to tackle the new job roles which modern organizations demand.

It is difficult to quantify and evaluate the impact of each of these input criteria on any specific organization. Suffice it to say that in general senior management will consider most, if not all of them, in formulating their policy.

There is one influence which has not yet been mentioned and which perhaps dominates the rest: the availability of finance. Money is the life blood of all organizations and is of crucial importance in goal formulation. Credit facilities, and the cost of credit, are major considerations. Government financial incentive schemes are of significant importance in relation to decisions such as the geographical siting of an organization. The accuracy of decisions taken in relation to the financial factor is crucial. Survival of the organization is generally dependent on its ability to show a positive financial return at the end of a given period of operation. We are talking here of profit. The term 'profit' is not restricted to manufacturing organizations. In the public sector profit is achieved when an organization is able to do more with the budget it receives. In this sense it is possible for formal work organizations to be so structured and operated that more services are made possible within the finite limits of a specific budget allocation. Thus their efficiency is a form of profit. Public organizations are increasingly becoming more accountable for the way they utilize financial resources. The student should be cautious of concluding at this stage that goal setting is purely a one-off, analytical process. The input factors identified are indeed the issues which policy-makers need to consider, but the influence of views outside the policy-making body, both internal and external to the organization, will have a considerable impact on the policy goals arrived at. Thus the views of trade unions, environmentalists, etc. will have a part to play in the balancing process in policy negotiations. Policy making is an interactive process which requires continued adaptation to meet changed circumstances.

1.8 PROCEDURE FOR CONVERTING THE INPUTS INTO OUTPUTS

In the private sector the group concerned with assessing the various input factors, and thereby determining the formal policy for the organization, is the board of directors. A board of directors is a committee which varies in size according to the size of the organization. In the large public companies they can be as large as 25 members. Usually each director has a functional responsibility. This means that each one heads a specialist functional area such as personnel, marketing, finance, production, and research and development. This is not necessarily so; some company directors have no functional responsibility, and many have only a part-time involvement with the organization.

Leadership of the board is as important as the leadership in relation to informal groups or pressure groups. Individual directors are really very little different in certain aspects of their behaviour from the factory or office worker. There is always the danger that any functional executive director could press the interests of his particular department regardless of the larger overall organizational interests. In addition, directors will vary in their interpretation of what is best for the organization and, in consequence, there is always likely to exist a multiplicity of goals even in the board room. Strong leadership by the chairman is essential in order that the board reaches decisions on a clear and comprehensive statement of policy for the organization. This statement of policy represents the formal direction for the organization.

In the public sector the issue of policy making in relation to the operation of national and local government organizations is nothing like as clear. Perhaps the greatest confusion stems from the role of permanent and elected officials. In our democracy the separation of the legislative from the executive function is, in theory, quite clear, but in reality is nothing like as clear-cut. First of all the complexity of modern government, both at national and local levels, makes it almost impossible for elected officials to have either the knowledge or experience to decide all policy matters. Secondly, in the implementation of policy, policies are, in fact, being made. Because of this, Mattei Dogan expresses the view that the senior public official requires two essential attributes, political sensitivity and technical skill, in order to reach decisions which are not only technically correct but also politically acceptable.

There is little doubt that the scope and technical complexity of modern government is having an effect on the role and function of permanent officials in the public sector, bringing them more into the policy-making arena in most European countries. In France, for example, where economic planning has come to represent a major part of the government's overall strategy, the higher civil servants play a crucial role in its success. This fact leads Shonfield to the conclusion that modern government seems to be most successful in a non-participative environment, which could pose a threat to democratic government and therefore goal formulation in the future.

The policy-making function of the top permanent officials in the public sector is both complex and subtle: complex because of the wide variety of tasks undertaken by the bureaucracy, and subtle because of the common law setting. Although British senior civil servants are more involved in this policy-making process today than they have been in the past, they are in no position to make up for the defects so frequently ascribed to the workings of the Palace of Westminster. Elected officials are still charged with the major responsibility for policy direction, and hence the goals of government departments are inextricably linked with the processes of politics.

There is a major problem in understanding the processes of goal determination even when we narrow the issue down to the top policy-making positions in both private and public organizations. The major influence on goal formulation may not necessarily be reflected by the concrete decisions made in a board room, the Cabinet, or a County Hall, but in the making of 'non-decisions', that is, the decisions taken by people to limit the information provided for the policy maker and thereby either reducing decision making to safe issues or giving the policy decisions a specific bias. This charge was, in fact, levied by the official Labour Party evidence presented to the Fulton Committee reviewing the British civil service in the mid-1960s. The Labour Party stated that ministers were often presented with a restricted set of policy alternatives, all of which were satisfactory to the public service organizations presenting the information.

1.9 FORMAL GOALS: STATED OR UNSTATED?

The reader could have drawn the conclusion that formal goals are always clearly stated by organizations. This is not the case. Many organizations have no clearly defined objectives at all, apart perhaps from the universal one of making a profit in the case of commercial organizations. The problem for organizations without clearly stated goals is that they have no way of knowing where they are going, or of knowing whether or not they have arrived! They may have devoted much time, energy and precious resources to perfecting unnecessary activities or more efficient ways of producing a product with little or no contribution to or relationship with profit. There are distinct advantages for an organization in setting out its objectives. These advantages are well stated by J. O'Shaughnessy as follows:

(i) Where objectives are absent or misunderstood there is a danger that action will be taken in pursuit of ends which no longer contribute to them. Setting them out formally facilitates their communication within the company and such communication lessens the risk of misunderstanding.

(ii) If objectives are made explicit, any conflicts among them are more likely to be discovered, with consequent attempts at reconciliation.

(iii) Explicit criteria for judging overall company performance are provided, unless the formal statement of objectives is merely for 'propaganda' purposes and conceals the true ones.

(iv) Objectives are based on forecasts, and it is by considering the future that setbacks and opportunities are anticipated.

But once these objectives have been stated it must not be forgotten that organizations develop needs of their own. The result is that organizations produce a range of unstated goals which sometimes dominate the formal goals. There are many examples to demonstrate this. Look at:

1. The total bill for social security benefits and the ratio of the amount of money paid out in benefits to the amount paid to administer the payments.
2. Examples of fund raising organizations, and compare the net amount available as charitable funds in comparison to the cost of the organization set up to raise the funds.
3. Administration costs to medical costs in the health service, or administration costs to teaching costs in the education service, and so on.

1.10   ORGANIZATION GOALS: UNITARY OR PLURALISTIC PERCEPTION?

The traditional view of organization structures talks of the need to ensure that the sum total of the efforts of individuals within the organization is in accord with the corporate task, and that the responsibility for achieving this is in the hands of management. This perspective assumes that management can mould all the employees into a single unified team with a single goal – the stated aims of the organization. For the period for which each individual is employed there is no conflict between the aims of the worker and aims of the organization. Each employee plays a part, like the different positions in a football team, towards the ultimate success of the organization. This is called the unitary perception of the nature of people working in an organization. Many have taken, and still take, this perception and have both organized and managed using it as the basis for their theories and practices.

The classical writers, referred to in Chapter 2, clearly see organizations with a single focus of authority and, by implication, one focus of loyalty. As a result they have developed prescriptive organization models which include such elements as hierarchies of authority of the pyramid type and payment systems based on the perception that people are motivated solely by financial rewards. The important implication of this unitary perception is that it leads to a general view that the vast majority of people who go to work clearly accept the job role and all its conditions; they do not challenge the leadership of management or look to rival leadership; they work towards the goals stated by the organization; and at the end of a week or month collect their wage packet or salary cheque as a reward. This perception does not admit to the existence of individual goals running contrary to those of the organization. There is no need for them to exist! The few that challenge the organization, or adversely affect its operations, are classified as troublemakers who should be brought into line. The predominant attitude of management to the trade union movement, particularly in the early stages of its development, clearly illustrates this perception in action. The trade unions were seen as having no purpose or justification and therefore needed to be severely controlled ('stamped out' was the original plea).

On the other hand, many take the view that organizations are not made up of unified teams of workers at all, but are at best groups of people with varied interests which are often divergent. This perception leads to an organizational model which abandons ideal prescriptions concerning the right way to organize. Instead, it focuses on ways in which many interests and objectives can be kept in a satisfactory state of equilibrium, satisfactory in the sense that the purpose of the organization remains more or less acceptable to the formal leadership. Such a perception admits to the legitimate existence of many sources of leadership and many focuses of loyalty. As a consequence, an organization is seen as containing a whole hierarchy of goals, often of a conflicting nature (Fig. 1.2).

These two perceptions are important in that they represent two extremes of the way people can be viewed in organizations. Such perceptions are important since it is largely on the basis of perception that we form our judgements. Thus if we view people in organizations in a unitary way, then the organizations we design will contain distinctive characteristics based on this belief; for example, hierarchical control systems based on a single focus of command; clearly defined departmental roles and individual job roles; and a dependence on almost unchallengeable goals. The organization will have a mechanistic appearance, all the parts fitting together like the component parts of a machine. Each part fulfils its function in a prescribed way, such that the overall function fits a clearly stated specification. If, on the other hand, we hold a pluralistic perception, the organization we design is less likely to hold on to these rigid characteristics and will be likely to have the flexibility to modify in order to meet differing situations: it is

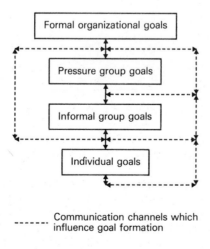

Figure 1.2   *Hierarchy of goals*

seen as a living organism with an organic nature. Thus organizations are seen as needing the ability to adapt to change, both internal and external, and rigid job role definition and goal definition are seen as examples of negative factors hindering an organization's powers of adaptation.

The importance of this perception issue cannot be overstated. It is analogous to a frame of reference against which we take decisions. Alan Fox in his research paper to the Royal Commission on Trade Unions and Employers' Associations stated that 'the importance derives from the fact that the frame of reference we employ determines (a) how we expect people to behave and how we think they ought to behave, (b) how we react to people's actual behaviour, and (c) the methods we choose when we want to change their behaviour'. It is clear, therefore, that a unitary perception would view the existence of individual goals quite differently from a pluralistic one. An individual expressing goals contrary to those stated and expected by the organization would be viewed as unacceptable and requiring corrective action, perhaps of a disciplinary nature. The pluralist would take the opposite view in that he would accept the goals as perfectly legitimate, and would search for ways of incorporating the individual goals into the organization without doing harm to either.

1.11 SUMMARY

In this chapter we have examined the concept of goals in relation to the activities of formal work organizations. We have seen that great difficulties exist when trying to describe the nature of these goals. On the one hand goals exist at a number of levels from those of individuals to the stated goals of the whole organization. On the other, we have seen that some goals are clearly stated and others hidden.

We have briefly examined some of the levels at which goals can be seen to exist in formal work organizations. Every individual employee brings unique personal goals which may range from simply wanting to do the job for which he is employed in the prescribed way and to receive the agreed payment at the end of the week or month, to wanting to disrupt the structure of the organization in order to obtain a greater say in the decision-making process, a greater share in the wealth of the organization, and perhaps a change in the nature of ownership and control.

We have seen that individuals form two kinds of grouping within the structure of the formal work organization – formal groups and informal groups. These groups have goals, some of which are clearly stated and communicated openly, while others remain suppressed or deliberately hidden. Informal group goals can become the goals of formal groups. A dissatisfied group of workers can, for example, take a grievance either through a procedure laid down by the formal work organization itself, or place the grievance in the hands of a trade union. We have seen that trade unions are examples, themselves, of formal organizations which generally act as pressure groups. In addition to trade unions we have examined the importance of pressure groups in relation to the activities of formal work organizations.

At the level of the formal work organization itself, goals are usually determined by small groups of senior executives in private enterprise organizations, and by committees in public sector organizations. These groupings of people decide on the corporate goals for their organization. In reality, the corporate goals are at best only the goals of those who decided them; the problem is to ensure that they become the goals of those employed by the organization. In other words one of the biggest problems facing formal work organizations is that of ensuring that individual employees accept the specification for the jobs they are asked to do, understand how each job contributes to the achievement of the corporate objectives, and do everything possible to see that these are attained.

The chapter has limited its focus to objectives at the policy-making level, since goals at other levels, for example, departmental and section level, will be examined in later chapters.

1.12   THE BANK HOUSE PROBLEM: A CASE STUDY IN ANALYSING OBJECTIVES

Aim

The aim of this study is to illustrate a situation where conflicting forces influence the process of determining policy goals. The situation described here demonstrates some of the problems of formulating policy goals in public sector organizations. The tables and figures are included to show the kind of conflicting needs which confront public-sector decision-makers.

Objectives

1.   To illustrate a policy decision.
2.   To provide the reader with a goal determination exercise.
3.   To provide a realistic situation where conflicting needs have to be assessed in determining a policy decision.
4.   To illustrate the inevitable part that personally held values play in the process of decision-making.

Tasks

1.   Information analysis. The tables and figures at the end of the case study contain considerable data. The reader should analyse these data and determine what is relevant to the specific issue in question.
2.   From the information suggest the alternative uses to which Bank House could be put. Identify the major reasons which support each of these.
3.   Identify the use you think is most appropriate, and draft a full recommendation to the Director of Social Services.
4.   Identify the values you have considered to be most important in influencing your assessment of the situation. How might your values differ from those of other interested parties?
5.   What pressure group influence would you anticipate being involved in such a decision? In what circumstances do you think the views of pressure groups would be regarded as legitimate and influential?

6. Contact the appropriate agencies and update the information contained in the tables and figures.
7. Identify any other information needs you think are appropriate and obtain these from reliable sources.

(This study is based on a situation developed jointly by J. G. Capey and A. Sutton of Wigan Social Services Department, for an in-service training course for management staff.)

The Problem

Castlefield Metropolitan Borough have recently completed construction of a building known as 'Bank House'. The accommodation was developed for use as a children's home, catering for 15 children aged 5–16 years. However, the present economic climate is forcing local authorities to reconsider their past decisions on resource allocation and review their strategy for the future. As a result, the social services department is reconsidering its decision to use Bank House as a children's home. Some members feel it could be used more appropriately as a hostel for the elderly, while others think it could be used as a hostel for the mentally ill.

To consider these alternatives and investigate other possible uses the director has established a working party, of which you are a member. Your working party's terms of reference are: to advise the Directorate and the Social Services Committee on the most appropriate use of Bank House.

North West

The North West Region comprises the whole of Lancashire and Cheshire together with the High Peak district of Derbyshire. It is an area of 3083 square miles, and contains a population of 6.8 million which is expected to grow to 7.4 million by 1991, and to about 8 million by 2001.

Density of population varies markedly. For example, North Lancashire includes a part of the sparsely populated area of the Lake District, while the River Mersey has on its banks nearly 5 million people in the Merseyside and Greater Manchester conurbations separated by an area which already contains large and growing towns. There is extensive suburban development in the north-east and north-west of Cheshire. North-east Lancashire has a declining population. Taken as a whole the North West Region has a higher proportion of its area (some 25 per cent) in urban use than any other region, and its density of 3.4 persons per acre is greater than that of any other region in the country. The South East, by comparison, has a density of 1.8 persons per acre.

Following the population boom in the nineteenth century as a result of the industrial revolution, industries on which the economy of the region had been founded – coal, ship-building, cotton – began to decline. As a result the North West has experienced a net loss of population because of migration almost every year since the First World War. The rate of natural increase in population has been consistently below the average in England and Wales since 1918. This has mainly been due to the relatively high death rates which have outweighed the effects of birth rates which are only slightly above the average for England and Wales.

The region's population of working age has actually been declining, while employment growth has also been at a rate well below the national average. Between 1953 and 1963 the number of employees working in the region increased by only 51 000, or 1.8 per cent compared with 9.1 per cent in Great Britain as a whole. While in the same period manufacturing jobs declined by 4 per cent and primary industries decreased by nearly one-third, there was a considerable employment growth in the service sector within the region. Construction and the service industries increased their share of the North West's total employment from 47 per cent to 52 per cent (compared with the national figure of 56 per cent). Even here, however, the growth was slower than the national pattern – 10 per cent as against 15 per cent. Given a constant rate of employment growth it seems unlikely that within the next ten years, sufficient jobs will be created to match the internal increase in the region's labour supply, and certainly not enough to allow for a reduction in unemployment. The region as a whole has a considerable legacy of outworn and obsolete development, both residential and industrial.

Greater Manchester

Two conurbations dominate the North West – Greater Manchester and Merseyside. In 1971 nearly 2¾ million persons lived in the area of the Greater Manchester Council (GMC).

The GMC is composed of ten metropolitan districts (MDs), listed in Table 1.1. (For the purpose of this study they have been given imaginary names.)

The declining population of the inner districts, Minchaser and Sallyham, contrasts with the growth of the remaining districts. But population change is only one indicator, and the differences can be summarized by using seven indicators to produce a table of the 'most privileged' and 'least privileged' districts.

The indicators have been converted into ranks. The 'best off' scores 1 and the 'worst off' scores 10. The seven indicators are:

(a) Many men in professional and managerial jobs.
(b) Few men in semi-skilled and unskilled jobs.
(c) Many aged 15–20 in full-time education.
(d) Few houses unfit.
(e) Few men out of work.
(f) Many acres of parks, playing fields per 1000 population.
(g) High rateable value per head.

Table 1.1 *The ten metropolitan districts of the GMC*

	1951	1971	1975	1981
Castlefield	279 250	320 930	309 600	335 400
Binlot	253 830	259 550	263 300	275 900
Bagfold	151 400	174 620	180 400	195 100
Raeburn	170 700	203 130	211 500	218 400
Sallyham	305 950	278 990	266 500	266 200
Minchaser	703 220	543 870	506 300	488 700
Ottle	221 310	223 980	228 400	222 800
Tribank	202 240	227 960	226 700	230 100
Sedgham	223 730	292 230	294 100	296 700
Wildhead	204 730	220 860	222 800	227 300
County	2 716 260	2 729 040	2 709 600	2 756 600

The ranking of these indicators (see Table 1.2) shows that three districts – Ottle, Castlefield and Sallyham – are poorly placed, and that three districts do consistently well – Bagfold, Tribank and Sedgham.

Table 1.2 *Indicators of privilege in the ten metropolitan districts*

District	(a)	(b)	(c)	(d)	(e)	(f)	(g)	Final ranking
Sedgham	1	2	1	3	2	1	3	1
Tribank	2	1	2	2	3	4	1	2
Bagfold	3	3	3	1	1	2	9	3
Binlot	4	5	4	5	6	3	5	4
Wildhead	5	4	9	4	5	9	7	5
Raeburn	5	7	6	6	7	5	10	6
Minchaser	8	5	5	10	10	6	2	6
Ottle	7	10	8	9	4	7	6	8
Sallyham	10	7	7	8	9	9	4	9
Castlefield	8	9	10	7	8	8	8	10

Castlefield Metropolitan Borough

Castlefield Metropolitan Borough was formed with local government reorganization in April 1974 by the amalgamation of Castlefield County Borough, 12 neighbouring urban districts and Leedle Municipal Borough.

Castlefield Social Services, which is the subject of this exercise, is administered from a headquarters base, and has a total staff of 1879 consisting of residential, day and domiciliary service, fieldwork service and administrative staffs.

The range of residential services and some of the day care services can be found in Table 1.3. The department has an establishment of 83 basic grade social workers, which includes 13 social workers operating within a medical social work setting. The total range of service offered is similar to that of social work departments existing in the present economic climate and operating within Northern Industrial Urban Areas.

Trends and Forecasts

Barbara Castle, as Secretary of State for Health and Social Services, in 1975 said,

> The demand for the future development of our health and personal social services will always outstrip our capacity to meet it, therefore, it is essential at any time to work out our priorities carefully, but at this time when the growth of public expenditure must be severely restrained it is all the more imperative that we should choose the right priorities and plan how they can be realised.

Central government is not alone, however, in attempting to cater for the future, as careful planning is an essential prerequisite for the success of any organization, either statutory or voluntary. Therefore, one can find a plethora of statistics, trends and forecasts which can and should be used to identify needs and illustrate priorities. The extracts given here represent only a small percentage of the range of relevant research material available. However, they do provide sufficient information for a quantifiable base to be used for some decisions.

Table 1.3   *Residential and other services mainly for the elderly and handicapped (United Kingdom) (000s)*

	Persons aged 65 and over						All persons					
	England and Wales				Scotland	N. Ireland	England and Wales				Scotland	N. Ireland
	1961	1974	1975	1976	1976	1975	1961	1974	1975	1976	1976	1975
Residents (on 31 December) in accommodation of:												
Local authorities, etc.	66	98	102	106	8	2	74	105	108	112	9	3
Voluntary organizations	10	15	16	17	5	1	13	21	20	22	6	1
Home nursing—cases attended	431	—	76	75	—	—	882	—	167	168	—	15
Home helps—cases attended	249	513	562	603	—	12	328	596	648	691	52	—
Meals on wheels—persons served during one week	—	177	180	183	—	4	—	181	185	186	20	4
Chiropody—persons treated	—	—	85	89	—	—	—	—	92	95	—	—
Overall population (millions)	5.5	6.9	7.0	7.1	0.7	0.2	46.2	49.2	49.2	49.2	5.2	1.5
Total persons registered as												
Blind	65.1	76.6	77.9	79.0	—	—	96.7	105.6	106.7	108.4	9.1	2.5
Deaf	3.7	6.1	6.3	7.2	—	—	23.8	27.1	26.9	29.0	2.2	—
Other handicap	53.2	348.9	411.2	472.4	—	—	151.1	588.7	677.1	766.7	31.5	11.0

Sources: Department of Health and Social Security; Welsh Office; Scottish Education Department, Social Work Services Group

The 1976 Consultative Document, *Priorities for Health and Personal Social Services in England*, stated that the growing proportion of the population aged 65 and over will place an increasing strain on most of the health and personal social services. The main objective of services for elderly people is to help them remain in the community for as long as possible. It is, however, important to provide hospital and residential care for old people unable to live independently, and to improve hospital facilities for early diagnosis, intensive treatment and rehabilitation.

Subject to local circumstances, the following national targets are suggested: expansion of the home nursing services by 6 per cent a year, of the chiropodist services by 3 per cent a year, and of home helps and the meals service by 2 per cent a year; an increase in the number of local authority residential places by 2000 per year, to be concentrated where local needs are greatest, and of day centre places by 600 a year; an additional 1150 hospital geriatric beds a year, and the provision of a progressively increasing proportion of geriatric beds in general hospitals; provision of 2000 beds a year in community hospitals for old people, including those with severe mental infirmities, to replace provision in unsatisfactory long-stay hospitals.

Effective joint planning between local and health authorities is particularly important. The voluntary sector will continue to have a major role to play in the provision of services for the elderly.

However, it is inevitable in a time of economic restraint that financial brakes are to be applied to public expenditure, and David Ennals in the Consultative Document *The Way Forward* reappraised these targets and stated that:

There has been little criticism of the long-term aims set out in the Consultative Document. But considerable doubt has been expressed on whether it is practicable to achieve them within the suggested time-scale. While the Government has ensured that there will continue to be at least a modest rate of increase in resources for these services in the country as a whole, I appreciate that we cannot hope to make significant and rapid changes in the desired directions without a more rapid growth of resources. On the one hand, we need to channel extra resources to those parts of the country with greater than average health needs which have been poorly provided for in the past. On the other hand, we need to improve the care of children, the elderly, the mentally ill, the mentally handicapped and the physically handicapped as well as to finance important new developments in therapy. A more rapid rate of growth, both of revenue and capital resources, must depend on an improvement in the general economic situation. I hope we shall not have to wait too long.

It is not only the limited rate of growth of revenue which prevents us making rapid change. Much of what can be done is conditioned by what has already been achieved. New buildings may need to be provided and professional skills redeployed. Plans (particularly those involving major buildings) launched several years ago are coming to fruition and we must make the best possible use of them. Inevitably the capacity for change varies in different parts of the service and in different parts of the country.

In view of all these constraints, it would be easier for us to postpone the effort involved in moving to new priorities until the impact of past plans has been absorbed and until it is possible to provide a more rapid growth of resources. But this would be wrong. We must be clear about the role we are all trying to take even though our progress will be uneven. National policies must be clearly stated. The public, the authorities, the professions and all who work in health and social services expect a clear lead from the government on the way forward.

I am convinced that there is scope for making fast progress in the desired directions by making better use of the resources which we have already.

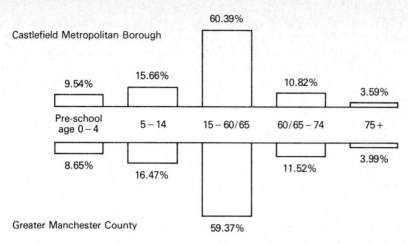

Figure 1.3 *Age structure of Castlefield Metropolitan Borough and the Greater Manchester County population*

Old people are major users of most of the health and personal social services. The primary care and acute hospital services are very important to them. But those services which are mainly or entirely used by the elderly will have to meet a particularly sharp increase in demand. Moreover, social and environmental changes such as smaller housing units and increased job mobility have tended to reduce the ability of younger people to care for the elderly in a family environment. In the last ten years the number of people aged over 65 has increased by more than 1 million. They now total more than 6½ million, which is over 14 per cent of the population, and nearly one-third of them live alone (see Fig. 1.3 and Table 1.4). The projections indicate a continuing increase in both the numbers and proportions of old people in the population with a particularly rapid increase projected in the number of people aged 75 and over. Over the next 20 years, the over 75s are expected to increase by nearly one-third, from 2⅓ million to just under 3 million. People aged over 85 are at present about one in 100 of the population, and nearly half of those who are in the community live alone; by the year 2001 their proportion is projected to increase to about one in 75. The 1976 Consultative Document stated:

Home helps: In 1974 there were about 41 000 whole-time equivalent home helps, i.e. six per thousand elderly. The guideline is for a ratio of 12 per thousand.

Meals: About 600 000 meals are served each week through the meals on wheels services and day centres and clubs. The guideline is for 200 per week per thousand elderly (about 1 300 000 overall).

Table 1.4 *Proportion of households consisting of people of pensionable age living alone*

Area	Percentage
Castlefield Metropolitan Borough	11.63
Lancashire	12.84
GMC	12.79
Great Britain	11.66

Day centres: In 1974 there were about 23 000 day centre places available to the elderly and the younger physically handicapped. About half of these are used by elderly people, giving about two places per thousand elderly. The guideline is three to four places per thousand.

Residential facilities: In 1974 there were about 125 000 local authority places available for elderly people and for the younger physically handicapped and others, including places supported by local authorities in voluntary or private homes. Of these, about 120 000 were occupied by people aged 65 or over, i.e. about 18.5 places per thousand elderly. The guideline is 25 places per thousand elderly.

Domiciliary services: The more these can be expanded, the more the pressure on residential accommodation and on hospitals can be eased.

The demand for services among the elderly is more closely related to the size of the population of the very old, those in their eighties and nineties, than to the size of the population of those aged 65 and over. The ageing of the elderly population could, for example, result in demand for residential care rising by as much as one third over the last quarter of this century. Services for the elderly are likely to be under increasing pressure as a result of demographic change.

The Department of Health and Social Security (DHSS) states that the main aim of services for the physically handicapped is to enable them to lead as full and useful a life as possible by providing appropriate support services and care within the community.

A high rate of expansion would be beneficial for home aids and adaptations and certain other services provided under section 2 of the Chronically Sick and Disabled Persons Act 1970, which make an important contribution to the mobility and quality of life of the physically handicapped.

Further local community day centre places should be provided. Attention should be paid to the needs of the blind and the deaf for social work support.

Of the local authority services, purpose-built residential accommodation for the younger disabled is a key provision for those who are unable to remain in their own homes but do not need to be in hospital. There are 33 residential homes provided by local authorities for this group under Part III of the National Assistance Acts, and according to latest information authorities intend to build a further 15. It is suggested that local authority provision of residential accommodation should increase by 2000 places per year, the large majority of which are likely to be required for elderly people. For those under 65 the need is greatest and thus the priority highest for those most severely handicapped, including the multi-handicapped and those in the 40–60 year age group.

Local authority day centres are important in helping handicapped people to remain in the community. It has been estimated that about 600 day places should be provided annually.

The domiciliary services which help the physically handicapped to remain in their own homes suitably adapted, or in special housing, have grown considerably in recent years, and there is a need to develop these further in quality and type. Aids and adaptations, and certain other services available under section 2 of the Chronically Sick and Disabled Persons Act 1970, are particularly important for the physically handicapped, and there is strong pressure for further expansion of these services. Given the great contribution they make to the mobility and quality of life of physically handicapped people, it is suggested that a high rate of expansion would be justified. This increase in expenditure nationally would yield considerable benefits, and though those local authorities which have already made good progress may have less ground to catch up, there are others where a larger expansion is needed. The expansion of these services (particularly in localities where they are at present underdeveloped) would be suitable for consideration by joint care planning teams, and might be a suitable use of joint finance.

The 1976 Consultative Document *Priorities for Health and Personal Social Services in England* stated that 'the long-term aims for services for the mentally handicapped remain those proposed in the White Paper, *Better Services for the Mentally Handicapped*: provision of a satisfactory environment either at home or in residential accommodation; avoiding unnecessary segregation; developing ability by education and training, and support for families'. Full implementation of the White Paper targets was envisaged as taking place over a 20-year period.

There are estimated to be about 110 000 severely mentally handicapped people in England and more than 350 000 with mild mental handicap. In 1974 nearly 60 000 were in residential care, 9000 in local authority homes, 50 000 in hospitals and over 10 000 in lodgings, foster homes, etc. The general aims of services for mentally handicapped people are to ensure that they have a satisfying environment (which should as far as possible be within the general community), and to provide education, social stimulation and purposeful occupation and employment so as to develop and exercise all the skills they can acquire.

The long-term aim is to achieve the pattern of services proposed in *Better Services for the Mentally Handicapped*:

1. To provide a satisfactory environment whether at home, in hospital or in residential accommodation.
2. To avoid unnecessary segregation.
3. To provide education, training and occupation to develop ability.
4. To support families and help them to cope for as long as possible.

Full achievement of the White Paper proposals by the early 1990s implies that by 1985 there would need to be some 22 000 places in local authority homes compared with the 1974 figure of 9500, and about 60 000 places in training centres compared with about 32 000 in 1974.

The national development group agree that priority for the expansion of local authorities services would best serve the interests of the mentally handicapped; the development of training services which, despite rapid expansion in the past few years, are still not available for many mentally handicapped people living with their families is particularly urgent. Within the residential programme priority should be given to enabling children to be kept out of hospital care: the number of local authority places for mentally handicapped children, though increasing, is not rising fast enough to match the undoubted priority for this category. There is also a possibility of accommodating a small number of children in the other ways, for example, by fostering.

Each year an estimated 5 million people consult their general practitioner with a mental health problem. Mental ill health is also a factor in many of the cases presented to local authority social service departments. Most mental health problems are dealt with by the primary health and social services, but even so some 600 000 people receive specialist psychiatric care each year.

Specialist services for the mentally ill are at present based mainly in large mental illness hospitals, often some distance from the communities they serve. The government's long-term strategy for the further development of both health and personal social services is set out in a White Paper, *Better Services for the Mentally Ill*. The main services needed by mentally ill people should be available locally in each district, so that people can, as far as possible, receive treatment while continuing to live at home. Inpatient treatment in hospital, or residential care in a local authority home or hostel, should be provided only for those who cannot otherwise be helped effectively. The emphasis in such treatment and care should then be on helping the individual to cope with life in a community again to the fullest possible extent; even if a degree of more or less permanent support and care is needed the aim should be to give as much opportunity as possible for independence and self fulfilment.

One of the government's broad objectives for strategic planning over the next 25 years is: 'to increase local authority social services residential and day facilities, fieldwork, and domiciliary care, for the mentally ill'. At present these fall far short of what is needed, so that many patients stay in hospital unnecessarily or are discharged to unsatisfactory conditions in the community.

The most serious deficiencies in existing services for the mentally ill are in local authority social services, where in 1974 there were fewer than 4000 residential places, and only just over 5000 day places, against an estimated national requirement of 12 000 and 30 000 places respectively. This does not necessarily reflect a lack of concern by authorities, a good many of whom could point to mental illness schemes for which they had requested loan sanction in the past few years but which the central government of the day had felt unable to approve. Even with a prospect of a sharp reduction overall in local authority capital schemes, it is essential that capital expenditure for mental illness should be increased, not only as a proportion of a total but in absolute terms, if there is to be any real progress either in meeting existing urgent needs or in developing the new pattern of services.

There is especially urgent need for more day care, which is at present (as the above figures show) the least adequately provided of all services for the mentally ill. Its availability may be a critical factor in determining the success with which a person recovering from mental illness is able to readjust to life in the community. A need to develop a range of suitable residential accommodation in the community for people who have been mentally ill is scarcely less pressing, and for this also an increased capital programme is suggested.

For both day care and residential services (but especially the latter) faster growth is achieved by concentrating on forms of provision with a lower capital cost, and it is hoped authorities will use all the means in their power to increase their services to the maximum for each pound of capital available. This can be done, for example, by the use of adapted rather than purpose-built accommodation, where suitable premises are available; for day centres, sharing facilities with other groups with similar needs to the mentally ill or making premises serve more than one function, for example as a day centre during the day and as a community centre or youth centre during the evenings. Close contact between the health services and the social services department, and between both and voluntary organizations, is of supreme importance in providing an effective service within the resources available. The arrangements for joint financing of community social services schemes are particularly relevant to the development of services for the mentally ill.

In 1969 the Seebohm Committee stated that at least one child in 10 will need special education, psychiatric or social help before the age of 18. At present not more than one child in 22 gets such help, and many are now getting the wrong help: taken into care for lack of day nurseries or home helps; into approved schools when early identification might have led to a solution of problems; into schools for the physically handicapped or delicate, when a school for the maladjusted would be more appropriate; into hospitals for the mentally subnormal when they could be living at home if their parents were given more support.

We need now to ask ourselves if these conditions still apply and what needs to be done in the future.

It is a key objective of the personal social services to support the family. Where children are concerned, the main objective is to help families provide a satisfactory home for the child, and to enable children to stay with their families except where it is against the children's interests. Many of the services provided specially for children are required when the child's home no longer provides a satisfactory environment, either temporarily or permanently, or when the child has no family of his own and it is necessary to provide a substitute family or, in some cases, residential care. The main interest at present is, however, in developing forms of help which minimize the need to take the child away from the family.

Day care for pre-school children has an essential role in alleviating the effects of social deprivation in the child's formative years. Local authority facilities are concentrated on those who have priority need. They have long waiting lists. Private arrangements, voluntary agencies and employers provide a significant and growing proportion of day care services, for example play groups and childminders.

Meanwhile, there is substantial unmet need for residential care. This may to some extent be due to unsatisfactory use of the places which are available. But some homes are badly run down, others are in the wrong place, too far away from the community they serve, and there are serious shortages of specialized accommodation, particularly secure accommodation, both for remand and for treatment. Growing numbers of young people, including 14-year-old girls, are having to be remanded in prison service establishments because secure community homes places are not available.

The philosophy of the Seebohm Report, under the Local Authority Social Services Act 1970 which established the new local authority departments, was that services should be developed to identify and respond to the differing needs of families and individuals in the community, irrespective of how they arose. Client groups specifically considered in this document by no means account for all the community's needs for personal social services. Families in need of help often present a mixture of problems which sometimes find expression in marital violence, alcoholism, juvenile delinquency, or in other ways. The personal social services have to decide how to respond to a large and varied range of problems which are themselves interwoven with forces affecting society more widely.

The Consultative Document, *Priorities for Health and Personal Social Services in England*, projection of resources and demands in the period 1980–5 stated:

> The number of elderly people will continue to increase, though as a whole the increase will be less than in the next few years because the number of people in the 65 to 74 age group will fall. However, the number of people aged 75 and over will continue to increase (at around 1.8 per cent per year), and since it is they who have the largest need for services, those programmes which provide care and treatment for the elderly will continue to face increasing pressures, and are likely to require a significant proportion of any available growth. The number of women of childbearing age is also increasing, and if, as suggested in the central projection of the Office of Population, Censuses and Surveys, birth rate increases as well, the number of births and children under five will rise rapidly. In this case services for younger children and families, and perhaps also the maternity services, will need to expand if standards are to be maintained. If on the other hand the birth rate follows the OPCS continuing low projection, then the number of births and children under five may remain below the 1973 level, and the number of children may continue to fall. In this case there may be scope for further reduction in the maternity services, and for some economies in the health services used by children; however, the number of children in care, and families in need of support, may continue to rise even if the birth rate remains low.

Unemployment

The mid-1970s have seen a level of unemployment not known in the UK since the Second World War. This unemployment is particularly severe among young people. Since 1975 the Government has initiated a number of measures to mitigate unemployment, many of them specifically intended to help unemployed young people. In particular, schemes involving almost 100 000 jobs were approved for aid under the Job Creation Programme between October 1975, when the programme began, and August 1977. By no means all of the increase in unemployment can be attributed to a fall in the numbers employed. The number of people in employment has decreased in the last three or four years, but at the same time the total size of the labour force, that is, the total number of people in a job or looking for one, has increased. Thus unemployment has been added to in two ways.

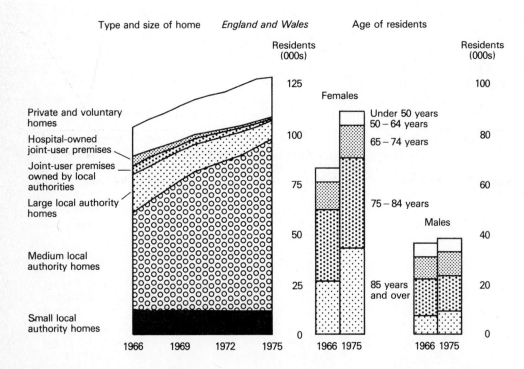

Figure 1.4 *People supported by the local authorities in residential accommodation. Sources: Department of Health and Social Security; Welsh Office*

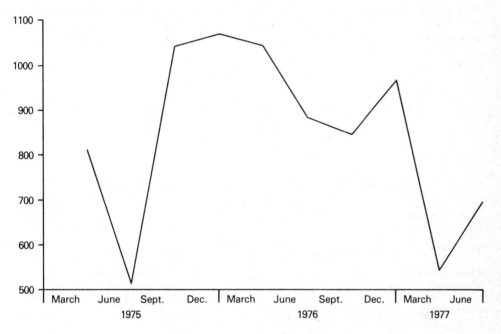

Figure 1.5 *Number of applications for aids/appliances received quarterly: borough totals 1 January 1975 to 30 June 1977*

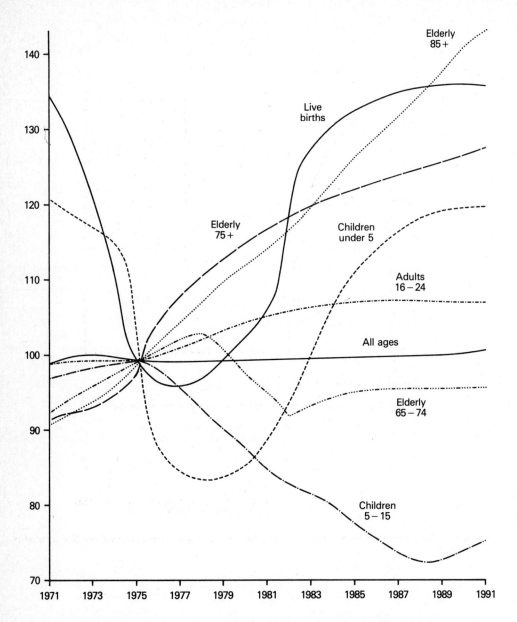

Figure 1.6   *Population changes (England). Source: Department of Employment*

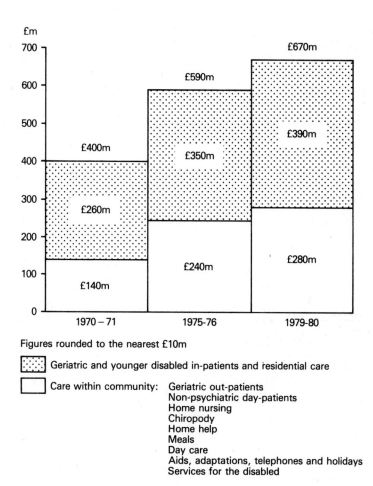

Figures rounded to the nearest £10m

Geriatric and younger disabled in-patients and residential care

Care within community: Geriatric out-patients
Non-psychiatric day-patients
Home nursing
Chiropody
Home help
Meals
Day care
Aids, adaptations, telephones and holidays
Services for the disabled

Figure 1.7 *Services mainly for the elderly and physically handicapped, current expenditure (£m November 1974 prices)*

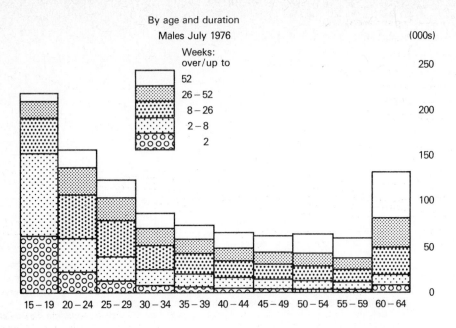

By age and duration
Males July 1976

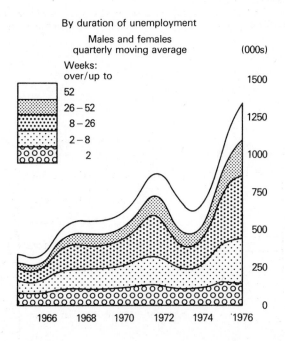

By duration of unemployment

Figure 1.8 *Unemployment (per thousand population). Source: Department of Employment Gazette*

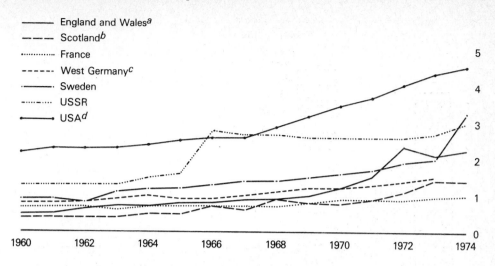

Figure 1.9 *Divorce rates (per thousand population): international comparison.*
[a] The Divorce Reform Act 1969, amending the grounds for divorce and judicial separation and facilitating reconciliation, came into force on 1 January 1971.
[b] The Divorce (Scotland) Act 1976 extended the grounds for divorce in Scotland to be similar to those applying to England and Wales although the change does not affect the data in this chart.
[c] 1974 data not available.
[d] Data and estimates are based on divorces and annulments reported by a varying number of states.
Sources: UN Demographic Yearbook; Population Trends, Office of Population Censuses and Surveys

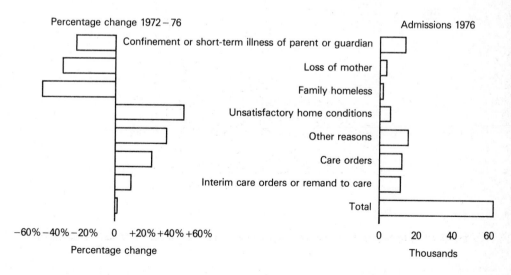

Figure 1.10 *Circumstances in which children are received into care of local authorities in England and Wales.*
Sources: Department of Health and Social Security; Welsh Office

Table 1.5 *Social Services Committee costs 1976–77*

	Children's homes (for 10 children or less)										Children's homes (for 11 children or more)			Hostel for adolescent girls
	1	2	3	4	5	6	7	8	9	Total 9 homes open all year	A	B	Total 2 homes open all year	X
Places available	9	6	10	10	9	8	8	8	8	76	18	22	40	8
Average number of places occupied	7.6	5.4	6.9	7.4	8.6	5.6	5.3	6.1	7.0	59.9	16.1	18.9	35	7.4
Percentage occupied	84%	90%	69%	74%	96%	70%	66%	76%	88%	79%	89%	86%	87%	92%
Net cost	£22 912	£14 614	£20 388	£23 098	£22 920	£20 283	£21 590	£18 080	£23 960	£187 845	£47 684	£54 292	£101 976	£26 629
					Weekly cost per child					Average weekly cost per child	Weekly cost per child		Average weekly cost per child	Weekly cost per child
	£	£	£	£	£	£	£	£	£	£	£	£	£	£
Employees	35.26	36.92	38.30	32.69	27.98	41.32	44.96	27.89	32.47	34.75	37.22	37.62	37.44	40.39
Maintenance of buildings and grounds	4.04	4.51	4.05	7.70	10.85	1.33	3.34	0.79	1.34	4.55	2.68	3.88	3.33	2.91
Fuel, light, cleaning materials and water	2.40	1.62	2.24	3.27	1.85	4.18	4.52	3.87	2.95	2.91	3.61	3.24	3.41	4.27
Rates and insurance	1.40	0.76	1.14	0.92	0.59	1.94	2.06	1.45	1.56	1.27	0.86	0.94	0.90	2.22
Furniture and equipment	1.30	0.54	0.38	2.16	1.22	2.02	3.57	0.65	1.00	1.39	1.03	1.28	1.16	0.83
Personal needs of children	2.41	1.87	2.05	1.70	2.50	2.55	3.33	3.01	2.92	2.46	2.38	2.13	2.25	3.06
Provisions	6.13	5.08	4.82	5.80	5.30	6.69	6.31	6.68	7.29	5.98	6.36	3.66	4.90	6.16
Clothing	1.95	1.58	1.08	1.54	1.30	2.25	1.95	1.71	1.67	1.64	1.65	1.08	1.34	1.15
Laundry	0.12	0.22	0.09	0.24	0.19	0.00	0.01	0.00	0.01	0.11	0.19	0.09	0.13	0.04
Postage and telephones	0.39	0.57	0.26	0.33	0.29	0.61	0.58	0.55	0.50	0.44	0.45	0.26	0.35	0.74
Other expenses	0.05	0.07	0.02	0.38	0.04	0.19	0.06	0.39	2.22	0.39	0.04	0.28	0.17	1.58
Gross cost excluding capital items	55.45	53.74	54.43	56.73	52.11	63.08	70.69	46.99	53.93	55.89	56.47	54.46	55.38	63.35
Less: Income other than charges for maintenance	0.94	1.41	0.92	0.67	0.91	1.36	1.28	0.93	1.44	1.07	2.22	1.64	1.91	2.14
Net cost excluding capital items	54.51	52.33	53.51	56.06	51.20	61.72	69.41	46.06	52.49	54.82	54.25	52.82	53.47	61.21
Add: Debt charges	3.64	0.00	3.14	4.00	0.19	7.54	8.86	10.85	13.46	5.51	2.60	2.13	2.35	7.94
Net cost including capital items	58.15	52.33	56.65	60.06	51.39	69.26	78.27	56.91	65.95	60.33	56.85	54.95	55.82	69.15
1975–76 net cost including capital items	43.80	45.67	39.52	35.94	33.88	53.75	52.86	59.70	45.59	44.50	43.05	56.79	49.18	61.41

Table 1.5 *(cont'd)   Social Services Committee costs 1976–77*

| | Reception, observation and assessment centres | | Homes for the elderly | | | | | | | | | | |
	Y	Z	A	B	C	D	E	F	G	H	I	J	K
Places available	21	57	51	50	51	51	49	51	39	31	38	40	51
Average number of places occupied	18.9	44.4	47.0	48.0	47.1	48.2	45.9	44.1	37.7	25.6	35.9	38.6	46.4
Percentage occupied	90%	78%	92%	96%	92%	94%	94%	87%	97%	82%	94%	97%	91%
Net cost	£95 779	£208 063	£89 678	£80 629	£77 177	£94 894	£85 891	£106 732	£63 157	£76 244	£113 487	£94 274	£95 855
	Weekly cost per child		Weekly cost per resident										
	£	£	£	£	£	£	£	£	£	£	£	£	£
Employees	56.43	57.98	22.72	20.67	19.97	22.84	19.39	24.10	20.44	33.42	31.07	29.70	23.33
Maintenance of buildings and grounds	6.69	2.55	0.81	1.08	2.07	1.99	1.34	1.99	2.12	11.76	18.22	1.34	1.15
Fuel, light, cleaning materials and water	7.32	6.13	3.69	2.83	2.54	3.47	3.20	3.86	3.37	2.41	2.97	2.88	3.53
Rates and insurance	2.38	2.11	1.46	1.21	1.29	1.62	1.36	1.07	1.49	1.49	1.43	1.85	1.48
Furniture and equipment	0.88	1.13	0.29	0.46	0.37	0.43	0.33	0.20	0.23	1.24	0.84	0.34	0.88
Personal needs of residents	1.79	0.43	0.16	0.14	0.12	0.08	0.12	0.07	0.06	0.14	0.11	0.04	0.07
Provisions	6.85	4.63	3.79	3.71	3.32	3.23	2.97	3.26	2.86	4.09	3.29	3.87	3.78
Clothing	0.96	0.64	0.03	0.20	0.18	0.15	0.13	0.10	0.13	0.00	0.19	0.07	0.00
Laundry	0.32	0.11	0.23	0.47	0.30	0.23	0.26	0.26	0.14	1.12	0.95	0.87	0.31
Postage and telephones	0.72	0.86	0.08	0.08	0.09	0.10	0.17	0.18	0.12	0.18	0.14	0.09	0.13
Other expenses	1.37	1.94	0.07	0.04	0.10	0.10	0.05	0.12	0.04	0.16	0.06	0.11	0.04
Gross cost excluding capital items	85.71	78.51	33.33	30.89	30.35	34.24	29.32	35.21	31.00	56.01	59.27	41.16	34.70
Less: Income other than charges for maintenance	2.71	1.78	0.57	0.37	0.42	0.47	0.50	0.60	0.42	0.24	0.36	0.31	0.44
Net cost excluding capital items	83.00	76.73	32.76	30.52	29.93	33.77	28.82	34.61	30.58	55.77	58.91	40.85	34.26
Add: Debt charges	14.28	13.23	3.86	1.64	1.46	4.01	7.05	11.77	1.58	1.45	1.78	5.95	5.33
Net cost including capital items	97.28	89.96	36.62	32.16	31.39	37.78	35.87	46.38	32.16	57.22	60.69	46.80	39.59
1975–76 net cost including capital items	78.04	68.79	30.23	29.41	25.55	30.66	30.35	37.00	27.85	36.94	36.46	41.98	32.32

Table 1.5 *(cont'd)* *Social Services Committee costs 1976–77*

	Homes for the elderly (cont'd)					Homes for mentally handicapped (adults)							Home for physically handicapped	
	L	M	N	Total 14 homes open all year	Holiday home	a	b	c	d	e	f	Total 6 homes open all year	Resi-dential care	Day care
Places available	32	61	51	646	16	6	10	28	25	28	25	122	22	35
Average number of places occupied	30.7	58.1	47.6	600.9	12.5	4.0	9.4	25.0	22.9	24.2	23.8	109.3	9.6	19.9
Percentage occupied	96%	95%	93%	93%	78%	67%	94%	89%	92%	86%	95%	89%	44%	57%
Net cost	£80 608	£111 500	£109 800	£1 279 926	£54 366	£12 245	£24 038	£55 345	£56 434	£50 504	£57 503	£256 069	£146 699	
	Weekly cost per resident			*Average weekly cost per resident*	*Weekly cost per resident*							*Average weekly cost per resident*	*Weekly cost per person*	
	£	£	£	£	£	£	£	£	£	£	£	£	£	
Employees	28.30	22.72	22.61	23.78	41.45	39.12	25.11	23.16	25.77	23.53	25.35	25.02	89.70	
Maintenance of buildings and grounds	2.67	1.48	6.52	3.41	14.96	1.67	2.93	3.85	1.75	0.93	2.04	2.21	5.21	
Fuel, light, cleaning materials and water	4.50	2.45	2.91	3.17	3.54	3.42	3.25	4.85	4.62	4.90	3.74	4.38	10.83	
Rates and insurance	1.67	1.39	1.50	1.43	1.67	2.72	2.19	0.41	0.19	0.27	0.36	0.56	0.32	
Furniture and equipment	0.41	0.88	0.23	0.50	1.29	0.36	1.37	0.41	0.25	0.65	1.06	0.65	1.94	
Personal needs of residents	0.12	0.08	0.08	0.10	0.37	0.28	0.07	0.13	0.08	0.15	0.13	0.12	0.06	
Provisions	4.39	3.62	2.99	3.48	8.08	5.01	4.16	5.62	5.49	5.21	5.16	5.25	5.16	
Clothing	0.21	0.15	0.20	0.12	0.00	0.27	0.12	0.24	0.34	0.43	0.30	0.30	0.01	
Laundry	0.29	1.18	0.20	0.48	0.44	0.00	0.22	0.31	0.27	0.36	0.38	0.31	0.77	
Postage and telephones	0.23	0.09	0.16	0.11	0.88	0.80	0.38	0.19	0.22	0.21	0.15	0.23	0.78	
Other expenses	0.11	0.10	0.05	0.08	12.37	0.09	0.16	0.17	0.32	0.23	0.25	0.23	13.26	
Gross cost excluding capital items	42.90	34.14	37.45	36.66	85.05	53.74	39.96	39.34	39.30	36.87	38.92	39.26	128.04	
Less: Income other than charges for maintenance	1.01	0.26	0.60	0.46	1.88	0.50	1.41	1.27	1.00	0.82	1.17	1.08	16.43	
Net cost excluding capital items	41.89	33.88	36.85	36.20	83.17	53.24	38.55	38.07	38.30	36.05	37.75	38.18	111.61	
Add: Debt charges	8.47	2.89	7.40	4.63	0.48	5.11	10.42	4.34	8.99	3.99	8.66	6.73	36.12	
Net cost including capital items	50.36	36.77	44.25	40.83	83.65	58.35	48.97	42.41	47.29	40.04	46.41	44.91	147.73	
1975–76 net cost including capital items	42.24	31.02	33.60	32.76	71.42	54.69	43.80	34.16	39.35	31.67	38.56	37.46	134.00	

Table 1.5 (cont'd) *Social Services Committee costs 1976–77*

	Adult training centres					Total 5 centres open all year	Day nurseries				Total 4 nurseries open all year
	P	Q	R	S	T		aa	bb	cc	dd	
Places available	100	45	60	60	45	310	50	58	50	50	208
Average number of places occupied	74.3	52.9	45.2	52.0	58.6	283	33.2	45.2	45.4	50.9	174.7
Percentage occupied	74%	100%	75%	87%	100%	91%	66%	78%	91%	100%	84%
Number of days open	229	250	241	234	224	Av. 235.6	244	244	253	244	246.3
Net cost	£60 928	£70 649	£54 952	£69 070	£47 328	£302 927	£72 350	£55 652	£58 518	£53 071	£239 591
	Weekly cost per trainee					Average weekly cost per trainee	Weekly cost per child				Average weekly cost per child
	£	£	£	£	£	£	£	£	£	£	£
Employees	12.38	15.97	16.09	16.84	12.79	14.60	28.93	21.65	18.47	17.75	21.04
Maintenance of buildings and grounds	0.70	4.54	0.93	0.82	0.21	1.43	0.53	0.74	0.59	0.35	0.55
Fuel, light, cleaning materials and water	0.64	1.19	1.57	1.90	0.85	1.18	1.85	0.80	1.11	0.87	1.10
Rates and insurance	0.10	0.15	0.14	0.16	0.12	0.13	0.71	0.19	0.51	0.19	0.37
Furniture and equipment	0.06	0.07	0.20	0.05	0.05	0.08	0.17	0.17	0.16	0.19	0.18
Training and educational consumable materials	0.09	0.54	1.07	0.65	0.25	0.47	0.17	0.13	0.10	0.12	0.13
Provisions	0.80	0.55	0.53	0.43	0.52	0.58	1.69	1.38	1.25	1.73	1.50
Incentive payments to trainees	0.24	0.25	0.25	0.25	0.25	0.24	—	—	—	—	—
Postage and telephones	0.05	0.06	0.10	0.05	0.08	0.06	0.13	0.06	0.05	0.06	0.08
Other expenses	1.42	1.60	1.68	3.10	2.25	1.97	3.19	0.15	0.07	0.08	0.68
Gross cost excluding capital items	16.48	24.92	22.56	24.25	17.37	20.74	37.37	25.27	22.31	21.34	25.63
Less: Income other than charges for maintenance	0.26	0.33	0.92	0.91	0.34	0.52	0.09	0.04	0.16	0.02Dr	0.06
Net cost excluding capital items	16.22	24.59	21.64	23.34	17.03	20.22	37.28	25.23	22.15	21.36	25.57
Add: Debt charges	1.68	2.12	3.56	5.03	1.01	2.55	7.40	0.00	3.30	0.00	2.27
Net cost including capital items	17.90	26.71	25.20	28.37	18.04	22.77	44.68	25.23	25.45	21.36	27.84
1975–76 net cost including capital items	16.36	20.71	21.20	25.39	14.85	19.23	22.73	18.90	22.35	16.84	29.02

Table 1.6 *Chronic sickness: by socio-economic group, age, and sex, 1974 and 1975 (Great Britain) (Rates per thousand)*

	Males					Females				
	0–14	15–44	45–64	65 or over	All ages	0–14	15–44	45–64	65 or over	All ages
Persons reporting limiting long-standing illness										
Professional	36	66	161	239	88	28	79	134	286	84
Employers and managers	50	74	162	336	122	26	72	161	412	119
Intermediate and junior non-manual	40	83	274	363	148	20	66	200	417	148
Skilled manual and own account non-professional	45	85	237	397	138	35	93	202	419	132
Semi-skilled manual and personal service	47	84	265	373	155	25	95	260	437	197
Unskilled manual	56	112	390	377	226	44	115	264	419	246
All persons	46	83	234	366	140	29	84	209	424	155

Source: General Household Survey, 1974 and 1975

Table 1.7 *Allowances and services provided for the disabled (England)*

	Households assisted (000s)				Total cost per case (£s) 1975–76
	1972–73	1973–74	1974–75	1975–76	
Services provided by local authorities					
Telephone installation	16.6	21.8	22.0	14.8	
Telephone attachments	0.7	1.1	1.6	1.6	42.00
Telephone rental	12.2	28.8	47.1	69.0	
Television (supply)	2.2	2.5	2.2	1.6	
Television licence	4.3	6.5	16.0	38.5	
Radio (supply)	0.8	0.9	0.5	0.5	9.70
Other personal aids	118.2	142.5	159.4	191.2	
Adaptations (all property)	28.4	39.2	41.3	48.6	71.80
Holidays[a]	80.9	89.8	104.8	101.4	37.80
Allowances provided by central government					Weekly rates
Attendance allowance:					
Higher rate	77.0	90.5	98.6	106.9	10.60
Lower rate	—	40.1	59.7	79.0	7.10
Mobility allowance	—	—	—	7.0	5.00

[a] Relates to persons, not households.
Source: Department of Health and Social Security

Table 1.8 *Planning figures for services for the mentally handicapped compared with existing provision*

	Places for children (age 0–15)			Places for adults (age 16+)		
	Required		Provided	Required		Provided
Type of service	Per 100 000 total population	Total England and Wales 1969	Total England and Wales 1969	Per 100 000 total population	Total England and Wales 1969	Total England and Wales 1969
Day care or education for children under five	8	3 900	500	—	—	—
Education for children of school age						
In the community:						
(a) for children with severe mental handicap living in the community	56	27 400	23 400	—	—	—
(b) for children coming by day from hospital	6	2 900		—	—	—
In hospitals:						
(c) for in-patients	7	3 400	4 600	—	—	—
(d) for day patients	6	2 900	200	—	—	—
Occupation and training for adults						
In the community:						
(a) for adults living in the community	—	—	—	130	63 700	24 500
(b) for adults coming by day from hospital	—	—	—	20	9 800	100
In hospitals:						
(c) for in-patients	—	—	—	35	17 200	30 000
(d) for day patients	—	—	—	10	4 900	200
Residential care in the community (including short-stay)						
In local authority, voluntary or privately owned residential homes	10	4 900	1 800	60	29 400	4 300
Foster homes, lodgings, etc.	2	1 000	100	15	7 400	550
Hospital treatment						
For in-patients	13	6 400	7 400[a]	55	27 000	52 100[a]
For day patients	6	2 900	200	10	4 900	500

[a] NHS beds allocated to mental handicap.

Table 1.9   *Local authority personal social services, average level of provision and current expenditure per head (November 1975 prices)*

Service	Population base	Level of provision (per 1000 appropriate population)			Occupancy rate	Cost per occupied place, available place, meal or staff		Expenditure per head of population	
		Departmental guidelines	1975–76	1979–80		1975–76 £	1979–80 £	1975–76 £	1979–80 £
			Available places			Occupied place			
Residential									
Elderly	65 years+	25.0	18.1	17.9	95%	1210	1290	20.8	21.9
Younger disabled	15–64 years	—	0.45	0.46	95%	1210	1290	0.52	0.56
Mental handicap, adults	16 years+	0.78	0.28	0.35	95%	1240	1310	0.33	0.44
Mental handicap, children	0–15 years	0.44	0.17	0.24	86%	3240	3440	0.47	0.71
Mental illness	Total	0.19–0.30	0.10	0.12	90%	920	980	0.08	0.10
Children	0–17 years	—	3.5	3.9	84%	3340	3730	9.7	12.1
						Available place			
Day care									
Elderly	65 years+	3–4	2.6	2.7	—	560	560	1.5	1.5
Younger disabled	15–64 years	—	0.59	0.63	—	560	560	0.33	0.36
Mental handicap	Total	1.5	0.77	0.97	—	720	740	0.56	0.72
Mental illness	Total	0.60	0.10	0.19	—	560	560	0.06	0.11
Day nurseries	0–4 years	—	8.3	10.8	—	1010	1010	8.4	10.9
			Staff (WTE)[a]			Staff (WTE)[a]			
Other services									
Home helps	65 years+	12.0	6.5	7.1	—	2210	2210	14.3	15.7
Social workers	Total	—	0.44	0.49	—	4590	4690	2.0	2.3
			Meals per week			Meal			
Meals	65 years+	200	119	132	—	0.34	0.34	2.1	2.3
Boarding out	0–17 years	—	—	—	—	—	—	1.2	1.3
Aids, adaptations, etc.	Total	—	—	—	—	—	—	0.26	0.27
Intermediate treatment	5–17 years	—	—	—	—	—	—	0.08	0.17
Other LA services	Total	—	—	—	—	—	—	0.59	0.58
Administration	Total	—	—	—	—	—	—	2.5	2.6

[a] WTE = whole time equivalent

Table 1.10 Receptions into custody on remand: by age and ultimate disposal (*England and Wales*)

Type of disposal and age[a]	Males				Females			
	Percentages			Receptions 1976 (numbers)	Percentages			Receptions 1976 (numbers)
	1972	1975	1976		1972	1975	1976	
Found not guilty or not proceeded with								
Age 14–16	1.8	0.9	1.2	53	3.7	3.3	3.2	10
17–20	2.3	2.2	1.9	330	3.6	3.1	2.3	33
21+	4.7	4.4	3.6	1270	4.7	5.0	4.5	106
Given a non-custodial sentence								
Age 14–16	40.1	36.9	31.9	1435	64.9	68.0	60.2	189
17–20	43.0	42.5	37.3	6294	78.4	70.0	65.4	921
21+	47.7	45.9	41.4	14550	71.2	65.1	60.4	1426
Given a custodial sentence								
Age 14–16	57.3	58.0	63.0	2832	29.1	20.0	27.7	87
17–20	53.1	51.0	53.5	9039	15.0	19.0	22.6	319
21+	44.6	42.4	41.1	14456	21.5	22.6	21.9	517
Sentence or result of trial not known								
Age 14–16	0.9	4.2	3.9	178	2.2	8.6	8.9	28
17–20	1.5	4.3	7.2	1217	2.9	7.7	9.6	136
21+	2.8	7.3	13.8	4856	2.5	7.3	13.2	312
Total (=100%) (numbers)								
Age 14–16	3061	5337	4498		134	420	314	
17–20	17600	20069	16880		1304	1679	1409	
21+	34398	38385	35132		1968	2498	2361	

[a] Age on initial reception into remand custody.
Source: Home Office

Table 1.11 *Mental illness hospitals and units: discharges and deaths by age and duration of stay, 1975 (Great Britain) (000s)*

	Age group								All
	0–14	15–24	25–34	35–44	45–54	55–64	65–74	75+	ages
Discharges									
Under 1 month	0.8	14.9	25.1	21.6	19.2	12.7	9.2	5.9	109.5
1 month but under 1 year	1.6	9.5	14.6	13.2	14.7	12.2	10.6	6.2	82.6
1 year but under 5 years	0.1	0.5	0.7	0.6	0.8	0.6	0.7	0.7	4.7
5 years but under 15 years	—	—	0.1	0.2	0.3	0.3	0.3	0.2	1.3
15 years and over	—	—	—	—	0.2	0.3	0.4	0.3	1.3
Total all durations	2.5	24.9	40.6	35.6	35.1	26.2	21.2	13.3	199.3
Deaths									
Under 1 month	—	—	—	—	0.1	0.3	0.8	1.7	3.0
1 month but under 1 year	—	—	—	—	0.1	0.4	1.3	3.0	4.9
1 year but under 5 years	—	—	—	—	0.1	0.3	0.9	2.6	4.0
5 years but under 15 years	—	—	—	—	0.1	0.2	0.4	1.1	1.8
15 years and over	—	—	—	—	0.1	0.3	0.6	1.0	2.0
Total all durations	—	—	0.1	0.2	0.5	1.4	4.0	9.4	15.6

Source: Mental Health Inquiry, 1975, *Department of Health and Social Security*

Table 1.12 *Unemployment in the United Kingdom (000s and rates)*

							1977	
	1971	1972	1973	1974	1975	1976	Qtr 1	Qtr 2
Unemployed (excluding school leavers)								
Males	655.5	715.2	510.2	504.4	749.5	975.2	1031.5	981.5
Females								
married	45.7	52.5	37.9	33.1	69.4	113.5	139.8	144.9
non-married	74.7	87.2	63.0	62.3	114.3	176.7	204.5	185.7
Total	775.8	854.9	611.0	600.1	929.0	1270.3	1375.8	1312.1
Unemployed school leavers	16.3	20.7	7.7	15.1	48.6	88.4	42.0	82.5
Unemployment rate (percentages)								
excluding school leavers	3.4	3.7	2.6	2.6	3.9	5.4	5.6	5.6

Source: Department of Employment

Table 1.13 *Census of population reports and population projection of children 0–19 years in the UK (000s)*

	Census enumerated		Mid-year estimates			Projections		
	1951	1961	1966	1971	1976	1981	1986	1991
Boys								
0–4	2215	2162	2451	2310	1925	1646	2010	2289
5–9	1885	1954	2181	2400	2282	1902	1622	1985
10–14	1682	2206	1956	2174	2387	2268	1886	1607
15–19	1564	1870	2158	1984	2184	2400	2281	1900
Total under 20	7346	8192	8746	8868	8777	8216	7799	7781
Girls								
0–4	2111	2051	2339	2192	1814	1555	1899	2163
5–9	1804	1862	2060	2278	2164	1792	1532	1875
10–14	1629	2102	1850	2057	2266	2149	1776	1516
15–19	1611	1825	2077	1876	2068	2277	2158	1785
Total under 20	7155	7840	8325	8403	8313	7773	7365	7339

Source: Census of Population Reports and Population Projections 1976–2016, The Registrar General's mid-year estimates of the population, *Office of Population Censuses and Surveys*

Table 1.14 *Circumstances in which children came into the care of local authorities (United Kingdom) (000s)*

	England and Wales					Scotland	Northern Ireland
Admissions to care of local authorities	1972	1973	1974	1975	1976	1976	1975
Section 1 of the Children Act 1948							
No parent or guardian, abandoned or lost	1.1	1.3	1.4	1.6	1.3	1.8	0.03
Death of or deserted by mother (including child illegitimate mother unable to provide)	7.8	7.5	7.1	6.1	5.4	1.3	0.33
Incapacity of parent or guardian	21.1	20.3	17.6	15.8	15.2	2.9	0.32
Parent or guardian in prison or remanded in custody	0.9	1.0	0.9	0.8	0.9	0.2	0.01
Family homeless (eviction or other cause)	3.0	2.8	2.4	1.7	1.3	0.4	0.03
Unsatisfactory home conditions	3.5	4.4	4.7	4.9	5.2	0.2	0.15
Other reasons	6.2	6.7	8.0	8.7	10.2	0.4	0.04
Court orders							
Court orders (Children and Young Persons Act 1969)	9.6	9.3	10.0	11.3	12.0	0.1	0.17
Court orders (family proceedings)	0.3	0.5	0.5	0.7	0.9	0.5	—
Total admissions to care	53.4	53.6	52.7	51.6	52.4	16.1	1.09
Interim care orders or remand to care	10.4	9.9	10.2	10.7	11.6	—	0.03

Sources: Department of Health and Social Security; Welsh Office; Scottish Education Department, Social Work Services Group; Northern Ireland Office

Further Reading

1. Maslow, A. (1964) *Motivation and Personality*. New York: Harper & Row.
2. Weber, M. (1947) *The Theory of Social and Economic Organisation*. New York: Oxford University Press.
3. Brech, E. F. L. (1957) *Organisation: The Framework of Management*. London: Longman.
4. Dogan, M. (1975) *The Mandarins of Western Europe*. New York: Halsted Press.
5. Etzioni, A. (1964) *Modern Organisations*. Hemel Hempstead: Prentice-Hall.
6. Fox, A. (1966) *Industrial Sociology and Industrial Relations*. London: HMSO.
7. O'Shaughnessy, J. (1966) *Business Organisation*. London: George Allen & Unwin.
8. Roberts, G. K. (1970) *Political Parties and Pressure Groups in Britain*. London: Weidenfeld & Nicolson.
9. Shonfield, A. (1974) *Modern Capitalism*. Oxford: Oxford University Press.

2

Organizations: Theory and Models

GENERAL OBJECTIVES

After reading this chapter and, where necessary, the appropriate references the student should be able to analyse relationships between organizational goals, structures, processes and development through the application of appropriate theoretical models and concepts.

LEARNING OBJECTIVES

The student should be able to:

1. identify major questions raised by principal theories/approaches to organizations;
2. analyse inter-relationships between organizational goals, structures and processes, indicating factors influencing organizational structures and design, and relationships between behaviour and structure;
3. attempt to diagnose deficiencies in a particular organization's structure.

In Chapter 1 we examined the concept of goals in formal work organizations without analysing the relationship of those goals to the structure of organizations. In this chapter we shall look at a number of views related to the problem of how to organize. In particular, it will be the aim of this chapter to identify questions raised by the principal theories/approaches to organizations. These questions will be principally concerned with the inter-relationships between organizational goals, structures and processes. The business student should be provided with a degree of diagnostic knowledge to enable him to make judgements in relation to the deficiencies of organizations with which he is familiar.

2.1   WHAT IS A FORMAL WORK ORGANIZATION?

Edgar Schein (*Organization Psychology* (1965)) defines a formal organization as 'the rational co-ordination of the activities of a number of people for the achievement of some common explicit purpose or goal, through division of labour and function, and through a hierarchy of authority and responsibility'.

It is important to note that this definition refers to the co-ordination of activities and not the co-ordination of people. It is apparent therefore that when Schein settled on this initial definition he was to some extent thinking along similar lines to the views of Weber who, as we saw in Chapter 1, talked about defining job roles rather than the activities of people in order to control the effects of the goals which individuals inevitably bring with them to their work. On the other hand, it is difficult to believe that such a differentiation will in fact result in the control both writers advocate. Chapter 1 has attempted to show the interlocking nature of individuals, and informal and formal groups within work organizations. If this interlocking structure does in fact exist, it seems impossible to separate as distinctly as Weber does the concept of organization from the behaviour of people.

Schein admitted that this definition is not totally adequate, but is a reasonable starting point in trying to determine the characteristics, and therefore the key structural points, of an organization. This was the starting point taken by F. W. Taylor in designing his 'scientific' model of management and by Weber in his 'ideal bureaucratic model'.

Taylor aimed for a work organization which would achieve greater efficiency and effectiveness than those existing in his day. He made two primary assumptions:

1. that people are motivated by financial rewards;
2. that organizations must consist of the following prescribed characteristics:
    (a)   a clearly defined division of labour,
    (b)   the employment of highly specialized personnel, and
    (c)   a distinct hierarchy of authority.

Taylor approached the design of his blueprint for an organization in a systematic way. His model was based on a thorough analysis of the work to be done in an organization. In order to perform this analysis he, together with F. B. Gilbreth, developed techniques of studying work, including method study and work measurement. Using these analytical techniques, Taylor studied men handling pig-iron at the Bethlehem Steel Company in America. As a result of this study he developed four main principles in relation to the design and structuring of work organization. He believed organizational design should be based on:

1. An analysis of the work to be done in the organization in order to determine the most efficient method of doing it. Basically this analysis involves breaking jobs down to the smallest workable element and structuring the organization of work around the efficient operation of each of these elements.
2. Careful selection of people who can best perform the work associated with the individual job elements determined above.
3. Close supervision of the people recruited to ensure that they perform their work as prescribed from the analysis in 1 above.
4. Clearly placing accountability in the hands of management.

Taylor used these principles to redesign the work organization at the Bethlehem Steel Company. As a result, the tonnage of pig-iron loaded increased from 12½ to 47½ tons per man.

From his studies Taylor developed both a motivation theory and the foundations for an organizational theory, the 'classical' model.

2.2   TAYLOR'S MOTIVATION THEORY (SCIENTIFIC MANAGEMENT)

Taylor's motivation theory focuses on two aspects: the physical capabilities of employees, and economic incentives linked to work performance. The major premise on which
this approach is based is that if material rewards are closely related to work efforts, the
worker will respond with the maximum performance he is capable of.

Thus Taylor concentrated his researches on analysing the ways in which people perform work and on the physical characteristics of the human body. From this developed
the science of ergonomics. Taylor's aim was to view machines and the people operating
them as a complete system. The operatives were as much a part of the machine as the
control handles, buttons, cogs, cutting tools, etc. In other words people function as
appendages of the machines they use. This directed the search to find measurements
related to the physical limits of human performance in dimensions such as loads, pace
and fatigue. Once these limits were determined it was merely a matter of linking payment systems as closely as possible to an output level that an average human being could
be expected to produce. From this belief developed the search for methods of measuring work, a search which has continued to the present day.

2.3   CLASSICAL ORGANIZATION THEORY

The classical model is based on three fundamental characteristics:

1.   division of labour
2.   unity of command
3.   a set of principles which influence the relationship between division of labour and
     authority.

The classical writers (primarily L. Gulick and L. Urwick) needed no convincing in relation to the principle of division of labour, the value of which had been demonstrated by
Adam Smith in 1776. Smith had shown that in an example concerning the manufacture
of pins, one man performing all the processes himself could produce only 20 pins
per day. By dividing the labour into a number of simple tasks (i.e., wire drawing,
straightening, cutting) output was increased to 4800 pins per worker per day. The major
premise on which division of labour is based is that the more a particular job can be
broken down into its smallest component parts, the more specialized and the more skilled a
worker can become in carrying out his part of the job. The classical administration
theory is based on the conclusion that the more skilled the worker becomes in fulfilling
his particular function, the more efficient becomes the whole organization. The only
problem which the classicists saw resulting from this division of labour was the co-
ordination of all the different functions that resulted. They therefore saw the need for a
management control system based on the principle of unity of command.

By unity of command was envisaged a control system stemming from a single decision
point. It was recognized that one individual has a limited scope in terms of his ability to
control the work of others effectively. Therefore there is a need for a hierarchy of control positions based on the span of control limitations of individuals and the overall size
of the organization. Thus the concept of a pyramid of control is developed (see Fig. 2.1).

The first of the classical principles influencing the relationship between division of
labour and authority relates to methods used to group workers together. Specialization
was considered to be the guiding principle: all tasks of the same or similar purpose
should be grouped together. Departments and divisions should be formed from

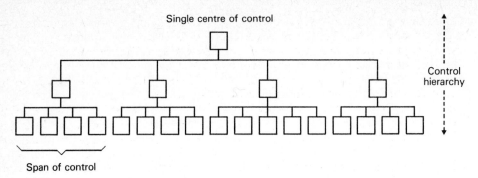

Figure 2.1   *Pyramid of control*

the groupings relating to sub-goals of the corporate goals of the total organization. From this develops the concept of functional departments we know today, e.g. production departments, personnel departments, marketing departments, etc.

The second principle was that specialization should be related to the type of clientèle, and the division of labour modelled accordingly. Thus, in the case of a motor-car manufacturer producing both cheap and expensive models there would be a need for two organizational hierarchies relating to the two different product classes.

The third principle relates to an organization which has aspects of geographical separation. All jobs in a specific geographical area should be grouped together. Under this principle it was considered to be perfectly reasonable for units of the army, navy and air force based overseas to be under one single command.

Questions Raised by the Classical Model

The following are examples of many questions raised which the student might well spend profitable time debating with his colleagues.

1. Is it legitimate to be as prescriptive as Taylor and the classical writers advocate? (Taylor stated the principles which he considered ought to be the basis for the structure of formal work organizations. He formed these principles on the basis of two fundamental sets of factors:

    (a)   a basic set of organizational assumptions, and
    (b)   the use of a set of analytical techniques to both design and measure work methods and outputs which he considered to be perfectly legitimate.

    If these factors are in any way questionable there must be doubts concerning the validity of the model. To be prescriptive the model would have to be constructed on a firm basis of unchallengeable issues.)

2. Is scientific analysis of work the only issue to be considered when looking at specialization? It cannot be denied that the techniques of analysis developed by Taylor and Gilbreth have had most widespread and useful application right through to the present day. On the other hand, can the results of method study and work measurement be considered in isolation? The student is asked to consider the effects of individual differences between people; the variable availability of manpower; the culture of the environment (e.g., is what is possible in the USA equally possible in the

UK or Russia?); the ecology and climate of the environment; politics; unions; and technological change in relation to the choice of structures for an organization.

3. Is it legitimate to view people as appendages to machines? The behaviour of people in work situations is examined in Chapter 4. At this stage it is valuable to consider the possible implications of people working with machines. In what ways does boredom affect performance? This is an example of the sort of question we might well be asking. What factors influence work performance other than the physical capabilities measured by Taylor? The student should consider how health, financial problems, family problems, political sympathy and similar issues might have a bearing on an individual's attitude to, and therefore performance of, his job role.

4. Is division of labour of the type prescribed by classical writers the most efficient way of performing a work function? There is no doubt that Adam Smith obtained significant increases in output by introducing a divison of labour into his work organization. But does something like the law of diminishing returns come into play if one adopts the classical belief of breaking work down to the smallest workable elements? How small a job are we going to ask people to perform? Are there negative effects which result from high repetition of simple tasks which Taylor did not consider?

2.4   THE HUMAN RELATIONS MODEL

The human relations model had its birth in the studies of Elton Mayo at the Western Electric Company, Chicago, between 1927 and 1932. Mayo did not set out to challenge the scientific model, but rather to perfect it. The initial aim was to improve the classical model by understanding the relationship between specific structural arrangements and work output. If the working conditions, for example, were improved would the workers' output increase? This question represented Mayo's initial focus of attention. He experimented with improvements such as the level of illumination, hours of work, and the number of rest pauses.

The experiments were performed at the Hawthorne Works of the company. Initially, the results of the experiments suggested support for the classical model, for in every case output increased. But the results were perplexing for output not only went up in the workrooms with better lighting, but also in the control room. The results became even more confusing when the physical improvements were withdrawn. When the lighting was reduced in intensity from 10 to 3 foot candles in the experimental room, production actually increased instead of decreasing as Mayo had anticipated. Similarly when the rest pauses were withdrawn and the hours put back to their original level, output increased to the highest level recorded by the experimenters up to that stage in the exercise.

To ensure consistency in terms of experimental findings, and therefore the conclusions to be drawn from them, observations were continued for several years. The most significant conclusion Mayo drew was that at least equal attention should be given to the behaviour of the people doing the work as to a detailed analysis of the work to be done. No simple and direct relationship was found to exist between the physical working conditions and the rate of production. No evidence was obtained to support the hypothesis that increased output follows from a relief of fatigue.

What Mayo did observe was the existence and importance of small groups within the formal organization. The women working in the Relay Assembly Test Room were friendly and talked and gossiped throughout the working day about personal matters. The supervisor (who was also a research worker) had become accepted as an important member of this small social group, and the whole group developed an identity within the purpose of the formal organization. On the other hand, the 14 men engaged in wiring and soldering the telephone switchboards in the Bank Wiring Room demonstrated different characteristics: they were isolated from the other groups of workers and subjected to special study. They were therefore also isolated from other group-imposed output restrictions and should, if Taylor's assumptions were correct, have worked as hard as they could. The payment system was designed to test Taylor's motivation theory, and a piecework payment system was designed specifically linking output with payment levels. Therefore the harder the men worked, the more payment they would have received. In fact the group developed a norm which they regarded as the level of output for a proper day's work. Any worker exceeding this norm was ridiculed. There was a strong feeling among the men that they should not allow the foreman to know what output they were actually capable of achieving. The basic feeling was that if too much output was achieved pay rates would drop and redundancies would occur, and if too little was produced they might also risk losing their jobs. As a result effective control of the group was exercised by the group itself, and not by the representative of the formal organization, the foreman.

As a result of his Hawthorne Studies Mayo concluded:

1.   That the amount of work carried out by a worker is not determined by his physical capacity but by his social capacity.
2.   That non-economic rewards play a central role in determining the motivation and happiness of the individual worker.
3.   That the highest degree of specialization is by no means the most efficient form of division of labour.
4.   That workers do not react to management and its norms and rewards as individuals, but as members of a group.

Mayo's conclusions have significant impacts on the following organization design issues:

1.   *Division of labour and specialization.* The Hawthorne Study suggests that the scientific model principles apply only to the point where the role expected of a human being is satisfying and self-respecting. To achieve this, organizations should consider the extent to which work can be broken down into simple elements and still remain satisfying to workers. Secondly, the physical layout of the work organization cannot be thought about without giving some consideration to informal relationships between people. The Relay Assembly Room study suggests the need to structure work situations so that workers can form satisfying relationships with each other and with the management of the organization. (Students should consider any mass production system structured on flow-line principles with which they are familiar. Are there any symptoms which may relate labour relations problems to the nature of the work situation?)
2.   *Leadership.* The organization cannot ignore informal leadership impacts on the setting and enforcing of group norms. The scientific model assumes that the leadership required in the formal work situation rests solely in the hands of management. The Bank Wiring Room study indicated that informal leadership influences can be much stronger than the influence of management. The implication here for the design of organization is that the structure cannot ignore leadership influences outside the formal control hierarchy. This must seriously question the classical unity of command notion. Thus, no matter how carefully we study the tasks to be performed, work out the best methods of performing the tasks, train people to do the work in accordance with these methods, define responsibilities and apply close

supervision, the human factor can have a negative influence unless the organization recognizes its existence.

3. *Communication*. Important implications for the systems of communication in organizations resulted from both studies. In the Relay Assembly Room the supervisor (who as you will remember was a member of the experimental team) fully explained matters to the workers and reassured them. This factor was highlighted by the workers when the results of the experiments were analysed. They stated that the good relations built up between themselves and the supervisor were partly because of the care taken to communicate with them. They also stated this was untypical of their normal supervision. Their interpretation of this was that management was especially interested in them and therefore they responded with that extra effort and commitment. On the other hand, the Bank Wiring Room study illustrates the effect of communication breakdown. The work group had determined output levels which they thought management would have regarded as acceptable. In fact management were trying to achieve higher output levels but consistently failed to break through the communication barriers set up by the group.

It is apparent, therefore, that the human relationists are arguing that organizations should be viewed as social environments which stimulate individuals to strive towards organizational goals. The framework of their arguments rests on the following beliefs:

1. That social grouping will tend to stimulate co-operation at the expense of organizational conflict. If these social groupings are in large part engineered by the organization then the co-operation and effort of the group will be directed towards supporting the organization. The evidence of the behaviour of the workers in the Relay Assembly Room is often stated to support this belief. If, on the other hand, the social grouping is allowed to develop on its own without any influence from the organization then the resulting group effort can very easily run counter to the interests of the organization. The Bank Wiring Room study is stated to be evidence of this. It is not suggested that conflict will be removed, but that destructive conflict where individuals are constantly working against each other and against the goals of the organization will be minimized.
2. That these engineered social groupings will, to a large extent, achieve the goals of the organization, whilst being satisfying to individual members of each group.
3. That, as a result, organizations so structured will achieve an optimum state of equilibrium between the goals of the organization and the goals of individual workers. As a consequence the organization is likely to experience positive human behaviour, such as high productivity, rather than negative behaviour, such as high absenteeism.

These beliefs are based on the one over-riding assumption that the most satisfying place to work will also prove to be the most efficient. The human relations approach adds a further dimension to the factors which need to be considered in the design of work organizations: the behaviour of people as individuals, as members of groups, and as individuals performing job roles which attempt to specify required behaviour patterns.

The human relationists argue that consideration of the behavioural dimension is necessary because rational allocation of work and authority, as advocated by the classical approach, does not necessarily meet with the approval of the people being asked to do the work. The fact that the methods and processes have been scientifically analysed and rationally designed does not mean that they will be accepted. For instance, scientific rationality of the classical type does not consider boredom and frustration. Machines can accommodate simple repetitive tasks with consistent efficiency, but many people find such tasks intolerably boring, so much so that the frustrations produced can and do lead to aggression. This aggression often has serious negative consequences for the organization. Many people believe that the lack of satisfaction produced by modern mass production methods has been responsible for a great deal of the industrial relations problems of the industrialized western world, particularly during the last half century.

By combining the classical and human relations approaches we obtain important insights into what an organization really is. These insights suggest the existence of two systems within what might appear to be one system. These two systems are called the formal organization and the informal organization. The first is that structure which the classical approach concentrates on, i.e., the organizational design produced by management. It is that organization which is identified and described by the dimensions of division of labour, hierarchy of supervision and control, systems of rules and regulations, and patterns of administration. The second is the system identified by the human relationist. It is concerned with the pattern of relationships which exists between the people who work in the formal work organization in addition to those prescribed by job roles. The informal organization is concerned with understanding relationships and behaviour which result from the interaction of people and work within the formal organization. Above all it is concerned with understanding the determinants of human behaviour in a work setting. Why are some individuals more effective than others as leaders? Is informal leadership different from the leadership required by a formal job role? What factors produce boredom, frustration and aggression? How important are the informal groups to the formal organization? (These questions are examined in Chapters 4 and 6.)

Questions Raised by the Human Relations Approach

1. What effect is consideration of the human relations school likely to have on the classical organization dimensions? For example:
   (a) Is the pyramid structure shown in Fig. 2.1 likely to be affected, and if so, because of what issues?
   (b) Is the selection process of people for management positions likely to be affected?
   (c) Will the selection of people for all posts be affected by human relations considerations?

Let us look at these questions briefly. If the human relationists are right, the most important structure is a harmonious working group who have both an intrinsic interest in and control over the work they are doing. This means, first, that the groups should have sufficiently demanding and interesting work to perform in order to minimize boredom and frustration. Secondly, it means that the group has a sufficient level of delegated authority to control the majority of the work activities for which it is responsible. In order to achieve these two characteristics the pyramid structure would have to be flattened (i.e., the number of levels reduced) in order to reduce the fragmentation and to increase the authority of each level. Such a flattening would, as a consequence, simplify the communication networks and increase the chance of attaining integration of the goals of different groups into a corporate goal for the organization.

The Hawthorne studies demonstrated the importance of both formal and informal leadership in the behaviour of working groups. The conclusion is that the relationship between the group and its leadership is a crucial issue, particularly if the dominant leadership position rests with the group and not with the formally appointed manager or supervisor. The important question is: Would involvement of members of the working group in the selection of its supervisor or manager increase the chance of the person appointed being accepted as the leader of the group?

Similarly, changes in group membership are an important issue. Will a newcomer fit in and be accepted by the others in the group? Will the group's cohesiveness continue? Should the group members be involved in the decision to introduce a new individual to the group? These are some of the questions which the human relations approach to the structure of organizations raises.

2. How accurate is it to view an organization as a possible large, happy family in which all the members are working harmoniously together? The student should consider such issues as technological development and the human side of the organization. Is it likely, for example, that the introduction of automation which results in the loss of jobs will also lead to a happy, harmonious set of relationships among the employees in an organization? Similarly, will leadership and explanation produce an understanding and positive response from the workers involved, particularly those whose jobs are lost?

3. Is the human relations approach equally applicable at all levels in an organization? In other words, the student should consider whether groups of shopfloor workers react in similar ways to groups of senior managers in the boardroom of a private company. In what ways is the behaviour likely to be different, and for what reasons?

2.5 STRUCTURAL FUNCTIONALISM

To many people the harmony concept of the human relations approach is unacceptable. It does not seem reasonable to conceive of a formal work organization consisting of many groupings of different individuals all working together harmoniously towards a common goal. There are far too many different and divergent individual goals existing in society for this to be the case. At best we can only hope to minimize the extent to which the goals of individuals run against the goals of the organization. This is the view of the structuralists who argue that the human relationists have presented a very distorted picture of the nature of work organizations.

The structuralists argue that most organizations are large and complex social units consisting of many interacting sub-units. The goals and interests of these sub-units, for example, groups of production workers, supervisors, managers, office workers, are widely variable. They are sometimes in harmony, but more often than not they are in diametric opposition to each other. For there to exist the happy family idea suggested by the human relationists the goals and interests of the sub-units would have to be acting in common accord – a highly unlikely state of affairs. For example, it is unlikely that senior management will have the same view as shopfloor workers over such issues as pay increases, distribution of profits and the fringe benefits which should accompany employment. The structuralists argue that the human relations model at best is referring to possible ways of making work more pleasant, and thereby possibly reducing the extent of conflict over such issues. They argue that we can never design an organization where individuals working for a third party will find work a wholly satisfying activity.

The structuralists' view revolves essentially around the belief that formal work organizations inevitably alienate workers. This inevitable alienation process results from:

1. The fact that the majority of workers have no share at all in the ownership of land, buildings, machinery or the products or services provided by the work organization. This means that most individuals cannot have the same degree of involvement in the organization as would be the case if ownership was wholly or partially theirs.

2. The trend towards increasing specialization in formal work organizations reduces the opportunity for most individuals to have a complete picture of what is going on in them. In many cases, particularly in the large manufacturing organizations and government departments, specialization is so great that the resulting high fragmentation of individual job roles makes work seem almost meaningless to the individuals employed in them.
3. The fact that irrespective of the extent to which authority and responsibility are delegated to subordinate groups in a formal work organization, workers are inevitably controlled, and not in control of what they do. They do not determine how their efforts will ultimately be utilized, nor do they have sufficient influence to alter fundamentally the conditions under which their work is performed.

What we need to be aware of, say the structuralists, is the extent to which a formal work organization can be modelled in order to minimize the alienation which results. The classical approach provides us with a prescriptive and most useful model for the structure of the formal work organization, that is, the need to determine objectives and specifications for work, methods of grouping, authority systems and control systems. The human relations approach provides ideas for making the lot of the individual worker more pleasant and acceptable, thereby minimizing the conflict produced by the alienation process.

Functionalism is concerned with the concept of order in formal work organizations, and in particular how order seems to prevail in both organizations and society irrespective of the changes in personnel which are constantly taking place. In particular the question of how people manage to coexist in organizations and society is the key issue. In other words, the structural-functionalists are seeking to understand the relationship between the parts and the whole in an organization, and in particular to identify how stability is, for the most part, achieved.

Structural-functionalism evolved from the Hawthorne studies. It is argued that Mayo and later writers missed the following essential issues:

1. An analysis of the perceived conflicts of interest which were evident amongst different groups of workers at the Western Electricity Company.
2. An analysis of the unintended actions and results that were constantly occurring.

The first issue is of importance since we need to know much more about the goals of individuals and groups in an organization, and the factors which contribute to a wide diversity of interests, values and beliefs. Until our knowledge is greater we are in danger of over-simplifying the nature and behaviour of organizations, and of drawing conclusions from available evidence which are incomplete or at worst wholly inappropriate. For example, the significance of the norms of the informal group in the Bank Wiring Room was missed by the human relationists. The importance of informal norms and goals is that they result from the beliefs and perceptions of individuals making up groups and, as W. I. Thomas once stated, 'If men define situations as real, they are real in their consequences'. The conclusion here is that we need to take into account conflicts of interest and differing value bases if we are to begin to understand organizations.

The second issue concerns the common organizational phenomenon of results and functions within an organization being quite unintended by management. This issue is obviously very closely related to the first since the Bank Wiring Room example is also an example of an unintended outcome of managerial decision-making. The men's output levels were not the ones intended and expected by management. Robert Merton studied this phenomenon of unintended consequences, and produced some very valuable insights into organization theory. Merton's most significant points are that:

1. Behaviour is not always what it seems (the output restrictions operated by the men

in the Bank Wiring Room were not an attempt to sabotage management as they might at first have seemed).
2. The consequences of actions may be very different from those intended.
3. Very often what is thought bad shows up on analysis to be vital.
4. Many accepted functions may in fact be harmful to the organization.
5. A functional alternative may perform much better than the structure actually in operation.
6. Conflict in fact has a latent positive function, for example, it is a spur to vital adaptation and change, very often performs a necessary safety valve function, and often contributes to the maintenance of organizational stability.

Questions Raised by the Structural-Functionalist Approach

These questions should, if possible, be discussed in a group.

1. If the structural-functionalists are giving valuable insights into the nature and operation of work organizations, in what ways can these insights help in the day-to-day operation of an enterprise?
2. If the problem is that no situation is truly forecastable, what value are the observations made by Robert Merton to the practising manager?
3. Consider how the structural-functionalists would design an ideal model for work organizations. State the essential features of such a model.

At this stage you may find it difficult and somewhat confusing to answer these questions. You will find that the remaining theories and concepts developed in this chapter help to bring greater clarity to the points and views raised by the structural-functionalists.

2.6   THE SYSTEMS APPROACH

J. O'Shaughnessy describes a system as 'a set of interdependent parts which together form a unitary whole that performs some function'. The concept of a system is shown diagrammatically in Fig. 2.2.

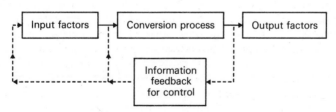

Figure 2.2   *Concept of a system*

A production department in a manufacturing organization can clearly be viewed in this way (Fig. 2.3). The input factors can be summarized as workers, money, machinery, materials, knowledge and skill; the conversion process is the process of actual manufacture where the raw material is processed by workers and machines; and the output the products of the organization, for example, motor-cars, pneumatic tyres, food products etc. The feedback of information is concerned with such issues as quality sampling, levels of production, breakdowns in production, and so on.

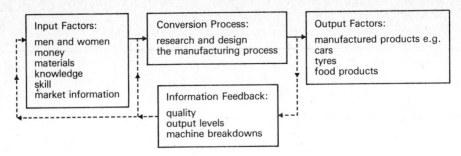

Figure 2.3   *Interrelatedness of factors within an organization*

Within this large system there are obviously many sub-systems, the activities of one worker's job being a system in itself. Similarly, the whole organization can be viewed as a sub-system of society.

The general concern of the functionalists is to understand the systems which make up an organization, and in particular the demands which a system makes on its component parts. This approach necessitates definition of the systems boundaries; the relationship of a system's component sub-systems; and the relationship of the system itself to other systems.

The Systems Boundary

Although it is relatively easy to describe the concept of a system it is nothing like as easy to specify the limits of any particular system. For example, it is quite possible to identify the obvious components of the system related to a single job role within a department, but this single job role will be part of a section system, which will be part of a department system, which will itself be a sub-system of the whole organization. Similarly, the organization itself will be a sub-system of several societal systems – the economic system, for example. The answer to the problem is in many ways related to the particular focus of study. If we study work in the way Taylor did, then the systems boundary surrounding each job role is much more definable than the systems boundary of the whole organization with its tentacles stretching out into all kinds of much more complex societal systems. Thus, when Taylor and Gilbreth were studying the behaviour of individual workers they determined the systems boundary as incorporating the machine plus its operator. The operator was seen as an integral part of the machine, and one could not be considered in isolation from the other. The application of the systems approach at this level is now fairly commonplace. Terms such as man-machine system are frequently referred to by ergonomists.

It is not always easy to be precise about the systems boundary even at this highly focused level. Systems are so interlinked that it is difficult to isolate one single system for study without giving weight to its interaction with other systems. Of course, this is a vicious circle concept for as soon as other systems are considered, the interaction of these with other systems is equally relevant. It is therefore necessary at times to acknowledge relationships between systems, but to separate systems artificially for study. What is essential is to recognize that the system has been artificially isolated, and that any conclusions should be tempered by this fact.

From an organizational perspective we need to study the sub-systems within an organization in order to understand the functions they perform in relation to:

1. The organization's ability to adapt to change;
2. The contribution of each sub-system towards goal attainment;
3. The integration of all the different functions within an organization into a corporate whole.

The Relationship of Individual Systems to Other Systems

It is apparent that we cannot consider individual systems as self-contained systems or *closed systems* as they are called, but as integrated into a whole network of interconnected systems. This concept is called the *open systems approach*. The open systems approach concentrates on attempting to show the dependence of one system on another. It stresses the interrelatedness of various phenomena, and reminds us that just to relate one narrow variable to another without taking account of the social context in which they function is illogical.

This is such a wide approach, with so many different variables, that simple answers cannot be expected; it is really a questioning approach, investigating structures, processes, interrelationships, roles, goals, behaviour, and so on. In attempting to obtain answers, business students add new insights into their level of understanding of the structure and functioning of organizations.

Organizations as Social Systems: Talcott Parsons

Talcott Parsons constructed a model of all the parts of a social system in order to try to identify the working forces and mechanisms. He attempted to show how a network of interlocking systems and sub-systems function, thus meeting the needs of each other. The essential need is the one identified by the structuralists: *order*. Parsons saw order being achieved by the interlocking of three systems – personality, cultural and social. He saw these systems as interlocking because there exists an over-riding *central value system* in society. This central value system is the very basis of society which provides its stability and continuity. Thus general behaviour is made more or less predictable and society persists despite changes in membership.

The term central value system means a set of beliefs or values which people hold and which form the basic element of stability in every society. Therefore, because the majority of people within the British cultural system would uphold most of the same common basic values, there is a binding force which holds that society together. This value system will change from country to country but will basically be constant within a particular and stable community. Individuals carry this value system with them in relation to every system with which they come into contact, including the family, memberships of clubs and societies and work organizations.

Parsons views organizations in the same way as a social system. He is concerned with trying to identify the central value system which ensures the continuance of organizations. In particular his search is for the relationship between the central value system and the attainment of organizational goals. His view is that integration is attained by the definition of roles within an organization. Organizational goals reflect in some way the goals of society, which reflect society's central value system. Therefore Parsons' conclusion is that the nature of individual job roles within an organization is determined in relation to the expectations which the individual role occupants bring to their job.

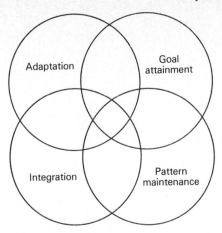

Figure 2.4   *Parsons' functional requirements of organizations*

Parsons also tried to explain the linking concept between an organization and society. He stresses that the primary linkage is the central value system which is common to organizations and the society in which they are situated. Against this central value system all organizations have *functional requirements*. Parsons identifies these as adaptation, goal attainment, integration and pattern maintenance. (See Fig. 2.4.)

By adaptation is meant the need for formal work organizations to be sufficiently flexible to accommodate change; integration relates to the need for effective linkage of all the parts of a formal work organization into a corporate whole; goal attainment refers to the accomplishment of objectives both by the individuals making up the organization and by the organization itself; and pattern maintenance refers to the maintenance of the dominant value system and the patterns of interaction it lays down. Thus stability is achieved through adaptation, operation and co-ordination of the component parts of work organizations.

The Practical Application of the Systems Approach

John O'Shaughnessy points out that in reality the objectives defined for any organizational or management study will determine both the boundaries of the system and the appropriate sub-systems. The primary focus of attention is the decision-making activity in formal work organizations, since decision making is the essential activity by which objectives and policies are determined. Decision making also determines the actions taken either to achieve or not achieve the objectives.

O'Shaughnessy defines the systems approach in a practical way. He sees it focusing on two inter-related functions: the decision-making activity and the communication activity. The essential features of an attempt to apply the systems concept in practice are summarized as:

1. Specifying objectives,
2. Listing the sub-systems, or main decision areas related to the objectives,
3. Analysing the decision areas and establishing information needs,
4. Designing the communication channels for the information flow,
5. Grouping decision areas to minimize the communications burden.

Questions Raised by the Systems Approach

1. The systems approach is stated to rely fundamentally on the identification of individual systems and the connection of these systems with other systems (a bit like a jig-saw). Is it possible to follow the process through to a meaningful conclusion? Try the process yourself in relation to any organization with which you are familiar.
2. For a meaningful understanding of the structural and functional aspects of an organization to be properly evaluated the system writers would argue that the systems interrelationships must be assessed. Is it possible to obtain and to handle all the information which would be necessary for this approach to be applied? Do human beings yet have the capacity and ability to conceptualize and apply such an approach in practice?
3. Discuss the communication implication of the systems concept. The jig-saw concept relies on making the various parts of an organization fit together, which implies a very sophisticated system of control and integration. Using your college or place of employment as a practical example, examine the existing communication networks and evaluate their ability to satisfy the systems approach.

2.7 THE IDEAL BUREAUCRACY MODEL: MAX WEBER

Max Weber is, in many ways, the most influential of the structuralists in that he was one of the founders and also produced a major contribution to the library of knowledge related to the structure and functioning of formal work organizations. His main focus of attention was the maintenance of order within the structure of formal work organizations, and in particular the distribution and acceptance of power amongst the various positions. He searched for a formula for organizational structures which would, on the one hand, control the individual members so as to obtain the greatest degree of effectiveness and efficiency and, on the other, would produce the minimum degree of unhappiness caused by working in a controlled environment.

One question above all held Weber's attention: 'Why do individuals accept authority?'. In other words he wanted to clarify some of the reasons why individuals will grant power and authority to others, and under what conditions. In some cases authority is not questioned for traditional, custom or practical reasons. For example, historically society has been based on an aceptance of a traditional hierarchy of authority from the monarch at the head, to lords of the manor, and country squires. This mode of acceptance is now tending to disappear. In other cases people obey a very strong, charismatic personality whose sheer personal presence gains acceptance. This method of gaining acceptance of authority is severely limited and cannot account for the wholesale acceptance of order in either organizations or society. Weber recognized a third method of gaining acceptance which he called rational-legal authority. This form of acceptance is based on the theory that individuals will grant to others the legitimacy to use power over them if the reasons are logical and conform to the framework of values which they hold. This means that people will obey instructions and rules if they are basically seen as being necessary in relation to a specific situation. Situations will vary and therefore the nature of accepted authority will vary. Thus the type of authority which will be accepted by soldiers at the front during active warfare will be different from that which a group of production workers in British Leyland, for example, will accept as being necessary or legitimate in the 1980s.

The important relationships can be shown in the form of a very generalized formula:

$$\text{Power} \quad + \quad \text{Legitimacy} \quad = \quad \text{Authority}$$
(The ability to   (The acceptance by individuals
get orders obeyed)   of the exercise of power)

Weber's theory is that legitimate authority is less alienating than coercive authority, that is, authority which is accepted out of fear. People will obey orders if the consequences of not obeying are sufficiently unacceptable, but this is not willing acceptance and the commitment to the tasks involved will usually be very minimal or even negative. Weber's conclusion, therefore, was that organizations should be structured on the basis of rational-legal authority.

The Rational-legal Structure: Rational/Pure Bureaucracy

For organizations to be effective and efficient they should be structured on the basis of rational-legal authority. To do this Weber formulated seven propositions relating to the structuring of legal authority systems:

1. The work of the organization should be clearly designed on the basis of defined, official tasks which are regulated by a system of rules.
2. The tasks should be arranged into functionally distinct spheres of operation so as to produce specific areas of competence. This means that organizations should be structured on the basis of division of labour, each division having the necessary authority to carry out its prescribed function through a system of rules which define the parameters of the function.
3. Individual job positions should be arranged hierarchically, each level supervising the level immediately below it. The limits of authority appropriate to each office should be clearly stated. This system of supervision provides control and ensures the compliance of job holders to the prescribed tasks.
4. Individual offices (job positions) may be regulated by technical rules or norms necessitating the appointment of specially trained people. Therefore specific training is normally associated with individual job positions, a feature which is important in the legitimizing of individuals occupying the office.
5. Individuals occupying job positions should not own any part of the means of production or administration.
6. Job holders cannot appropriate their office for personal gain. This means that an individual has no right of ownership of his job and cannot sell it to another when leaving.
7. The process of administration should be based on written codes of rules and systems.

Weber, in fact, did not define bureaucracy. He used the term generally, but, when wanting to be precise and for the purpose of clarity, he referred to his rational-legal structure as the rational/pure type of bureaucracy. He saw this model as possessing the characteristics of precision, continuity, discipline, strictness and reliability. It does not imply rule by officials, but rather rule through designated offices or functions.

Weber acknowledged the inherent tendency of bureaucracies to accumulate power, and to combat this problem he recommended the following:

1. *Collegiality.* Control by a committee-like structure made up of a wide variety of people. Membership may in fact consist of people drawn from outside the bureaucracy. A board of directors and a governing body of a school or college are examples of the type of structure Weber was referring to.
2. *Separation of powers.* The separation of powers into relatively distinct functional spheres. This means dividing responsibility for the same function between two or more individuals. Thus in the process of decision making compromises are necessary which limit the power of each individual.
3. *Amateur administration.* By this concept Weber meant a system of mixed administration in which generalist staff are supported by specialists. This provides an element of checks and balances where the generalists help to prevent the bias and possible empire-building of specialists. An example of a work organization possessing this characteristic is the British Civil Service.
4. *Representation.* Here we are looking at an organizational structure based in part on democratic principles. Thus the policy making and the overall control function related to government departments are in the hands of elected officials. The applicability of this concept to a business enterprise might be in the concept of worker participation in the decision-making process.

It is interesting to look at the manpower structure which Weber recommended in relation to his rational/pure type bureaucracy. Weber argued that his organizational model would ensure that staff are:

1. *Rule bounded.* That is, that they are subject to strict and systematic discipline and control in carrying out the duties of each post.
2. *Chosen on the basis of competence.* This means that individuals will be selected and appointed to specific positions on the basis of professional or technical qualifications.
3. *Guided by rationality in decision making.* The function of every position being clearly specified and recorded in writing.
4. *Part of a clearly defined career structure.* That is, that the organization will have a clear hierarchy of job positions with the ultimate control and authority in the top position.
5. *Impartial in their administration.* Individuals observe impersonal duties as defined by the rule book.
6. *Promoted* to higher posts on the basis of seniority and merit, based on the judgements of seniors.
7. *Employed in both a salaried and pensionable post.* The salary structure being graded in relation to the hierarchical structure.
8. *Employed in one job.* People appointed to a Weberian organization will be expected to make the post their sole occupation.

We should stress at this point that Weber was describing an ideal model similar to the way economists state the components of a perfect market. Neither exists in reality. Weber's model is a valuable yardstick for comparison purposes; for example, when examining the characteristics of several organizations, the model can be used as a datum for determining the extent to which they are bureaucratic in their activities. This is usually described as the degree of bureaucratization.

Questions Raised by the Bureaucratic Model

1. Will an organization designed on the basis of Weber's rational/pure type bureaucracy have the flexibility to adapt to changing situations and requirements? Or is there a rigidity which in fact hinders the effective operation of the organization?

Robert Merton examined this aspect of bureaucratic organizations and came to the conclusion that the attempts to impose order and control reduced the extent to which individuals occupying the various job positions exercised initiative and flexibility. In fact, the very structure of a bureaucracy attempts to control these behavioural characteristics on the pretext of obtaining greater predictability in decision making. Merton found that these controls tended to alienate job holders, who became almost totally reliant on the rule book for every decision, a rigidity of behaviour not really desired by the organization. In many bureaucracies this reliance on rules resulted in more and more rules and in consequence even greater behavioural rigidity.

2. The Weber model calls for a hierarchy of job positions with varying degrees of authority and responsibility delegated to each level. Organizational control is obtained, in theory, by the supervisory function of one level over the one immediately below it. Does this delegation of authority always obtain positive results for the organization?

Philip Selznick researched this question and came to the conclusion that delegation of authority and responsibility needs specialized and costly training of staff, which inevitably affects the scope of problems tackled. This leads to a need for more assistance and therefore more delegation. Ultimately, the delegation process is so widespread that there is difficulty in co-ordinating all the fragments into a single corporate organizational goal (see Chapter 1). Greater control is often seen as necessary to achieve this co-ordination. This control increases conflict and alienation which create renewed and reduced differences in goal achievement. These differences result in more specialization and more delegation – a vicious circle concept.

3. Does the increased use of general and impersonal rules in the organization reduce the effective internal communication throughout the hierarchical structure?
4. Does a rule-bound system produce only the behavioural characteristics it is designed to achieve? Or are there other consequences which are not at all intended?

These two questions form the focus of Alvin Gouldner's attention. He found that the demand for control laid down minimal acceptable standards in relation to each job position. This tended to produce a response in the individuals occupying the various positions which focused on a conformity to these mimimal standards, that is, individuals tended to do only that which was prescribed for the job position which they were occupying.

2.8 SUMMARY

This chapter has provided the student with a summary of the major theories and models relating to formal work organizations. It has attempted to show a link in relation to the development of organizational thinking.

The classical approach, although much criticized, is the only really prescriptive model, and identifies the basic issues with which organizational design should be concerned, that is with the determination of objectives and work specifications; methods of grouping; authority systems; accountability systems; and control systems.

Other theories have contributed to our insight into the complicated structures and relationships which exist in formal work organizations. These theories and approaches should not be viewed as alternative models, but as different and complementary contributions to our knowledge. They do not replace the basic issues raised by the classical writers, but indicate to us the complexity of those issues. The human relations approach points out the complexities which result from the interactions of human beings in the context of formal work organizations. Above all, it describes the importance of the informal organization which inevitably exists within the structure of a formal work organization.

The structuralists are concerned with understanding the nature and component parts of order in organizations. The structuralists' view of formal work organizations is that they can never be designed so that the individuals working in them will find their work a wholly satisfying activity. This view revolves around the belief that such organizations inevitably alienate workers. The structuralists' concern therefore is to understand the extent to which an organization can be modelled in order to minimize the alienation produced.

The functionalists are also concerned with the concept of order and, in particular, how order seems to prevail in formal work organizations irrespective of the changes in personnel which are constantly taking place. In particular the question of how people manage to co-exist in organizations and society is the key issue. This leads to a search for an understanding of the relationships between the parts and the whole in an organization, and in particular to identify how stability is, for the most part, achieved.

The essential contribution of the structural-functionalists is a system of questioning, mechanisms of searching for answers. The systems approach represents a development of this search for answers. It is concerned with providing a framework for the accurate identification of the nature of specific problems and issues, and the sources of relevant information related to them.

The chapter concludes with an explanation of the theories of perhaps the most famous of the structuralists, Max Weber. Weber was primarily concerned with the acceptance of authority and the structure of organizations. He provided two important theories. The first relates to the reasons why authority is accepted by individuals (rational-legal authority); the second to the structuring of an organization on the basis of this authority (rational/pure bureaucracy).

Throughout the chapter questions have been raised. These questions have been answered to some extent in the text, but students should consider them in more depth, preferably in group discussion if this is possible.

Further Reading

1. Blau, P. M. & Scott, W. R. (1967) *Formal Organizations*. London: Routledge & Kegan Paul.
2. Etzioni, A. (1964) *Modern Organizations*. Hemel Hempstead: Prentice-Hall.
3. Landsberger, H. A. (ed.) (1970) *Comparative Perspectives on Formal Organisation*. Boston: Little, Brown & Co.
4. March, J. G. & Simon, H. A. (1958) *Organizations*. Chichester: Wiley.
5. Mouzelis, N. (1967) *Organization and Bureaucracy*. London: Routledge & Kegan Paul.
6. O'Shaughnessy, J. (1966) *Business Organisation*. London: George Allen & Unwin.
7. Pugh, D. S. (ed.) (1975) *Organisation Theory*. Harmondsworth: Penguin.
8. Schein, E. H. (1965) *Organization Psychology*. Hemel Hempstead: Prentice-Hall.
9. Silverman, D. (1974) *The Theory of Organisations*. London: Heinemann.

3

Organization: Functional Departmentalization

GENERAL OBJECTIVES

After reading this chapter students should be able to identify the role and function of the main functional areas within private and public work organizations. They should be able to assess some of the interactions between such areas, in particular authority relationships and communication systems. (The chapter concentrates on demonstrating the concept of functional departmentalization as seen through manufacturing organizations. Some reference is made to public sector organizations. The reader should develop the concept to apply it to different types of work organization.)

LEARNING OBJECTIVES

Students should be able to:

1. Compare contrasting organizations in order to identify the principal common functional areas.
2. Explain the role and operation of the principal functional areas.
3. Explain the need for specific organizational goals and planning and control activities designed to achieve them.

In Chapter 2 we examined some of the theoretical perspectives relating to the design and structuring of formal work organizations. In this chapter we shall examine in general terms the methods adopted in practice in both the public and private sectors of the economy to accomplish work goals. In this sense the chapter is concerned with looking at the main types of internal structures which have been developed so that work organizations in manufacturing industry, government and commerce accomplish their planned purpose.

The classical approach to the design of organizations, described in Chapter 2, identifies several basic issues which are critical to their effective operation. These include the determination of objectives and work specifications (including the effective communication of them to all who are employed in the organization), methods of grouping, authority systems, accountability systems and control systems. In practice, organizations have responded in individual ways to each of these issues, but it is still possible to examine them in a general way. The reader will be expected to compare this general analysis with the structure of any organization with which he is familiar.

3.1 THE DETERMINATION OF OBJECTIVES

The need for organizational objectives can be compared with the need to have a clear destination when travelling. Work organizations need to clarify their objectives in order to understand the direction they are taking, and the targets they hope to achieve. Where these objectives are not clarified there is a great danger that organizations will engage in activities which do not contribute to reaching the targets for which they were aiming. Without a clear statement of objectives it is difficult, if not impossible, to communicate the organization's targets to its employees. It is also difficult to judge the performance of both individuals and the organization as a whole, since there are no objective criteria with which to compare actual activities and results.

There are principally two levels of objectives in all formal work organizations: *policy objectives* and *executive objectives*. Policy objectives will usually be concerned with a number of issues including the relationship with the environment in which the organization is physically located (a relationship more fully discussed in Chapter 1), financial aspects, the products or services to be undertaken, the market for those products or services, the attitude towards staff relations, and a statement concerning the long-term development of the organization. In Chapter 1 we examined some of the issues associated with goal formulation at the policy level. These policy goals are usually defined in both short- and long-range terms after consideration of the internal strengths and weaknesses of the work organization, the threats and opportunities from the external environment, and the expectations of those to whom the organization is accountable (for example, shareholders, the national and local electorate, employees, and the customers or users of the service provided). Such policy goals are an attempt by senior management to optimize the potential of the organization's operations and activities through the best allocation of resources. In the private sector the senior management concerned with determining the policy goals will usually be the board of directors, whilst in the public sector it will be the responsibility of elected officials, supported by permanent officials (that is, civil servants, local government officials and managers of nationalized industries).

In order to specify these policy objectives in meaningful terms, all work organizations must attempt to forecast future developments. For example, in education it is necessary to forecast the expected birth rate to determine the number and sizes of schools needed, their location, the number of teachers, the facilities needed to train them, and the facilities needed to meet the educational demands of the future. In addition it is necessary to forecast the probable nature of the curriculum, and the numbers wanting to take advantage of post-school education on both a part- and full-time basis, and so on. Similarly, organizations in the private sector are concerned with forecasting to assess the potential of the market in relation to their goods or services. Thus the business organization is concerned with assessing any growth or decline in market demand for its products or services, any changes resulting from technological developments, and many other factors such as manpower considerations, financial considerations and the activities of competitors.

This forecasting activity is concerned with:

1. analysing present and past performance data and (often using sophisticated analytical techniques) making projections concerning probable future levels of operation,
2. analysing published information from such sources as government statistics, technical and professional journals, and the published information of companies and government departments,
3. carrying out independent research into the needs and tastes of the public, and
4. 'brainstorming' activity (that is, the creativity needed to generate new ideas) when the organization attempts to promote change and identify new solutions to existing problems and activities. (The government 'Think Tank' is an example of an organization's attempt to formalize brainstorming activity.)

These policy objectives provide the formal work organization with its principal aims and general guidelines relating to the methods of operation. They will usually have considered a wide variety of factors including the views of pressure groups, as indicated in Chapter 1. They can therefore be viewed as legislative in the sense that they lay down the framework within which the organization should attempt to operate. However, policy objectives need to be translated into a form which makes day-to-day operation possible. To function, therefore, the organization also needs a sub-system of executive objectives and a work structure designed to meet the policy objectives. In Chapter 2 we analysed a number of views relating to this. We shall develop these views by reviewing examples of organizational structures which the authors feel are a reasonable representation of those to be found in most sectors of the economy.

The type of structures adopted will influence the nature of the executive objectives, since these are usually related to specific functional structures within the work organization. Thus, in a manufacturing organization we can expect to find a structure with clear functional divisions such as finance, production, marketing and sales, research and development, personnel and industrial relations, purchasing and supply, transport, warehousing and distribution. There may be other divisions, but these examples serve to illustrate the point. The extent of this process of departmentalization will, of course, be related to the size of the organization -- the smaller the enterprise the less the need to subdivide into specialist sections or departments. Basically the aim is for an organizational structure which will maximize the attainment of policy objectives.

Whatever functional structure is adopted it is vital that an attempt is made to specify clearly how each functional division contributes to the attainment of the policy objectives. This means that the policy objectives must be translated into operational or executive objectives for each functional department. Profit objectives for a manufacturing company can be translated into selling objectives, that is, the number of individual items that have to be sold in a given period (usually one year) to generate the required sales income. This in turn is translated into a manufacturing requirement since goods cannot be sold until they have been produced. To produce these goods the organization requires buildings, machinery, materials and trained manpower. These requirements are translated into financial objectives (that is, related to methods of raising the required capital), purchasing objectives, and personnel and training objectives. The definition of these objectives is not a simple matter as many factors have to be considered and their effects calculated. For example, the production objectives cannot be stated simply in terms of units of production, but need to specify such matters as the cost of production. It is therefore obvious that the definition and development of executive objectives need to conform to an overall organizational planning process to ensure that the various parts link together into a whole, and that the whole conforms with the policy objectives. This planning process is usually referred to as *corporate planning*.

3.2   THE CORPORATE PLANNING PROCESS

Organizations vary in their specific approach to corporate planning, but there is a common underlying theme to most if not all systems. This theme can be summarized as follows:

1.   An assessment of organizational strengths and weaknesses. This implies an assessment of the knowledge, skills and abilities of all the people employed by the organization; an examination of the apparent purpose for the existence of the organization; an assessment of the nature and needs of the consumers of the goods or services; and an assessment of the activities of other similar enterprises if they exist.
2.   An assessment of the external environment. This implies an examination of the input factors identified in Chapter 1.
3.   Giving consideration to those who have an interest in the activities of the organization, for example shareholders, ratepayers and taxpayers.
4.   Clarifying policy objectives.
5.   Assessing the organizational structure and operating strategies most appropriate to the achievement of the policy objectives, together with an evaluation of alternative courses of action should the first choice fail.
6.   The development of detailed executive or operational objectives and plans related to their achievement in relation to each functional department.
7.   The translation of the departmental objectives into a more detailed series of objectives in relation to the activities of individual managers and first-line supervisors in each functional department.

Such planning is a continuous process and not a one-off activity. Information is constantly being circulated within the organization. This information will be very diverse in nature, but much of it will relate to the organizational activities of the organization. Managers need to become skilful in recognizing the relevance of the information being circulated and in taking appropriate action to amend plans as the need arises.

3.3   METHODS OF GROUPING

In assessing the organizational structure most appropriate to the achievement of the policy objectives many factors will be considered. Factors such as the size of the operation, the nature of its activities, the size and location of the markets, and the communications network are among some of the more obvious items, and others might include whether the operation is centralized or decentralized, physical constraints imposed by buildings or geography, and the capabilities of the labour force. Nevertheless it is possible to say that most organizations will be concerned with activities which include marketing, production, purchasing, research and development, personnel and training, and finance.

3.4 MARKETING

Marketing is a general term used to embrace a number of related activities. These activities include (i) assessing the characteristics of the market for the goods or services offered by the organization; (ii) determining ways of stimulating the market to purchase or utilize those goods or services; (iii) making provision for the movement of them to the consumer; (iv) making provision for an adequate after sales service; (v) deciding on the appropriate pricing policy and specific price levels for individual items; and (vi) deciding the conditions of sales.

Assessing the Characteristics of the Market

The primary aim of the marketing department is the successful sale of goods and services. Successful does not mean as many items as possible but refers to a sales level in line with the policy objectives. The reason for this is often basically very simple. Most organizations can sell only as much as the employees and machines can produce, and a level of sales over and above this can lead to great embarrassment. This embarrassment results from the fact that extra production may only be possible by the purchase and installation of costly plant and equipment, together with the recruitment of extra manpower. The costs of this may be too great and the organization may have to refuse the sales which have been generated. This can sometimes have damaging repercussions in the sense that the customer may react by taking all his business to a competitor. It is therefore vital that the marketing department has clearly determined executive objectives before it determines its own strategy for achieving them. (The student should note that policy objectives will exist at department level in the sense that they relate to the methods or strategy determined by it to achieve the overall executive objectives which have resulted from the policy objectives for the organization as a whole.) These executive objectives will, to some extent, provide certain limiting factors to the way the marketing department examines the characteristics of the market.

The predominant philosophy adopted today in relation to any assessment of the market is consumer-oriented. This has not always been the case, and may not be the case in some organizations today. Consumer-oriented means that the organization attempts to assess what the consumer needs and wants, and then designs its products or services accordingly. The aim is for customer satisfaction such that the order will be repeated. The alternative to this is a product-oriented approach where goods are produced with great concern for the right mixture of quality and cost, but with comparatively little concern for what the consumer needs or wants. In a sense the best approach is a combination of the two philosophies since goods and service must be provided to the consumer in the right mix of quality and price even though the goods and services are the ones needed and wanted.

Assuming a consumer-oriented approach is adopted, the organization needs to decide what aspects of the market it wishes to know more about. The overall market for all goods and services is immense, so what is needed is a method of narrowing down the focus of attention so that the information obtained is relevant to the nature of the organization's activities. This narrowing down is achieved when a business enterprise asks itself the fundamental question 'What business am I in?'. The answer to this question is not usually the responsibility of the marketing department but of the board of directors or other similar body. Nevertheless it is critical to the work which the marketing department undertakes since it will determine the systems boundary in relation to the search for appropriate market information.

Having determined the section of the market in which the organization is operating, it is the responsibility of the marketing department to obtain all the information it can in relation to it, to assess the opportunities that it presents. This means that the characteristics of the appropriate sector of the market must be determined. The market sector needs classifying according to various selected dimensions; this is called *segmenting the market*. This analysis is undertaken in order to understand the true nature of the market segment. It is necessary to know, for example, the size of the market according to various price levels. If the organization manufactures motor-cars, for example, it will be necessary to obtain information concerning the approximate numbers that sell at various price levels, and the share of this number that the organization can expect to obtain against the competition of other manufacturers. It may be necessary to segment the market more finely than this in order to obtain a more comprehensive picture, for example, the types of motor-car that the consumer wants (family saloons, sports cars, two-door models, four-door models, customized specials etc.), and it is the consumers' answers to these questions which the marketing department seeks.

In a highly competitive market it is essential to keep up to date with the activities of competitors and with any new and probable technological advances. The marketing department is, therefore, charged with the responsibility of obtaining information on the activities of competitors, and in particular on any changes that may be occurring in their share of the market. It is also responsible for detecting shifts in consumer tastes, and the possible impacts of these shifts on the potential of the market in relation to the activities of the organization.

The information obtained concerning the characteristics of the market will enable the organization to make the following decisions:

1. What goods or services to provide. This means that decisions are necessary in relation to the segment of the market the organization wishes to be in. In the example of motor-car manufacturing this decision may be a choice between comparatively low price and high volume – the ordinary family saloon – or high price and low volume – Rolls Royce, for example.
2. The level of provision. This means the volume of production or the range and level of services which the organization will offer. This decision will obviously be related to the market potentialities that have been determined for those goods or services.
3. The pricing policy to be adopted. The choice of market segment will determine the approximate price range for specified goods or services that the organization will charge. It will then have to determine whether it can sell enough at this price to cover costs and make a profit.

The student should remember that in making any of these decisions the organization has to decide its ability to provide the goods or services related to the identified market demand. This means an accurate analysis of the productive capacity (that is, machine output capabilities, limitations in plant capacity, the skills and abilities of the labour force, finance availability, etc.); organizational costings (that is, the costs of producing, selling, distributing, storing and administering the goods in relation to the total anticipated sales income); and the availability of all the materials related to the manufacturing process. This last point is highly pertinent in relation to rapidly diminishing mineral resources. We may in fact be entering a marketing era dominated by an ever-increasing shortage of resources which may significantly change future market characteristics.

Obtaining the Market Information

In order to obtain a clear picture of the characteristics of the market, the marketing department must develop methods of obtaining the market information. These methods are called *market research techniques* and fall into two broad classifications: desk research and field research.

Desk research is that activity which can be undertaken from within the organization. It is concerned with analysing information which is:

1. Generated by the organization itself, for example internal records such as sales details and histories, production information and cost information.
2. Intelligence reports from the sales organization. Sales staff are usually asked to make regular reports of the areas for which they are responsible, to include such information as the financial state of existing customers, changes in their buying habits, the products of competitors, etc.
3. Published information. An enormous amount of market information is available in published form, from government department circulars to the journals and reports of professional bodies. In addition information is produced by universities, polytechnics and colleges and other research institutions which is often of great relevance to the present or proposed activities of the organization. Organizations such as Chambers of Commerce and Employers' Associations are also important sources of valuable information.

Field research is concerned with obtaining information direct from the market. The two most commonly used techniques are questionnaires and structured interviewing. This type of research is undertaken by many organizations, particularly those concerned with the manufacture of goods, in order to obtain more information about the buying habits, preferences and trends of those people who actually make the decisions to purchase. Very often the research is specifically designed to establish why those who make purchasing decisions have preferences for some products rather than others, and is known as *motivation research*.

Stimulating the Market

Market research activity will provide information from which the organization will determine the characteristics of the market, and this assessment will result in the construction of a marketing plan. The marketing plan specifies the segment of the market to which the organization will sell, and this will lead to a specification of the limits to the product range. It will also provide an analysis of the intended future activity in the sense that it will give an indication of intentions to enter new markets or to extend the organization's share of the existing market. The plan will also be concerned with clarifying the organization's policy with respect to pricing, distribution, advertising and methods of selling.

All these issues have a close inter-relationship and great importance is attached to obtaining a well balanced and integrated policy and structure in relation to them. This is crucial in respect to the organization's attempts to stimulate the market to purchase its goods or services.

Pricing Policy

The method of pricing products or services is a difficult issue for all business organizations. The difficulty results from the large number of variables to be considered. For example, the following costs have to be calculated:

1. The costs of production. This means assessing the total costs incurred by the departments concerned with producing the goods or services. Some of these costs will be comparatively fixed (that is, they do not vary to any great extent with changes in the number of products manufactured, and this will include depreciation costs, interest charges on loans to purchase buildings and machinery, for example), but others will be directly variable with production levels.
2. The costs incurred by all the servicing departments (that is, the running costs of the purchasing function, the personnel function, research and development, transport and distribution, and the general administration activity); and
3. The costs incurred by the marketing and selling activity itself. The price levels that are determined must produce sufficient sales revenue to cover all of these costs plus a surplus which is the profit level.

This seems comparatively straightforward, but several other vital factors have been ignored. For example, at what price are competitors selling equivalent products? Are they selling equivalent products in every sense – quality, function, appearance, etc.? Does the customer value any of the differences such that it affects his decision to purchase? In addition, the marketing department has to calculate the expected sales for all items in the product range since sales volumes will usually have an important bearing on price levels due to the variable cost element already mentioned. It is often necessary to calculate the effect on sales volumes of variations in price levels in order to determine the optimum range in respect to profit potential.

Finally, the effects of advertising will have an important bearing. The return from advertising is calculated in the sense that the organization attempts to assess the changes in sales levels resulting from different levels of advertising. There is often a level beyond which the increase in sales volume does not cover the extra costs of advertising, and therefore the organization will wish to monitor this most carefully. Advertising can also affect the selling price, in that a good advertising campaign can often persuade the public and industrial buyers that a higher price is worth paying for a return in terms of such qualities as durability, reliability, appearance, comfort, etc.

The Selling Activity

The student should recognize that the market for goods and service is in a constant state of change, and in consequence there is a constant need for up-to-date information. Market research activity is, therefore, an on-going activity constantly striving to present the organization with reliable information. This information is analysed in order to assess the selling potential of existing products or services, and to determine the strategy in relation to the development of new ones. The development of new products and services is usually time-consuming and expensive. It may take years to develop new products, and it can take a considerable length of time to modify existing ones. It is impor-

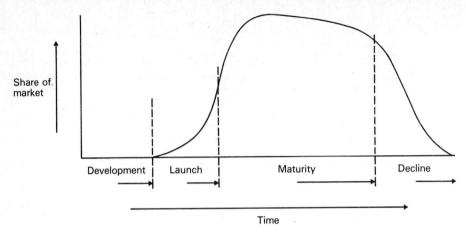

Share of
market

Development | Launch | Maturity | Decline

Time

Figure 3.1   *Life cycle of a product*

tant, therefore, that the organization engages in forward forecasting to be well prepared for future market needs. This forward information can be partially determined through market research activity, together with the projection of existing sales patterns using statistical techniques. The accuracy of the information obtained will be very dependent on the nature of the product or service, some having a very stable and consistent market pattern over time, others being highly variable and subject to wide variation.

No organization can expect its products to continue to sell at a consistent rate over time. New products have to be developed or existing ones modified to meet the changes in consumer tastes. These changes in tastes result from a wide variety of reasons, including developments in technology, new products introduced by competitors, the influence of social advertising (the fashion industry, for example) and the changes in the purchasing power of the consumer. Products will, therefore, have a *life cycle* from the development of the initial design through the market launch to maturity and then steady decline until the sales drop to a level where the products are withdrawn from the market. This concept is illustrated in Fig. 3.1. The sales department is responsible for monitoring the development of this product cycle, and in particular for identifying in advance when the decline is likely to occur so that modifications can take place or new products can be developed. The aim is for a steady share of the market, which may be following a planned steady increase. This concept is perhaps more easily explained diagrammatically, as in Fig. 3.2.

The selling activity can be organized in a number of ways. The dominant factor to influence the choice is the nature of the market. If the organization is selling to the *industrial market* it will need a different organization from that if it was selling to the *consumer market*. The term industrial market refers to that sector of the economy which does not sell direct to the public, and in which the buyer tends to be very professional, company buyers, who make comparatively large buying decisions, for example. The consumer market is therefore concerned with many more buyers but who make relatively small buying decisions, based on far less technical knowledge and expertise than the industrial buyer. In financial terms the industrial market is three to four times as large as the consumer market.

A salesman selling in the industrial market will usually be technically qualified as well as experienced at selling in order to communicate effectively with the professional buyers who demand technical information. His sales territory is likely to be large because of the comparatively small number of buyers in any one area. On the other

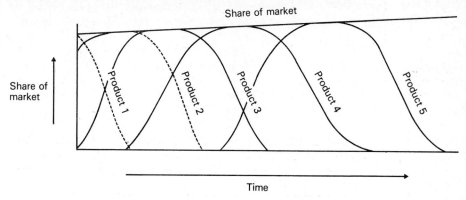

Figure 3.2 *New product development and market share*

hand, the salesman selling to the consumer market is less likely to be a specialist, and will have a much smaller geographical area to cover due to the heavier concentration of buyers in any one area. The organization of the sales force will vary from organization to organization.

The sales force not only sells the products to the buyer, but is also a source of valuable information. Records are kept of all information which the sales force acquires in the course of its activities. This information will refer to the activities and financial status of existing customers, and to the activities of competitors.

Organizations can also use other means to sell their products. These include the use of agents who sell the products of organizations under clear contract conditions in return for preferential ex-works prices, or an agreed remuneration based on the level of sales achieved. There are many examples of organizations which adopt this method, including the motor trade (many garages have an agency with a particular manufacturer such as BL, Ford, Saab, etc.), clothing manufacturers, certain high quality potteries, including Wedgwood, Doulton, Twyford, and many others. (The student should consider other examples, preferably in discussion.) Organizations selling overseas tend to use agencies to meet the problems of different languages, cultures, units of measurement, currency and credit control, and political and economic factors. In addition there is the remoteness of the market in relation to the organization and an overseas agent helps to bridge this problem.

Advertising and Sales Promotion

Advertising is concerned with motivating buyers to purchase or use the products or services of the organization. It is therefore concerned with giving information, persuasion, and with the creation of an image. Advertising is expensive and money can easily be wasted. It is therefore important that the organization develops a specialized advertising section, or employs the services of a professional advertising agency. Research into the effectiveness of advertising is a constant need, since up to half the money expended can be fruitless in terms of direct sales results. The problem is that it is very difficult to identify that part of the advertising activity which is relatively ineffectual, and that which is vital.

There are many choices open to organization in relation to advertising. First there is the choice of media. The number of publications on the market is enormous, from daily newspapers to highly specialized magazines, from small posters to large hoardings, and so on. Then there is the choice of other media such as radio and television, mail shots, telephone communication and specialized sales literature.

The effects of advertising have to be carefully assessed. On the one hand too little advertising can prove to be disastrous, whilst too much can prove to be equally fruitless. The effects created by the advertising may not be those desired or intended. The media chosen may not be reaching the right sector of the market and close liaison with the market research activity is of great importance. Above all the organization attempts to match its advertising activity with the nature of its product and the type of buyer or user aimed at. The essential goal is that of image creation. The organization tries to create an image which projects the organization's products or services as being just right in terms of price, quality, design, reliability, support, service, appearance, results, and so on.

Sales promotion is a term used to embrace all aspects of an organization's activities in relation to its attempts to increase sales, including advertising. It is usually used to refer to those activities which attempt to have a quick and often short-term effect, such as special offers, special displays, premium offers such as reductions in the price of other goods on proof of purchase of the organization's products (breakfast food manufacturers tend to use this method of sales promotion a great deal), and competitions.

The Distribution Activity

The methods of distribution are usually linked to the nature of the market. Organizations manufacturing industrial goods, for example, will usually choose to sell direct from the factory to the consumer, whilst consumer goods tend to be distributed through a whole range of different channels. The most commonly used channels for consumer goods are: wholesalers, who then redistribute the goods to numerous retail outlets dealing directly with the individual consumer; direct selling to retailers; direct selling to the consumer through retail outlets owned by the organization itself; house-to-house selling; mail order selling, and so on.

The issues which the organization has to consider in relation to distribution are how to bring the buyers and sellers together most effectively; how to create the most favourable attitudes; how to achieve the most effective transport and warehousing systems; and how to achieve the most efficient service to the consumer. The nature of these issues will vary between one organization and another depending on the nature of the product, the size of the organization, and the size and geographical spread of the market. Students will find it most interesting to take several well-known organizations and identify the distribution system they have chosen. The important issue is to analyse the reasons why the particular choice seems appropriate to the organization concerned. The reader should compare the way public services are distributed to the community as well as manufactured goods.

After Sales Service

Depending on the nature of the products produced and sold, organizations will often need to develop a good after sales service. Indeed, many organizations win sales on the strength of their after sales record, e.g. BL's Supercover scheme. What is needed is a speedy and reliable service to the consumer. This will involve consideration of the need for the storing of an adequate supply of spare parts, the employment of teams of repair and maintenance staff, and a responsive communications system by which the consumer can make the repair need known quickly and the service can be provided speedily. Again, the exact nature of the organization required will vary from company to company. The student should again examine the after sales organization of well-known manufacturers and examine after sales organizations in operation in relation to each.

Credit Control

The organization wants to sell its products or services in return for money – money which is needed for continued existence. It therefore needs to be certain that the customer can pay for the products purchased. This means that the marketing function attempts to establish the credit worthiness of both new and existing customers. New customers are generally asked to give proof of their credit worthiness in the form of references from banks and other organizations with which they have a trading agreement. Sometimes organizations will engage in their own research to establish the credit worthiness of potential customers. The credit rating of existing customers is established in two ways, by examining their record as payers, and by asking the sales force to look out for any signs of deterioration in their financial position. When doubts arise more detailed investigations are generally undertaken to ensure that payment can in fact be made for any goods sold.

It is usual practice to sell goods and services on specified periods of credit. Indeed, many customers would not buy without a credit period. In most industries there is a common period of credit applied throughout all organizations, although it is often prudent to give extended terms in order to win over and keep a good customer. Whatever credit limits are agreed, it is important to see that they are kept. Any extension in credit time is valuable working capital lost to the organization. Effective credit control mechanisms are therefore important. Close working relationships with the accounting function are vital in this respect.

Student Activities

Students can improve their knowledge and understanding of the marketing function by considering the following issues. The issues can form group discussion questions or individual research activities.

1. How will the organizational structure be affected if the organization adopts a consumer orientation rather than production orientation, and vice versa?
2. Examine the significance of the increase in the number of people employed in wholesaling and retailing between the middle of the nineteenth century and the present day.
3. Construct a chart to show the structure of the marketing function of any organization with which you are familiar.
4. Analyse the communication links between the marketing activity and other functional departments within an organization.

5. The marketing concept does not require that marketing executives run the organization, but rather that senior management be marketing orientated. How can a company secretary, a production manager and a personnel manager become marketing orientated?
6. Analyse the marketing activity of a central government department, the DHSS, for example, and compare it with a private manufacturing organization.

This list of issues is by no means exhaustive, but is merely an indicator of the kind of analysis that can profitably be undertaken.

3.5 PRODUCTION

The production function is concerned with making the products which the marketing function has determined it can sell, or the service needed to be provided. This production activity can refer to both manufactured goods and the preparation and provision of services. In Chapter 2 we examined some of the theoretical issues which are appropriate to the design of production organizations, particularly in relation to the manufacturing industry. In this chapter we shall look at some of the more typical systems of production to be found today.

The fundamental issue concerns the question of how to structure the various component parts of the production process in order to achieve the maximum effectiveness in terms of output and cost, together with work force contentment. The issue is further complicated by the need to consider changes in production requirements resulting from changes in market demands. This requires consideration of the need for research and development, new technologies, the purchase of new plant and machinery, the use of new materials, and the training of new and existing manpower. Above all there is the need to link developments to the availability of finance.

The three most generally applied systems are – particularly in manufacturing organizations – job production systems, batch production systems and flow of continuous production systems. These terms can be used to describe the manner in which public or commercial organizations structure their organizations in practice to provide their service to clients or the general public.

Job Production

Some organizations offer a service to individual customers, a service whereby the product or service is tailor-made to meet the client's specific requirements. Each job is individually planned to match the specifications of each order. This approach requires a highly flexible structure able to respond to changed circumstances from job to job. It also requires a highly qualified and experienced labour force in order to be able to respond to the changed needs with equal levels of quality and service. Some degree of standardization is often possible, particularly in the early or preparatory stages of production. The task of many organizations today, in the light of increasing competition, is the maximization of the extent of standardization in order to minimize the duplication of processes, components and organizational sub-sections.

Batch Production

Perhaps the most widespread approach to the structure of the manufacturing process is batch production. In this method the structure of the manufacturing process is designed around the production of a sizeable number, or batch, of identical products or components. These batches are usually made according to a plan based on the maintenance of a predetermined stock level of each item, customer demands being met from the stocks. There is a need for a close liaison with the marketing department in order to be prepared for changes in the market demand patterns. These changes will affect the size of the batches of any one item produced in order to maintain stock levels which will satisfy consumer demand. The major characteristics of this type of production system are a comparatively high level of skilled manpower; groupings of general purpose and specialist machines in order to achieve a degree of production flexibility which will allow several processes to take place at the same time; and seasonal variation in demand and supply patterns which has a corresponding effect on the nature and mix of items in production (for example, in the food industry canning and other food processing activities are affected by the seasonal supply of fruits and vegetables).

Flow or Continuous Production

This method of organization is adopted when production of individual items is required on a large scale. The term flow derives from the nature of the manufacturing system in that there is a logical flow from one operation to the next until the finished product is made. The number of different operations involved depends on the extent to which scientific (or classical) organization principles have been applied, that is, the extent to which the work involved has been the subject of detailed study and broken down into workable elements. The system requires careful planning and co-ordination since one link in the chain is totally dependent on the next, and therefore a smooth and regular flow is needed from one position to the next. There will be one single-purpose machine for each operation and these need to be kept in good working order continuously. Therefore, a system of planned continuous maintenance is required in order to prevent costly hold-ups. Operations may vary in complexity and length of time taken to complete. It is therefore necessary to plan the production process most carefully to ensure that there are enough machines at any one point to maintain the steady flow along the line. There are many examples of organizations using flow-line principles, including those engaged in the production of the most popular makes of motor-cars, and those manufacturing electric light bulbs. This method of production very often incorporates the use of assembly lines and conveyor belt production flow from one stage to the next.

Production Planning and Control

Whatever system of production is adopted there is a need for the co-ordination of activities in order to ensure that items are of the correct specification and type, and are produced at the lowest possible cost, bearing in mind quality and reputation considerations. There are two important stages in the planning process: the first is the preplanning stage, when the nature and quantity of products are determined in conjunction with the sales organization. This stage is also concerned with the determination of such issues as delivery dates and detailed product specifications agreed with the customers. The second – production planning – stage is concerned with determining a detailed set of operating specifications, concerned with the co-ordination of machines and the labour needed to operate them, the determination of output levels on a daily or weekly basis (sometimes the time-scale is extended depending on the nature of the activities involved), the achievement of a smooth operational flow with the elimination of bottlenecks, and the full employment of the labour force (this process is known as scheduling), and the communications of the detailed plans to the work force in the production departments.

Production planning is a very skilled activity requiring, in the majority of organizations, a detailed knowledge of the specifications for each item in the product range, a working knowledge of the production processes by which they are manufactured, and experience of planning processes. In addition, a detailed knowledge of the layout of the total manufacturing organization, together with the machinery associated with it, is required. Without this it would be virtually impossible for the planners to achieve an even distribution of work to various departments (shop loading), or even scheduling of the work-flow through them. In short, therefore, the production planning function is concerned with deciding the best production time schedules and completion dates, maximizing the utilization of expensive machinery, and ensuring the supply of raw materials and equipment needed. (Close co-ordination with the purchasing department is a crucial aspect of production planning.)

Production control is that activity which tries to ensure actual activities are conforming to those planned. It is therefore concerned with examining data from the production departments and comparing these with the plans. This comparison, often taken on a daily basis, will give an indication of the progress achieved in relation to that forecast, any variations requiring corrective action. This activity is usually called progress control or progress chasing. It can be complex, since the reasons why there is a variation between the actual and planned activities can be many, and include such problems as machine breakdown, power supply failure, a failure in raw materials supply, stoppage of work due to industrial action, absenteeism, design errors, planning errors, and so on. The aim of all organizations is to keep these problems to a minimum, but they will inevitably occur, demanding corrective action.

Inspection and Quality Control

Quality standards are difficult to define since the term quality has many possible meanings and interpretations. Most organizations determine their own quality standards in relation to the characteristics of the market, the capabilities of the organization, and the relationship between anticipated sales volume and profits. Quality standards and costs of production are therefore very much inter-related. The important aspect is that once the quality standards have been determined the organization needs to establish a mechanism by which they can be enforced. The issue of quality is not restricted to the finished product only, but is concerned with the activities at all stages of the manufacturing process. Scrap losses must be kept within acceptable limits, the work force should provide consistent output levels and quality levels, and so on.

The inspection function is responsible for the detection of variations from the specified standards at all stages in the manufacturing process, for identifying factors which may have contributed to the variations, such as faults in the initial design, bad workmanship, material faults, and machine limitations and malfunctions, and for communicating the implications of the variations to senior management. The implications will vary and will include increases to production costs which may not have been assessed in the price calculations resulting in a lower profit yield than expected, or the quality may not match that agreed with the customer and, therefore, consumer dissatisfaction can be expected. To minimize these effects, regular inspection of the quality standards of raw materials, of work in progress, of the processing system itself, and of the final finished product is usually undertaken.

The method of inspection will depend on the nature of the product and the manufacturing process, the quality standards which have been established in relation to it, and the need for inspection which has been determined over time, for example, certain aspects of a production process may have proved to be either very reliable or unreliable. In general, inspection can be either centralized, decentralized or a combination of both. Centralized inspection means that work is sent to an inspection department before progressing to the next stage in the manufacturing process. This has the advantage that the whole inspection function is together and standards can be more easily assessed and evaluated, records are centralized, supervision is easier, and the shop floor is not congested by the inspection activity. On the other hand, the method can (and does) result in delays to production while work is under inspection. The decentralized approach overcomes this problem, but has the disadvantage of needing space on the shop floor. The decentralized system has the great advantage of being on the spot, which means that both fault finding and corrective action are comparatively quick.

It would be economically, and sometimes physically, impossible to inspect every item at every stage of the production process. For example, in an armaments factory it would be impossible to inspect all the bullets manufactured since the final test of quality requires them to be actually fired, after which they are useless as ammunition. In other cases the finished product may be so inexpensive that stringent quality control makes no economic sense. In most cases, therefore, a system of sampling is necessary. Using statistical analysis techniques the selections and deviations are analysed. The statistical theory of probability is used, and from the sample trends can be calculated. Control is exercised by comparing the number of defective items in the samples taken against a control chart.

Production Plant and Equipment

The organization will usually need a building or buildings in which to perform the production activity. The factors which are considered when the choice of location decision is made cannot be described fully here, but a summary may well be valuable to the reader. The choice will depend on such issues as whether to rent or buy the buildings, the availability of government grant aid, the availability of suitable labour, wage rates, communication facilities (road, rail and air links), the proximity of commercial services, the availability of housing, and such issues as local by-laws, etc. The type of building is also an important consideration. The organization may require a custom-built factory designed specifically for the products manufactured, with consideration given to such issues as humidity control, ventilation, hygiene control, temperature control and so on. There may too be a preference for single storey or multi-storey buildings, depending on the nature of the manufacturing process. For example, the work flow may well make good use of a gravity-based feed process between stages which would require a multi-storey building.

Once the choice of building has been made, the organization has to consider the choice of plant and equipment. As has been indicated so far in this chapter the choice will to a large extent depend on the nature of the products and the type of production system adopted. Thus decisions are necessary in relation to the need for both special purpose and general purpose machines, their costs, taking into account the initial purchase price plus maintenance and depreciation costs and output performance capabilities. Space is usually at a premium, and the floor area will be carefully planned in order to accommodate the machinery in the most effective way possible. Other considerations will include the type of labour needed to operate the machinery (skilled, unskilled or semi-skilled), and the planned length of life of the individual machines.

The layout of the machines is also an important consideration in order to economize on the use of space, minimize heating, lighting and ventilation costs, provide for a logical and smooth movement between the separate stages in the manufacturing process, allow easy access for the supply of materials and semi-processed items, and the forward flow of items to the next stage of processing. Layout planning is also necessary to minimize the amount of movement of both people and mechanical transport, to facilitate ease of inspection and supervision, to isolate dangerous and noisy operations, and to ensure the general safety of the work force. There are two common approaches to this problem: to arrange the machinery to coincide with the sequence of processes related to the manufacture of a specific product (this method coincides with flow production systems); and to group machinery according to the functions for which they are designed irrespective of the nature of the final product (this method is usually associated with job and batch production systems).

3.6   THE NEED FOR EFFICIENCY AND EFFECTIVENESS

There is a constant search in a competitive economy for more efficient and cost effective ways of producing goods and services whilst maintaining a satisfactory service to the consumer. This search has led to the development of techniques for studying the work actually done (method study) and even the need for the work to be done. Such techniques as value analysis, which questions the need for the actual specifications being used in relation to the function a product is designed to perform, variety reduction, which questions the need for the variety being offered in the product range, and standardization in relation to the various component parts have been developed. In addition there is a constant need to examine the systems adopted in relation to the manufacturing processes and related services, and methods of improving the efficiency with which labour is utilized (these have ranged from pay incentive schemes to behaviour theories applied to the theories of management). For a detailed analysis of these techniques the student should refer to *Resources for Business Activity* which has been specifically prepared in relation to study area C of the Business Education Council guidelines for the core studies at Higher National level, and the texts listed in Further Reading at the end of this chapter.

3.7   PURCHASING

The purchasing function is basically concerned with buying supplies of defined quality, in stated quantities, at the right time, at the right place, and from the most economical sources. In a manufacturing organization, the purchasing need is predominantly dictated by the production function, whilst those concerned with selling a whole range of goods in the distributive sector of the economy will be influenced by the calculations of the sales departments.

The objective is not just to buy, but to buy well; not just to hold stock, but to manage the stocks so as to yield the most service for the minimum costs. The traditional view was to regard the purchasing function as an adjunct to the production activity, but this is changing, largely through a greater appreciation of the need to become more effective in the practice of management. As a result, the purchasing function is now recognized as an independent function of management, requiring specialist knowledge and training. Nevertheless the purchasing activity is closely bound up with the other activities performed within the organization. These inter-relationships can be summarized as follows:

1. With the production department. The principal aim is for a reconciliation of technical and commercial viewpoints in selecting supplies and suppliers, and for a regular interchange of information regarding production needs and supplies availability.
2. With the research and development department. The primary aim is for cooperation in determining changed needs and in the development of new materials and specifications.
3. With the sales department. The principal requirement is for effective communication of changes in demand patterns well enough in advance for the purchasing department to adjust its operations to meet the changed supply needs.

It is difficult to think of any section of an organization which does not have frequent, if not daily, contact with the purchasing function. The essential need is for co-ordination to achieve a coherent buying activity. Above all, there is a control need to ensure that departments do not by-pass the purchasing department by making their own contracts with suppliers. Much thought is necessary to ensure the effective co-ordination of the activities of the purchasing function with those of other departments and sections of the organization. Failure to achieve this can result in commitments which are not in the best interests of the organization, or unsatisfactory service.

Most purchasing departments have the sole authority to commit their organizations to purchase expenditure. Depending on the size of the enterprise this authority may lie in the hands of one person, or in one or more departments, often sub-divided into specialist sections corresponding to particular organizational needs. The precise limits of responsibility will be carefully defined in respect of negotiation and procurement, sub-contracting, progressing, invoice certification, stores, material control, receiving and inspection, and disposals. In most cases the financial limits are determined by budgetary control, so that spending can be monitored and controlled in line with other organizational activities.

The most common method of organizing the buying activity is on a centralized basis which will enable bulk buying to take place thereby maximizing bulk purchase discounts. It also allows specialization of the purchasing activity to be developed and a higher degree of uniformity in procedures together with standardization of purchased items. It has the disadvantage of not allowing flexibility, particularly in those organizations with a significant extent of geographical separation (local management is often much more aware of local demand and supply facilities), and being somewhat bureaucratic in its method of operation.

3.8 RESEARCH AND DEVELOPMENT

Our analysis of the marketing activity has indicated that work organizations exist in a rapidly changing environment, and that the products or services of any enterprise need to be constantly reviewed to be both in line with these changed needs, and competitive in relation to the products of other organizations. Organizations therefore engage in research activities to acquire a whole range of information related to their operations. We have already seen that some of this research is concerned with obtaining market information, but there is a great deal more concerned with the acquisition of technical knowledge related to processing techniques, materials and energy sources and application. This research is concerned with two aspects of the organization's activities. First, it is concerned with attempting to ensure that the existing operations are being performed as effectively and efficiently as possible within the limitations which inevitably restrict the operations of all enterprises (finance, space, etc.). This aspect of the research activity is concerned with developments in the methods of processing, the techniques applied, the materials used, and the specifications needed for individual items. Secondly, it is concerned with the attempt to break new ground. This new ground is not restricted to scientific and technological development, but is also concerned with behavioural research, for example, research into reducing boredom and frustration produced by modern production methods, or ways of resolving conflicts between the organization and its work force.

Research is classified under two categories: pure research and applied research. Pure research has the objective of extending the boundaries of human knowledge without necessarily having any practical application. This category is not undertaken by the majority of business organizations since they could not generally afford the financial outlay necessary as much of it will, of its own nature, be unproductive in commercial terms. Universities and other research establishments are more normally concerned with this. Business organizations are primarily concerned with applied research, with either general or specific applications in mind. The term development is used to describe the various activities engaged in to convert the findings of the applied research into practical terms related to materials, processes, products, equipment and systems.

The research and development activity presents great problems to an organization. First of all it is expensive both in terms of money and time. Secondly, it is often unproductive in terms of specific developments which can be incorporated into the manufacturing activity elsewhere. Thirdly, it is very difficult to predict the proportion of the work of research and development that will ultimately be converted into financial benefits. As a result it is very difficult for organizations to assess the extent of the total budget which ought to be devoted to this activity. It is very easy for organizations either to spend too much or too little with quite serious consequences in terms of ultimate profitability. Of course the extent of the need for research and development will vary according to the nature of the activities undertaken. Organizations with strong scientific or technological links will have the greatest need, and these include pharmaceuticals, electronics, chemicals, telecommunications and aerospace. And because of these difficulties it is often necessary to engage the services of external agencies specializing in the research activity, for example the Rubber and Plastics Research Association, and the government Scientific and Industrial Research Department. In some cases membership of a trade association may provide an opportunity of sharing the research burden. This sharing can vary from simply dividing the cost among the members, to establishing joint research schemes and establishments.

Research and development is closely enmeshed with the design function. The design function is basically concerned with balancing the ideal model for the product or service with the consumers' requirements and preferences. In its broadest sense, design is a term used to encompass all the activities related to the development of a product or service, from inception through all the developmental stages to the final model. The design activity, therefore, is an integrating activity that brings together all sectors of the organization concerned with product development, manufacture, sales and finance.

3.9 PERSONNEL

The personnel function is concerned with the employment and management of people. There is a great deal of confusion about the nature and operation of this function. Where an organization has developed a specific personnel department its purpose will be a service to mainstream departments concerned with the production and selling of its goods and services, and not a function which takes away the responsibility for the management of people from those directly responsible for their day-to-day supervision. Thus all managers and supervisors have a personnel responsibility as part of their job role. The need for specialist departments stems from the increasing complexity of employment conditions and systems, together with the ever-increasing need to make better use of people at work. This chapter will not explore the managerial responsibility for the face-to-face management of people, but will examine the nature of the specialist support function, usually called the personnel and training department.

The personnel function is concerned with the problem of manning the organization. It is, therefore, concerned with determining the quantity and quality of people needed for the effective operation of the enterprise. This information is determined on both a long- and a short-term basis. This process is called manpower planning, and is also concerned with the various means of ensuring that the manning needs identified are met. The number of personnel required derives from the volume of business which the organization intends to perform in the period under consideration. The sales forecasts can be translated into production targets, purchasing targets, and targets for all the other sections of the organization. Similarly, they can be translated into personnel needs, that is, the number of people needed by each section in order to achieve these targets. An examination of the existing work force will provide details of the capabilities and potential of the existing personnel which, when compared with the overall work load need, will indicate the recruitment needs of the organization.

Analysis of Work Roles

The nature of each job is determined by a process called *job analysis*, which is concerned with the collection of data related to the various aspects of each post. This information will reflect the nature of job roles and will vary from position to position. Thus, managerial posts are analysed to determine the true nature of the post in such terms as areas of authority, the number of subordinates supervised, the limits of authority, and the position in the control hierarchy. Shop floor posts in manufacturing organizations are analysed in terms of the sequence of operations performed, the methods of performing each operation, and an analysis of the time an average worker takes to perform the work. The information collected by the process of job analysis is presented in the form of a *job description*. This is a document which sets out the information in a logical and often summarized way. It is used for a variety of purposes, for example, it can be the basis for determining the characteristics of the person considered most suitable to perform the work. This is called the *personnel specification* and describes the characteristics of the ideal person for each job in such terms as age, education, qualifications, industrial training and previous work experience, and physical characteristics such as strength, eyesight, hearing and specific aptitudes including manual dexterity and numeracy.

Recruitment

Recruitment of labour includes giving consideration to the potentialities of the existing labour force. Internal promotion can be the most effective means of filling job vacancies. It is good for the morale of employees since they will see that the chance of personal advancement is open to them. It is also highly cost effective since training costs and other factors such as lost production are minimized. Where internal appointment is not possible external sources of recruitment have to be used. This requires considerable expertise since external recruitment is expensive, the sources of supply of suitable labour may be difficult to identify, the methods of contacting the sources may be difficult to isolate, the time-scale may be critical, and there may be extreme competition for certain types of employee from competitive organizations. External recruitment sources include the Department of Employment, employment agencies, schools, colleges and universities, the careers service and advertising.

Selection

Selection is the term given to the process of evaluating the abilities (attributes) of each job applicant. The job description and personnel specifications are important documents in this context. The selection process in most organizations includes the use of selection advertising (which attempts to attract only those applicants suitable for the post), application forms, references, aptitude and ability testing, personality tests, medical examination and interviewing. During the selection process it is important to understand fully the nature of the post to be filled, the types of human characteristics and qualifications most likely to match the job requirements, and the selection activities most likely to identify these from the applicants for a post. Since interviewing is a universally adopted method of making selection choices it is important to study it in considerable depth; and this is examined in Chapter 6.

Employment Conditions

The personnel department is responsible for determining the terms and conditions of employment in relation to particular job posts. This involves having a complete understanding of policies in relation to salaries and wages, holidays, sickness and welfare conditions and facilities, redundancy, employment terms such as the notice to be given by either side in the event of termination of the employment contract, and disciplinary procedures, grievance procedures and systems, and any other employment conditions which either the organization imposes unilaterally, or has agreed with trade unions via negotiation. From this list it will be apparent that a full understanding of existing and proposed legislation affecting the employment of people is required. In relation to this and other responsibilities it is important for the personnel department to keep a system of personnel records which give a complete employment history for each employee.

Labour legislation today provides employees with a degree of protection against unfair treatment by the employer never before seen in the United Kingdom (and many other countries as well). This has increased the responsibility of the personnel function since it must become both conversant with and skilled in dealing with tribunal and court proceedings.

Education and Training

All companies with a genuine concern for the people they employ will have induction procedures for new staff. This concern is twofold: a concern for the comfort and feelings of people new to the organization, who usually feel lost and uncomfortable during the first few days of a new job; and secondly a concern for the efficiency with which employees give a return for the salaries and wages paid to them. Induction courses will therefore usually include a programme of introduction to the facilities and procedures of the organization appropriate to the particular new employee. In addition they will include the preliminary introduction and basic training for the particular job to be performed.

The personnel department will also be responsible for developing longer-term training programmes for both newly-appointed people and existing staff whose development requires a course or courses of further training. The aim of these courses is to maximize the contribution of employees to increased productivity and efficiency, whilst at the same time increasing the opportunity for them to increase their own earning power. This training activity will vary in nature according to the training needs of the employees concerned. They may be totally devised and run by the organization internally. Alternatively they may be run by a consultant on the organization's premises, or externally at a college or university, a specialist training or research establishment, or a government training centre. It is also possible for other combinations to be used, for example, many educational establishments will provide in-plant training for organizations in relation to specific training needs.

All levels of personnel in an organization will need training from time to time, including top management and shopfloor representatives. The nature of the training need will vary from short programmes designed to develop new skills or to provide new information (for example legislation requirements) to long-term programmes of development, such as apprenticeship schemes and management development programmes. We have already seen that change, resulting from the research and development and marketing activities, requires the organization to engage in new activities which will generally result in a manpower retraining need. As the rate of change continues to increase so the manpower retraining needs of work organizations in all sectors of the economy increase.

In addition to specific training related to the job roles existing in the structure of organizations, many employers are willing to support their employees wishing to pursue courses of education, usually at a local college or through the Open University or correspondence schools.

Employer-Employee Relations

In Chapter 2 we examined the need for organizations to develop a system of rules relating to the conduct of individuals occupying various job roles. These rules are very difficult, if not impossible, for the organization to impose unilaterally, since most people both demand and are entitled to an opportunity of contributing to their specifications. Thus the organization must set up one of two means by which employees can have a voice in the making of rules: *joint consultation* or *negotiation*. In most organizations it is one of the functions of the personnel department to organize these activities. The responsibility involves the very exacting tasks of mediating, negotiating and conciliating between employees, trade unions and management. The personnel department is therefore required to have a thorough knowledge of collective agreements, conciliation and arbitration, the appropriate legislation, and the policy and rules of the organization.

Negotiation is perhaps the more exacting of the two means by which employees can have a voice in decision making, since it is a bargaining process which is expected to result in very definite outcomes, such as new pay agreements, changes in employment conditions, and changes in the rules of procedure between the two sides. The outcomes which relate to specific matters such as pay, holiday entitlement, fringe benefits and so on, are called substantive matters, while outcomes concerned with the nature of the negotiating process itself, and other rules governing the relationships between the employer and the employee, are called procedural matters. The atmosphere in which negotiation is carried out can sometimes be very hostile with the two sides taking opposite stances in relation to issues. On occasions this hostility, or failure to agree, leads to employees withdrawing their labour as a protest and a form of pressure to bring the employer nearer to their point of view. Where this action is taken by employees without the agreement of a trade union the strike is termed unofficial.

Consultation is not a bargaining process, and is not concerned with the process of joint decision making. Rather it is a process of communication whereby the employer can discuss issues with the employee, and vice versa. Because it is not a process of bargaining, joint consultation tends to lack 'teeth' and many consider it to be an ineffectual process as a result. It is therefore necessary for the personnel function to work hard to maintain and improve the effectiveness of the activity of joint consultation in order to foster positive relationships between the employer and the employee. It is not the intention of joint consultation to be merely a form of grievance-airing platform, but a genuine process of working together in order to attempt to solve problems of mutual concern. The process therefore imposes obligations on both the employer and the employee. The employer's obligation is to acknowledge fully the workers' right to be consulted and to recognize the value of their contributions. The employee's obligation is to recognize management's ultimate right to manage the organization. The more these obligations are recognized the greater the chance of employees' participating in the decisions that affect them at their place of work.

Remuneration

An important aspect of the activities of the personnel function is the responsibility of providing a full and accurate information service regarding the wage and salary structures operated by the organization. This involves careful monitoring of collectively negotiated pay agreements and salary scales, bonus systems and merit rating schemes. The personnel department is also responsible for ongoing research to maintain an up-to-date log of pay movements in the economy generally, so that the pay structure of the particular organization does not deviate from those of employers in similar industries.

Health, Welfare and Safety

The second half of the twentieth century has seen the introduction of legislation on a large scale to ensure that employees are provided with fundamental and prescribed conditions with respect to health, safety and welfare at work. In addition to the minimum levels prescribed by law, many employers provide facilities and benefits considerably in advance of the minimum. These benefits are provided as a result of many pressures, including the demand for higher living standards, the increasing competition for skilled labour and the greater contribution to organizational effectiveness, and generally result in a contented work force, a general concern for the health of people at work, together with the increasing realization by employers of their social responsibility.

The personnel department has the responsibility of ensuring that working conditions satisfy the minimum legal requirements, that adequate welfare services are provided, including such facilities as medical aid, transport, pension funds and perhaps assistance with temporary housing, and that adequate sports and social facilities are provided where appropriate. Perhaps the most acute responsibility rests in the area of ensuring safe working practices and procedures.

3.10 FINANCE

By now the reader may have formed the impression that the internal structure of work organizations has developed to become rather like the specialization of functions performed by the organs in the human body. In fact, this is not a bad analogy. Each of the organs has a specific function to perform to a prescribed level in order that the whole body performs well. In order to achieve this the separate organs need to be co-ordinated and controlled, hence the body has several control and co-ordinating mechanisms which include the blood system, the nervous system, and the endocrine system. In a similar way work organizations need control and co-ordinating mechanisms. The finance function can well be regarded as one of these essential mechanisms. Indeed, money has often been referred to as the life blood of all organizations. In this sense the supply and flow of money control the level of activity of the whole enterprise. Decisions have to be taken regarding the capital structure, the source and supply of funds, the determination of levels of return to shareholders (dividends), liquidity levels, investments, and so on. Perhaps above all, there is the need to determine operating activities in cost terms so that costed planned actions can be compared with actual results, and any variances fully analysed. This is the process of budgeting, a highly critical activity for all organizations in all sectors of the economy.

The finance function will be given a different title depending on a number of variables. Perhaps the most obvious is the difference between those in the private sector and those in the non-manufacturing areas of the public sector. In the private sector the function is usually divided into *financial accounting* and *cost accounting*, whilst in the non-industrial sectors of local and national government the whole activity comes under the general title of the *Treasury*. The reader should examine the titles given to the financial function of the organization with which he is familiar, together with any sub-divisions that may exist, and determine the essential function that is performed and its contribution to the effectiveness of the enterprise as a whole. (It is always helpful in investigations of this kind to use diagrams to illustrate the relationship with other functions.)

It is important for the student to appreciate the nature of the dependence of other functions on finance. For example, the new product development activity associated with marketing has to be financed until the return from goods sold meets the needs. In more general terms, activities in the research and development area require financing, sometimes without return. It is therefore important that an accurate check is made on the amount of finance made available to development activity; too much may lead to financial problems, but equally too little may result in the same problem in the long term as outdated products or services will result in a loss of income.

One essential feature of the accounting function is the recording process. All aspects of accountancy – financial accounting, cost accounting and financial management – are concerned with recording the financial transactions of the organization. The recording process has a twofold function: first, to record what has happened, and secondly, as an aid in determining what should happen. Information is collected and presented in the form most suitable to the various decision-making needs of management. The important features are that the recording process is comprehensive, covering all aspects of the organization's activities (for example, sales, purchases, costings, investments and so on); that the recorded information is classified in a prescribed manner; and that the information is readily accessible.

The important control function is provided in two ways. First, control is achieved by providing financial 'pictures' of the organization in terms of statements – for example, profit and loss accounts, balance sheets and operating statements. These give different financial perspectives; thus the profit and loss account summarizes the effects of all transactions for a prescribed period, whilst the balance sheet gives a static view of the financial situation of an organization as at a particular point in time. The second means is to provide a measurement system by which real activities can be monitored. This is the budgeting activity. Measurement is made possible by comparing real revenue and cost against budgeted revenue and costs, and the differences (or variances) are analysed and accounted for. The recorded financial information is vitally important in the process of budgeting for future activities.

It is only since the advent of the joint stock company that the accounting function has been called on to provide a basis for the managers of organizations to determine levels of solvency and profitability together with a means of informing such people as shareholders and auditors how the activities over a prescribed period have been conducted, and what the results have been. Increasingly management have to account for their activities to many bodies such as trade unions, government departments, ratepayers' action groups, creditors and, in many cases, the wider general public. It is in this sense that management uses accountancy techniques to explain certain aspects of its stewardship role. All people occupying a job role in which they are responsible for activities which utilize other people's property are in a position of stewardship. Accountability is the state of being liable to explain how resources have been used, and what results have been attained.

In short, therefore, the finance function of all organizations is twofold: first it is concerned with external stewardship and secondly with internal management. Most organizations use finance provided by other people such as shareholders, ratepayers, taxpayers and loans from banks and finance companies. The finance function is concerned with raising funds as necessary from the various sources available, and accounting to those sources how the funds have been applied. The second is a management function. Financial analysis of an organization's activities has proved to be one of the most effective ways of providing direction and control.

It is not the purpose of this book to introduce the reader to the various techniques used in accounting. The important focus here is an overview sufficient to provide the reader with an appreciation of the role of the finance function in relation to the other divisions of an organization. Perhaps in its simplest form this appreciation should be a realization that formal work organizations cannot function without money or credit. Money is simply purchasing power. The possession of money enables the organization to employ human effort, both mental and physical, and to obtain control and ownership of resources.

3.11 SUMMARY

The aim of this chapter has been to illustrate how work organizations are structured to achieve their objectives. We have taken a generalist approach in the sense that the description may not reflect any specific organization. Nevertheless it is felt that the generalization is sufficiently reflective of the typical structure found in business, commerce and even the public services to provide the student with a realistic base from which to understand and analyse the organizations with which he comes into contact.

The chapter has not been written to stand in isolation from the others. On the contrary, the reader must also consider Chapters 1 and 2 to attain a balanced perspective. Only by taking the three chapters together can a business student begin to appreciate the complexities associated with the structure and functioning of work organizations. The need for objectives is emphasized. Without these the structure of an organization is 'hit and miss'. Objectives have to be specified bearing in mind all the problems which were identified in Chapter 1. The description of the principal functional areas which typically constitute work organizations is an attempt to translate some of the theoretical organizational issues, discussed in Chapter 2, into a real form.

3.12 MARSH ENGINEERING LTD: A CASE STUDY

Aim

This is a simple study which requires the reader to think about methods of organization. It is also an attempt to bring to life some of the issues described in this chapter.

Objectives

1. To provide an opportunity for the reader to design an organizational structure and think about the inter-relationships and communication systems which must be satisfied for an organization to function efficiently.
2. To bring together the theoretical issues raised in Chapter 2 and the practical realities discussed in Chapter 3.

Student Tasks

1. Draw up an organizational structure, or structures, which you feel would satisfy the requirements of Marsh Engineering Ltd.
2. Indicate the objectives you have attempted to attain through the structures you have designed.

Reorganization at Marsh Engineering Ltd

Allied Industries Ltd is the headquarters organization of a large group of companies in the light engineering field. Group products are diverse, ranging from aluminium kitchenware to components for the automotive industry. In addition to many financial, commercial and technical services performed for the firm in the group, Allied Industries Ltd operates a central organization and methods department which is much used by the member companies.

Three months ago a new firm was added to the group, Marsh Engineering Ltd, an old established concern which Allied Industries is now in the process of modernizing. Part of this programme involves overhauling the company's organization structure and you, as a member of the central O & M department, have been given this task.

The work is going well and, after careful analysis, you have got as far as listing a number of management positions which you intend to retain in the new structure. These are as follows:

No.	Position title	Chart code
1	Accountant	Act
2	Assembly superintendent	AS
3	Buyer	B
4	Canteen manager	CM
5	Quality control manager	QCM
6	Cost and works accountant	CA
7	Chief draughtsman	CD
8	Cashier	C
9	Designer	D
10	Distribution manager	DM
11	Development and design chief engineer	D & D
12	Computer manager	CuM
13	Education and training officer	E & TO
14	Export manager	EM
15	Employment officer	EO
16	Foundry superintendent	FS
17	Foreman inspector	FIns
18	Goods inwards inspector	GII
19	Home sales manager	HSM
20	Managing director	MD
21	Market research officer	MRO
22	Chief motion and time study engineer	MTS
23	Maintenance engineer	ME
24	Machine shop superintendent	M/cS

No.	Position title	Chart code
25	Nurse	N
26	Personal assistant to managing director	PA
27	Progress chaser	PCh
28	Planning engineer	PE
29	Personnel manager	PerM
30	Production controller	PC
31	Production development officer	PDO
32	Secretary and chief accountant	S
33	Stores superintendent	SS
34	Safety officer	SO
35	Marketing manager	MM
36	Transport officer	TO
37	Toolroom superintendent	TS
38	Welfare officer	WO
39	Works manager i/c production	WM
40	Assistant works manager	AWM
41	Programmer	P

Allied Industries Ltd, believing firmly in standardization, follows the same pattern of having five main grades in the management of each of its firms:

No.	Management grade
1	Chief executive
2	Senior executive
3	Executive
4	Junior executive
5	Senior staff

The only personnel in the chief executive grade are the managing directors of the companies in the group, and all senior executives report to a chief executive. You have already decided that other grades will not necessarily be responsible to the grade above, thus a person in, say, senior staff grade may report directly to an executive, or perhaps even to a senior executive, depending upon circumstances. One of your main aims is to make the new structure a sound economic proposition.

Further Reading

1. Betts, P. W. (1980) *Supervisory Studies.* Estover, Plymouth: MacDonald & Evans.
2. Drucker, P. F. (1969) *The Practice of Management.* London: Pan.
3. Evans, D. (1981) *Supervisory Management.* Eastbourne: Holt, Rinehart and Winston.
4. Harding, H. A. (1970) *Production Management.* Estover, Plymouth: MacDonald & Evans.
5. Jervis, F. R. J. & Frank, W. F. (1962) *An Introduction to Industrial Administration.* London: Harrap.
6. Milner, D. & Taylor, M. (1981) *The Management of Work.* Eastbourne: Holt, Rinehart and Winston.
7. O'Shaughnessy, J. (1966) *Business Organisation.* London: George Allen & Unwin.
8. Pitfield, R. R. (1977) *Business Organisation.* Estover, Plymouth: MacDonald & Evans.
9. Woolcott, L. A. & Rose, C. A. (1979) *Business Organisation.* Amersham: Hulton.

4

People: The Needs of Individuals and Groups at Work

4.1   WHY DO PEOPLE WORK AT ALL?

In the first three chapters we have examined many aspects of formal work organizations, but perhaps the most important areas are those concerned with the behaviour of people. You are recommended to observe the different behaviour patterns of individuals at your own place of work or college. Note particularly the differences in individual attitudes to situations, the differing response to instructions, changes, or the nature of the work to be done. Notice the differences in work rates between different people, differences in work standards and, perhaps above all, differences in the behaviour of the same individual to changed situations. Compare your own attitudes and opinions with those of your colleagues. You will undoubtedly notice many variations. Some behaviour will be positive and supportive of the organization, some will be in conflict, and perhaps some may even be negative and destructive. These differences raise many questions which are vitally important to our understanding of the functioning of formal work organizations.

Why do people work at all? This question is crucial to our understanding of the behaviour of people in work organizations. Notice the way in which this question is phrased. It does not ask 'Why do people go to work?' but 'Why do people work *at all?*'. Work in this sense really means any kind of mental or physical exertion, whether performed in employment, in the home, in sport, in the garden, on holiday, or anywhere else. So the question could really be rephrased as 'Why do people engage in any kind of mental or physical activity?'. In order to begin to answer the questions the reader is asked to perform a simple exercise.

Exercise

This is best performed in the following stages:

1. Identify several situations, either at home, work or at leisure, where physical or mental activity is undertaken. (This should be relatively easy since we are doing something which entails mental or physical activity most of the time.)
2. Describe clearly and briefly the activities performed, for example the activities chosen might be reading a novel at bed-time, playing tennis at the weekend, eating or preparing a meal, and so on.
3. Identify and write down the apparent reasons for performing the activities identified in 2 above. Again, these might be something like the need to eat and drink, the enjoyment and relaxation of engaging in sporting activity, the sheer necessity of engaging in activity in preparation for later activities – shopping and food preparation preceding the food consumption stage, and so on, or some other similar explanation.
4. Now perform the same exercise with some of your colleagues, friends or fellow students. The aim should be to list the different activities which a number of people identify as work using the wider definition we have now adopted. It is also important to list the reasons they identify for performing them.
5. Examine the lists to see if any consistent pattern is emerging.

It would not be surprising if you came to the conclusion that there appears to be a connection between some kind of human need and a related activity designed to satisfy that specific need. Try to illustrate this relationship diagrammatically. (You will probably come up with something similar to that shown in Fig. 4.1.) Perhaps the most important

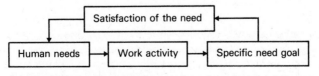

Figure 4.1 *Relationship between human needs and activity*

question relates to the result of the work activity undertaken – does it satisfy the need to which it was related? This provides the all important feedback loop which tells us whether or not to continue with the activity, or even to make a modification if the original is failing to produce the intended result. Thus we can add a feedback loop to our diagram. This gives us a preliminary model which we can use to investigate the question more fully and rigorously.

This chapter is concerned with examining theories relating to human behaviour and, in particular, theories which help us to become clearer in relation to the model of behaviour we have already produced. The main focus of the chapter is then on a second question, 'How does our knowledge of the behaviour of people generally help us to understand their behaviour in the formal work situation?'.

The relationship between work activity and the satisfaction of need was examined thoroughly by Abraham Maslow, who presented his conclusions in his paper *A Theory of Human Motivation* (1943). Maslow's main conclusion was that there exists a wide spectrum of different human needs ranging from the very simple and basic to the highly sophisticated and complex, and that human behaviour is directed towards the satisfaction of these needs. He maintained that the process of satisfying needs is continuous, and that as soon as one need has been satisfied, another takes its place.

Although the individual needs throughout the spectrum are probably too numerous to identify, Maslow argues that it is possible to group them under five general classifications, each classification being a collection of similarly based needs. The classifications correspond to different stages along the spectrum from basic to highly complex. Thus the first classification corresponds with all needs fundamental to the continuance of life, including the need for food, water, shelter and warmth. At the other extreme, the fifth classification relates to human creativity, the need to use fully the levels of skill and ability possessed by individuals, that is the need for self-fulfilment. This is shown in Fig. 4.2 and Table 4.1.

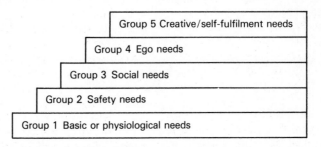

Figure 4.2   *The hierarchical relationship of human needs*

Having provided a basis for the grouping of human needs, the next part of Maslow's theory is perhaps the most important. He argues that these groupings are in fact in a hierarchical relationship to each other and that the lower level needs have to be satisfied before the next or subsequent levels begin to have an effect. Thus, to take an extreme example, imagine a situation in which an individual has been without food and water for a considerable length of time. The dominant force acting on that individual will be the need to satisfy the need for food and drink. This same individual may be highly accomplished in art or science but his desire to use his skill or knowledge will be temporarily lost whilst he strives to satisfy the basic physiological needs necessary for the continuation of life. This extreme relationship is simply an exaggerated view of the situation in everyday life. In this sense the desire to eat is a function of the length of time

Table 4.1 *Classification of needs based on Maslow*

Classification	Description
Level one: physiological or basic needs	Needs essential to the continuance of life. The grouping includes food, water, heat, sleep, etc.
Level two: safety and security needs	Needs essential to self-protection. The grouping includes shelter, insurance, restrictive practice, rules, etc.
Level three: social needs	The need for friendship and acceptance. This grouping includes companionship, affection, friendship and support.
Level four: ego or esteem needs	The need to be held in esteem by others. The needs grouped here include recognition, respect and status.
Level five: creative/self-fulfilment needs	The need to make full use of individual skill and abilities. The needs grouped here include achievement.

since food was last consumed. The effect of hunger on other activities, therefore, is proportional to the extent to which we actually feel hungry. There is a like relationship between all the needs. This implies that in an environment where all the need levels have the opportunity of coming into play (in an economy sufficiently developed to provide for the minimum levels of physiological and safety needs), there is not, in fact, a strict hierarchical relationship but an oscillating effect of needs constantly coming into play, being satisfied and replaced by other needs. Human energy is therefore expended on a constantly changing basis in an attempt to satisfy all or just some of the needs.

If we now change the original question slightly to 'Why do people go to work in a formal organization?' we are likely to receive a straightforward answer like 'To earn sufficient money to provide for the family'. Try the question out yourself on anyone you know who is employed in a factory, shop, office, or any other type of formal work situation. Let us now try to understand the answers given in relation to the need based model suggested by Maslow. What people might be saying is that they accept a contract to work in a formal organization in order to receive, in return, the means by which the social and physical needs of both themselves and their families can be satisfied. So the pay packet is rightly a very important feature of the work contract – it provides the means of purchasing food, drink, and all the other goods and services associated with a normal way of life in a developed economic system. It seems reasonable therefore to accept this answer to the question of why people physically leave their homes to travel to attend a formal organization designed to accomplish work activities. But does it satisfactorily explain what these same individuals actually do during each working period? Does the size of the pay packet determine the level or quality of work individuals perform? And does it explain the level of commitment people have to their work?

It is important to understand the difference between the reasons why people actually attend a formal work organization and what they do when they get there, and to obtain as much knowledge as possible about the behaviour of people in formal work organizations to understand how they actually function. If we are trying to establish why people do or do not perform work as prescribed by the organization, we should perhaps investigate if there is any relationship between the nature of the work to be done and individual needs of the people asked to do that work. For example, if we examine the tasks individuals are required to perform on a mass production line we are likely to find them repetitive, consisting of a fairly limited number of operations. Thus the time to learn the job is short and its cycle times (i.e. intervals at which the job is repeated) are equally short. On the basis of the organizational principles developed by F. W. Taylor (see Chapter 2) the output per worker is expected to be high. But problems may arise in the individual's reaction to the work. Do all workers react in the same way? Do they find the work satisfying? Are they looking to the work to satisfy their social, ego or self-fulfilment needs? If they are, to what extent does the work satisfy these needs? To what extent do they find the work boring and frustrating? How does such boredom and frustration find expression?

It is likely that these questions will produce different answers from different individuals. Nevertheless, an analysis of working days lost due to industrial action in British industry does seem to show a marked concentration in those areas with a high utilization of mass production processes. It is therefore most important that we try to establish whether or not there is a relationship between the behaviour of people in a formal work organization and the work they are actually asked to perform. Because we are dealing with a social rather than a physical science, any conclusions we draw are subject to the constraints of observation rather than controlled experimentation. What is important is that the student of business becomes aware of the possible relationships between the nature of the work to be done and the behaviour of the people actually doing it. It may be that the work, in fact, produces a conflict of needs in that an individual finds his work produces problems resulting from a desire to satisfy two or more mutually exclusive needs, for example, the need for a salary or wage to satisfy many personal and family needs, and the need for satisfaction, achievement and self-esteem. Where such needs are in conflict, the resultant behavioural response is often anxiety, irritability, frustration and even such organic symptoms as headaches, muscular pain, stomach pains, and so on.

4.2　NEED SATISFACTION AND MOTIVATION

The importance of Maslow's needs based theory is not that it is a prescriptive panacea for the treatment of all people in a formal work setting, but that it provides an important insight to be considered when we attempt to understand the behaviour of individuals or groups of individuals within work organizations. For the businessman it is important to assess the framework of values possessed by his employees – the concerns and issues they consider to be important. In this way it is often possible to find work activities which the organization requires which can be matched with the value systems and capabilities of individual employees. This approach requires the realization that the behaviour of people must be assessed on an individual basis, since people have their own unique behavioural characteristics. One person's set of values and needs may be dismissed as valueless and irrelevant by another.

Look back at the simple exercise you performed at the beginning of this chapter and consider the type of work situations which give you the greatest personal satisfaction. It is likely that you will identify several situations quite easily. The problem for the business manager is that he must be able to identify these types of situations in relation to people other than himself, that is the people he manages. A second problem arises, since there is often an inbalance between what the organization can offer and what individuals would like to be doing. There is often no alternative work to give an employee who is bored and frustrated with his existing job role. But even in this situation it is important that the businessman realizes the possible causes of an individual's boredom and frustration and consequent behavioural manifestations.

In the past, many managers who have perceived boredom, frustration, poor performance, lateness and absenteeism in their employees have concluded that they are naturally lazy and will avoid work if they can, and because of this these individuals are incapable of self-control and direction; they are unreliable and often irresponsible. Such a conclusion would lead to an obvious management style, one of coercion with a strict rule book and pattern of working, and penalties for stepping out of line (the ultimate penalty being dismissal). But what if this perception is wholly or even partially incorrect? What if the problem is the work itself, and not the nature of the person doing the work? In such cases the management style adopted could merely exacerbate the problem by generating even greater levels of resentment and aggression.

The value of Maslow's theory is that it requires us to question our first conclusions about the apparent nature of individuals, and to consider the relationship between work and behaviour before drawing generalized conclusions about the behavioural characteristics of a particular individual, or groups of individuals.

4.3   INDIVIDUAL DIFFERENCES

The basic problem with people, as far as the formal work organization is concerned, is that they are not robots. Robots behave in a predictable way depending on what they have been programmed to do. People, on the other hand, are all different. They have certain hereditary characteristics determined by a genetic programme which many believe prescribes the basic personality traits of each individual. This genetic programme, given to a baby by its parents, determines the physical characteristics such as colour of eyes, hair, skin, height and so on. It also provides the beginnings of the individual behavioural characteristics as well. The genetic programme is only the beginning: for man and woman are both the victims and the products of the environments into which they are born and grow up.

At this stage we would like you to try another exercise. Again we would suggest the exercise might best be performed as a group discussion, but this should not prevent a meaningful attempt by the individual reader.

Exercise

1.   Identify groups of forces or influences which act upon an individual in his development from a new-born baby to adulthood, and which are likely to have a significant effect in shaping the personality and behavioural characteristics of the adult.
2.   Discuss the nature of the influence of each of the forces you identify, and list the different ways in which you think each could have an effect in shaping the behaviour of the individual.
3.   Discuss the relevance of these differences for the business organization.

Your deliberations are likely to come up with a list that includes such influences as the immediate family, the social environment of early childhood, the geographical location with its own particular cultural characteristics, the nature of the locality (rural/urban, large/small, etc.), the social groups with which the individual associates (clubs, societies, friends, etc.), the various educational experiences, the mass media, differences in physical and intellectual capabilities and aptitudes, the working group, trade unions, the formal work situation and the treatment received from managers and super-visors, and so on. The interplay of these variables will gradually shape and reshape the values and beliefs held. By values and beliefs we mean the matters an individual regards as important, both physical and social. The variables will produce in the individual the basic framework by which he determines what is right and wrong, good and bad, and so on, for him.

It is therefore important that any businessman be aware that an organization consists of a group of individuals all with their unique set of values and beliefs and therefore needs. Some of these will correspond with the values held by the individuals managing the organization, whilst others will be in opposition. The business organization has to determine what attitude and response will be taken to people who express opposition to the goals and directions of management. We have seen in Chapter 2 a variety of differ-ent formal responses ranging from a strict definition of job roles and procedural rules of the classical approaches to organizational design (scientific approach and Weberian bureaucracy) to more open participation of all members of the formal organization in determining the direction of formal goals.

4.4   FRUSTRATION AND AGGRESSION: PROBLEMS FOR THE ORGANIZATION

Simply stated frustration is the name we give to the state of discontent an individual experiences if he is unable to achieve his desires. This, of course, varies in intensity according to a whole variety of different influences. Take, for example, the possible state of boredom many people feel in performing a simple repetitive task over and over again. The extent of boredom in the same individual will vary from day to day, depend-ing on his state of health, family circumstances, social relationships, personal activities, achievements, and so on. Nevertheless, bearing in mind that boredom is variable, even for the same individual, it usually results in a state of frustration. Research has shown that in both animals and humans unrelieved frustration develops into aggression, which often demonstrates itself as anger.

Anger is a physical phenomenon which can be measured in terms of increased heart rate, raised blood pressure, and so on. The individual seeks release from these tensions by taking either direct or indirect action against whatever it is he perceives as the cause of the frustration. The action taken is often irrational and destructive. On the other hand, the action taken could be positive if the individual tries to find a solution to the problem. This action may be to look for an opportunity which will provide a less repeti-tive and simple job, or to redirect his attention to an alternative goal. Many workers on a production line have developed the ability to perform the job tasks quite satisfactorily whilst engaging in a second diversionary type of activity with the other people making up the working group. (This activity may take the form of a discussion circle or a singing group, for example.)

The negative responses have four common forms: physical or vocal aggression, regression into forms of childish behaviour, resignation and fixation. By resignation we refer to the response where individuals perform the absolute minimum in order to retain the job position. In the case of fixation the individuals continue with the same behaviour pattern long after it should have become obvious that the activity will have no positive results for the person concerned.

It is therefore important for the student to realize that the work the organization requires an individual to perform may produce frustration, and that such frustration can be the result of a variety of causes, including:

1. disagreement between the individual and management about how the job can best be performed;
2. the repetitive and undemanding nature of the job itself;
3. the rules of the organization which the individual may consider too restricting or unnecessary;
4. the apparent irrelevance of the job task in the eyes of the individual;
5. the relationship that exists between the individual and the management of the organization.

It should be apparent therefore that in the operation of any type of business organization employee frustration can have serious consequences for the effectiveness of its activities. In some ways certain levels of frustration are inevitable: the frustrations which are so common in relation to salary and wages systems, or the frustrations of subordinate relationships, and so on. From a business education point of view the aim is to have a sufficient knowledge and understanding of the causes of frustration to be able to make a reasonable attempt at minimizing both the causes and the effects. So far in this chapter we have raised some important issues which should help in this goal of minimizing frustration, namely the matching of job design to individual talents, aptitudes and ambitions, greater care in selecting people for specific job roles to ensure that the job/person match is made as well as possible, recognizing that many, if not most, people need some form of recognition for their contributions, and greater organizational appreciation of the individuality of all employees and the importance of individual differences.

In looking at this list more closely it becomes clear that they are all interlinked in the sense that they are different expressions of human relationship situations. In this sense we are looking at the effects of the different human relationships that can exist within a formal work organization. Some of these relationships are prescribed by the organizational design. This is the *formal work organization* with its prescribed job roles and hierarchical relationships. Other relationships are not formally prescribed at all, but are the result simply of people meeting and forming friendship circles, support groups, and so on within the confines of the formal organization. These relationships are called *informal work organizations*.

4.5 INFORMAL WORK ORGANIZATION: IMPLICATIONS FOR MANAGEMENT

From your readings in Chapter 2 you have seen that research has shown that the informal work organization can be as influential as the formal one, as shown in Mayo's Hawthorne Studies. In some cases the influence can be supportive of management, as Mayo found in the Relay Assembly Room, but it can also be the reverse, as was seen in the Bank Wiring Room. The important issue is that people employed by an organization will form into social groupings themelves. They will talk to each other as they work; and will also meet at break and meal times and, as the relationship develops, they may meet outside work in their own time. These relationships can be devoted to personal issues, for example, discussing personal experiences and sharing personal joys or sorrows, but they can focus also on organizational matters, such as personal grievances, conditions of employment, management attitudes, and so on. How often have you met with fellow employees or fellow students at a break period and grumbled about pay or work difficulties, or a manager's or supervisor's attitude to you, or a lecturer's behaviour or attitude, and so on?

It is also important to recognize that while this informal social group may be restricted to the people working in close proximity within the same section or department, it can expand into a wider grouping bringing together people from different sections and departments. Thus people meeting at lunch or in the social club may represent different organizational activities, and their discussions can range across many aspects of the formal work organization. Employees can compare notes to see if their grumbles and grievances are shared by people working in other areas. When these grumbles and grievances grow to such an extent that the group members feel some significant action should be taken, there is considerable research evidence to show that the informal group becomes much more closely-knit and it is common for a spokesman or leader to be chosen to give direction. In some cases the informal group spokesman can become a powerful figure, even more influential than the officially-appointed supervisor or manager (again Mayo's Hawthorne Studies give evidence of this phenomenon). You can imagine the confusion and disharmony that results when the informal group leader and the officially appointed supervisor vie with each other for the allegiance of the group.

We have already seen that organizations form because people cannot achieve the same results working as individuals. The same is true of the informal or social group. Man is basically gregarious and needs the company and support of others to satisfy his social needs. Nevertheless, even though such needs exist, there is still the problem of individual differences, which inevitably result in a degree of conflict and frustration even in the healthiest of situations. Therefore in all human groupings, whether formal or informal, there is a need for *adjustment* to group norms if alienation is not to be the result.

Membership of the informal work group is not automatic. In most instances there are unwritten but accepted conditions which must be satisfied before an individual is accepted by an informal group. These conditions include a willingness to adjust to group norms, equality of status (it is most unlikely that individuals of different status would be accepted into the group circle), sharing in a common interest or common threat, and of course the obvious physical requirement of being geographically close enough to meet.

It is important that the positive nature of informal groups is recognized. People not only look to the work itself for satisfaction, but seek companionship and support from others at work. It is to the benefit of the formal work organization that cohesive social groups can form with the minimum of hindrance. If individuals enjoy the social intercourse that exists at work it is likely they will be motivated to attend more regularly, thus reducing such problems as lateness, absenteeism and labour turnover. The existence of a satisfactory informal organization (satisfactory in the eyes of the employees making up the social groups) can often make up for the dissatisfaction produced by the nature of the job itself. There is obviously a very fine balance here, for if the work is too unsatisfactory, either because of poor conditions or the work is so boring, then it is always possible that informal organization will develop into a pressure group with the goal of attacking the formal organization until the problems have been resolved. Hence management is constantly presented with the problem of ensuring that working conditions are good, that employment policies are fair and consistent, and that communications systems are effective, and so on.

4.6 PERCEPTION AND ATTITUDES

In this chapter great weight has been given to such terms as understanding, values, adjustments and tolerance. All these terms relate to the attitude each of us has towards each other. By attitude we mean the characteristics of the way an individual responds to another individual, an object or a situation. Attitudes are usually fairly well fixed in the make up of an individual and are therefore hard to change. Nevertheless, it is often possible to demonstrate that a person's attitude is the result of a limited interplay of forces, and that had other issues been considered, a different attitude might have been adopted: but the other issues may have been present all the time and the individual either consciously or subconsciously ignored them. Thus there is a close relationship between how we see or perceive a situation and our attitude to that situation. In the words of an American writer, 'if men perceive situations as real, then they are real in their consequences'.

Perception is the word given to the process by which we collect data via our physical senses (sight, hearing, touch, taste and smell) and then make sense of the data in the form of personal interpretations of what the data are telling us. This interpretation is influenced by earlier experience. It is a personal interpretation because all individuals are different and are therefore quite capable of perceiving the same set of sensations in different ways according to the particular experiences, motives and values each one possesses. Two individuals will often perceive the same thing differently, even in relation to a simple situation. It is no wonder then that when we move into the realm of human behaviour people form dramatically different conclusions about situations.

Let us take the example we referred to earlier, the situation where a worker performs a repetitive task of limited complexity, short operation cycle and short job learning time. Imagine two people observing the same employee. The first perceives the behaviour of the individual and notes in particular his apparent loss of job interest, the expressions of boredom, and obvious demonstrations of frustration and so on, and draws the conclusion that this particular employee is basically idle and unreliable. He is the type of individual who must be forced to keep his 'nose to the grindstone' and be continually kept under close supervision to ensure that his output is of both the quality and quantity required. The second individual observes the same worker at exactly the same time and notes the expressions of frustration and apparent loss of interest in the job. But he notices other facets of the individual's behaviour which suggest that in this case the peson is looking for a more demanding job role and greater involvement in the work of the section or department. His conclusion is that he must do something to help this person to get a more demanding job role. This might entail widening the existing job role, or giving him a completely new one. This second observer is not advocating close supervision or the use of discipline at all; on the contrary, he sees an individual who is quite capable of giving much more to the organization than that which he is being allowed or asked to do.

Why should these perceptions and consequent attitudes be so different? We are all inevitably products of our experiences. Any situation we meet is compared with our previous experiences. To use the description of Alan Fox of the University of Oxford, it is as though each of us has acquired a mental frame of reference against which we compare new experiences. We don't see new situations with an open mind at all, but already have expectations which are prescribed by our frame of reference. In relation to the behaviour of people our individual frame of reference determines first how we expect people to behave (this expectation may be different, for example, for people occupying different job roles or drawn from different social backgrounds or classes); and secondly, how we see and interpret the actual behaviour of any person or group of persons. We have already seen that it is common for different observers to see the same situation in different ways. What we are suggesting here is that the way we see is in many ways prescribed. We look for evidence that confirms our expectations. Thus in the simple example we have used, the first observer is likely to have held a frame of reference which classified most employees as basically idle, requiring constant supervision and control. When observing the behaviour of a new individual the first observer registered only those behavioural characteristics which tended to confirm his expectations. The second observer, however, held totally different expectations. Before making his observations perhaps he already expected the employee to be bored and frustrated in performing a relatively simple and repetitive task. Thus in his observations the behavioural characteristics which most particularly registered with him were those which confirmed these expectations. Thirdly, our individual frame of reference determines how we react to our observations. Our attitude to a particular individual or situation is now being formed. We have observed a situation and have drawn conclusions which are determining our attitude and response, and thus fourthly, our frame of reference in many ways also determines the methods we adopt to change other people's behaviour characteristics. Some choose discipline, close supervision and strict rules, whilst others decide on retraining, consultation, participation and shared decision making in respect to the *same* individual or group of individuals.

Douglas McGregor, in his *The Human Side of the Enterprise*, gives considerable evidence to demonstrate the universality of this perception-attitude-reaction interrelationship. McGregor observed many business managers carrying out their tasks, and in particular he noted the different ways in which they treated subordinates. From quite a large sample of observations he was able to identify that these managers fell into different groups according to the way they treated people. McGregor described the assumptions the managers must have made about their subordinates to have treated them in the way they did, and noted two extremes, one set of assumptions being described as theory X and the other as theory Y. (Remember McGregor is describing the assumptions he perceived other people to have made. He is describing two extreme frames of reference.)

Theory X

McGregor's description of the theory X frame of reference can be summarized as follows:

1. The average individual has an inherent dislike of work and will avoid it if he can; therefore
2. People must be coerced, controlled, directed and threatened with punishment to make them give adequate effort toward the achievement of organizational goals; and
3. The average individual prefers to be directed, wishes to avoid responsibility, has relatively little ambition and wants security above all.

In forming this impression, McGregor perceived organizational control being sought through the exercise of formal authority systems. Formal authority and physical coercion were the dominant methods used to achieve organizational targets. The behavioural consequences of unsatisfied needs in individuals were perceived as causes not effects; that is, it was regarded as the basic trait of the average man to resent work, and aggression was the natural expression of this resentment.

Theory Y

McGregor's description of theory Y is in many ways a mirror-image of the premises of theory X:

1. Work, both in its physical and mental form, can be as natural as play or rest.
2. Man will usually exercise self-direction and self-control in achieving objectives and targets to which he is committed.
3. Commitment to goals is a function of the rewards associated with their achievement.
4. The average human can learn to accept and even seek responsibility.
5. Many more individuals are able to contribute positively and creatively to the solution of organizational problems than do so.
6. The potentialities of the average person are not fully used.

It is not difficult to see that any manager having theory Y as his basic frame of reference will expect workers to behave in a totally different way from the manager holding a theory X frame of reference. The theory Y manager will encourage participation, and attempt to build a constructive team spirit on the basis of integration and self-control. The participation process will consist basically of creating opportunities, under suitable conditions, for people to influence organizational decisions that fundamentally affect them as individuals and members of particular groups, and to accept responsibility for their actions.

Of course these two expressions are descriptions of two extremes, as well as being generalizations. Neither may be an accurate description of any particular individual. It is in terms of generality only that theories X and Y are of immediate value. Does a particular manager or management team view the other employees of the organization as tending towards theory X or theory Y? The answer to this question will fundamentally affect the way the organization is managed. There is no basis for a precise prescription for the treatment of or approach to a particular individual. As we have seen, we must approach an individual as we perceive his make up, and no generalization can replace this need for individualized treatment. The important conclusion is that the question of how management treats people is largely determined by what it assumes the natural characteristics of people to be. The aim is for a close fit between the style of approach adopted by management and the nature of the individuals being managed. McGregor's own conclusion was that the theory Y frame of reference was the one which most nearly matched the true nature of most human beings; all that was needed was the right conditions and treatment for the theory Y behavioural characteristics to present themselves. Such a conclusion would obviously view the higher needs in Maslow's motivation theory as the most influential.

Support for McGregor's conclusion was provided by Frederick Herzberg, Professor of Psychology at the Case Western Reserve University, Ohio. Herzberg developed his theory after carrying out a motivational research programme amongst a group of accountants and engineers. The research programme was very similar to the approach used at the beginning of this chapter, that is, Herzberg asked his sample of professional workers to answer two simple questions: 'What events at work have resulted in a marked increase in your satisfaction with the job you do?' and 'What events at work have resulted in a marked reduction in your satisfaction with the job you do?'.

The answers given were analysed and some very interesting conclusions were drawn. The first was that the factors producing high levels of satisfaction were not necessarily the direct opposites of those causing dissatisfaction. For example, many people would express great dissatisfaction over working conditions but rarely would extreme satisfaction be generated because working conditions were particularly good. As a result of this a second conclusion was that the factors making up the working environment fell into two classes: those which basically produced satisfaction and were highly regarded as the reasons for a close relationship with the job, that is motivational forces or factors; and those which basically produced dissatisfaction if inadequately present in the working environment but which rarely were seen as intrinsically important to the person's quality of work, that is, they were rarely seen as the factors producing significant levels of satisfaction and were therefore not viewed as influential motivational forces. This second set of factors Herzberg called the maintenance or hygiene factors. The elements of the working environment which fell into each category of this two-factor theory can be shown as in Table 4.2.

It should be interesting to compare your own results and those of your colleagues with Herzberg's findings. Is there a close positive correlation?

Table 4.2   *Herzberg's analysis of factors for worker satisfaction*

Satisfaction factors	Dissatisfaction factors
Achievement	Pay
Recognition	Type of supervision
Responsibility	Relationship with others
Promotion prospects	Physical working conditions
The nature of the work itself	Fringe benefits
	Company policy
↑	↑
'Motivators'	'Hygiene factors'

Comparing Herzberg's theory with Maslow's shows that Herzberg's motivators almost exactly correspond with the two highest levels of needs identified by Maslow. Hence Herzberg is suggesting the same as McGregor, that the higher levels of needs exert the greatest influence on motivational forces. The lower levels are related to the conditions under which the job has to be performed – the hygiene or maintenance conditions. If these are not satisfactory they *detract* from the individual's attention to his job. Thus pay, working conditions and fringe benefits can cause much worry and tension in the process of achieving a level which is considered to be satisfactory by the work force at a particular time. A satisfactory outcome of pay bargaining does not necessarily produce improvements in the quality of work output, which also depends on other factors, such as the very nature of the work to be done, or the achievement factor, and so on. The significant conclusion is therefore that both sets of factors are vitally important, but that they perform different functions.

Of course Herzberg's theory is open to criticism. His sample was limited to groups of professional white-collar workers and his research methodology was also limited. But taking his work and conclusions together with the findings of others such as Mayo, Maslow and McGregor, there does seem to be a consistency in the type of conclusions being drawn. Herzberg did not carry out similar research with blue-collar workers and any conclusions must therefore be a theoretical extrapolation. Nevertheless, Herzberg provides us with further insights into the complex world of the behaviour of human beings, particularly at work.

4.7   LEADERSHIP

By now you will probably have become quite familiar with group work, either at your place of work or in your studies. Next time you are in a group try to act as an observer for some of the time and note the behaviour characteristics of the other group members. Note in particular the different levels of involvement. Who says the most? Who is the

...ost in *...ial?* Whose contribution was most sought by the other group members? *Why* *...* individual have more influence than another? Is it because of his know- *le* *...ary*, voice volume, sex, age, experience, or other factors? If you can, *...everal* group meetings where the same individuals are involved. Is the same *...on* always the most influential? If not, why do you think the influence centre changes?

From this introductory exercise you should be able to draw some basic conclusions regarding the nature of leadership in an informal group. Admittedly, the conclusions you draw will be on the basis of very limited information and uncontrolled observation, but this does not mean that the exercise is valueless. On the contrary, it will provide you with a tangible basis from which to make sense of and understand this section.

Many psychological and sociological studies have taken place to ascertain the nature of the leadership phenomenon. It seems that in every type of human grouping a leader is either appointed or evolves. In some informal groups more than one leader has been found. In some cases these leaders can be rivals striving for greater group influence, but in other instances it is common to find a shared role split on the basis of function and contribution. Study has also shown that in the informal group different leaders often emerge according to the circumstances at any particular time, the individual emerging as the leader being the person the group select as the one most able to cope with the prevailing situation.

Early approaches to the study of leadership took personality as the most important factor. This is not surprising since from very early times social systems have ascribed talents on the basis of very precise factors. For example, for a long time in Europe we ascribed leadership abilities on the basis of birth – a man of noble birth being considered much more capable of leadership than a person of lower status. Thus for many hundreds of years public offices, both military and civil, were allocated on such an ascriptive basis. The basic belief underlying ascription is that birth and family background predetermine the type of socialization and preparation an individual will receive for his adult role, and that middle- and upper-class family backgrounds provide a natural environment for the development of the talents and values needed for the preservation of stability, and so on. Such a belief neglects the fact that leaders evolve in all social classes and amongst all groups of people, therefore the focus on personality traits was as good a starting point as any.

The underlying belief among these early writers was that leaders were born and not made. Such a view can clearly be seen to have its roots in the old ascription belief. They made lists of the qualities they felt were essential for a person to be an effective leader. These lists included such qualities as intelligence, integrity, diligence, confidence, and so on. Of course such an approach is almost doomed to failure. First of all the list can become almost endless (try it yourself and see). Secondly, the lists are merely the personal views of the writers compiling them, and so are subjective ideas only of the qualities required by a good leader. Thirdly, the approach was not based on any controlled research and could not contribute anything significant to our understanding of the leadership phenomenon.

Perhaps one of the most influential earlier studies was performed by Ronald Lippitt and Ralph White under the guidance of the Gestalt psychologist, Kurt Lewin. The study was focused on the effect on the behaviour of groups (in this case groups of young people) of different styles of leadership. Three styles of leadership were used: authoritarian, democratic and *laissez faire*. The leadership was given by adults, and the group members were 11-year-old children.

The study had four fundamental objectives. The first was to study the effect of the three different leadership styles on both individual and group behaviour. The second was to study individual and group reactions to shifts from one type of leadership to another within the same group. The third was to seek for relationships between the nature and content of other group membership, particularly the classroom and family, and the reactions to the experimental social climates. The fourth was to explore the methodological problems of setting up comparative group tests to develop adequate techniques of group process recording, and to discover the degree to which experimental conditions could be controlled and manipulated within the range of acceptance by the group members.

The research procedure designed to fulfil these objectives involved setting up activity clubs of five youngsters each, who were matched for IQ, popularity, physical energy and leadership. The children were set to work on craft projects under the direction of adult leaders who had been thoroughly briefed as to the three styles of leadership they were to adopt. Leaders were rotated among the groups, each leader adopting each role, so that the effect of the individual leader's personality as such would be randomized.

In the authoritarian role the leader was strongly directive, taking primary responsibility for assigning tasks and working companions, and indicating as the need arose the steps to be followed (rather than outlining the total plan ahead of time). He praised or condemned the children's work arbitrarily and did not give reasons why he thought something good or bad. He was aloof from the group, demonstrated rather than participated, and gave frequent orders and commands.

In the democratic role, group discussion and decisions were encouraged by the leader. He tried to outline the steps necessary to reach the group's goals and to suggest alternative approaches. He left the children to work as they pleased and remained objective and 'fact-minded' in his criticism and praise. He was the most willing of the three types of leaders to joke, to discuss non-club activities, and in general to put himself on the same level as his charges.

Finally, in the *laissez faire* role the leader played a much more passive part than in the other two. He gave the group almost complete freedom to do as it wished, standing ready to help if asked for assistance but making very few suggestions. He was friendly rather than 'stand-offish', but did not attempt 'to evaluate negatively or positively the behaviour or productions of the individuals of the group as a group'.

The observation of the different groups' activity was far more detailed than anything attempted by Thrasher or Whyte. Four hidden observers, watching through peepholes, recorded group activity and conversation. Motion pictures were made so that the researchers (and posterity) might seek at their leisure evidence of sociological and psychological principles.

It was found that the three styles of leadership resulted in clearly distinguishable styles of group behaviour. When the groups were under democratic leadership, relations among members were more personal and friendly. More individual differences were shown, yet at the same time members were more 'group-minded' and looked at one another for mutual approval. There was less scape-goating, and a steadier level of work when the leader was (by design) out of the room.

The same groups under *laissez faire* leadership were notable for their lack of achievement. They asked more questions of the leader but lacked 'the social techniques necessary for group decision and co-operative planning'. Lippitt and White find it suggestive that 'two or three times . . . when the adult left, one of the boys exerted a more powerful leadership and achieved a more co-ordinated group activity than when the relatively passive adult was present'.

Authoritarian leadership evoked two patterns of reaction – one 'aggressive' and the other 'apathetic'. Both reactions shared a relatively strong dependence on the leader, but the aggressive reaction involved a rebelliousness and demanding of attention, and a mutual friendliness among members, which was lacking in the apathetic groups. The presence of internal solidarity rather than scapegoating in the aggressive, authoritarian groups is ascribed by Lippitt and White to the group's ability to channel its aggression sufficiently (towards the leader and the out-group), so that in-group tension did not rise to a dangerously high point. The underlying spirit of rebellion towards the leader and co-operation in out-group aggression seem to be the 'cohesive forces' in aggressive autocracy, while in apathetic autocracy, with its lower level of felt frustration, the shared submissiveness seemed to do away with all incentive to competition for social status.

When the group leadership changed from authoritarian to democratic or *laissez faire*, the previously apathetic groups indulged in 'great outbursts of horseplay between the members'. With regard to emotional freedom and 'letting off steam', the authors conclude that 'the adult restrictiveness of the benevolent authoritarian role and the environmental unstructuredness of the *laissez faire* situation were both found to inhibit greatly genuine "psychological freedom" as contrasted to "objective freedom" '. Thus the authors were able to arrive at the conclusion that psychological investigation of groups supports progressive democratic values.

The Lewin, Lippitt and White study was undertaken in the 1930s, and was perhaps more ideological than most contemporary small group research. Nevertheless, the study is regarded by many, including the present writers, as a landmark in the study of group behaviour and in particular an important milestone in the process of acquiring insights into the relationship between leadership and human behaviour.

The important focus of this book is leadership in the setting of a formal work organization. Repeated observations under controlled conditions have shown that leadership in informal groups usually evolves as response to the immediate needs of the group. In the formal organization setting people are appointed to job roles which incorporate a leadership responsibility for work groups. In this case the role is usually known as an official leadership position where the job role holder is expected to motivate and control his subordinates to perform work in a manner which contributes towards the achievement of goals which are regarded as desirable and possible by the senior management of the organization.

It is important to perceive clearly the difference between leadership in informal groups and formal groups. In the first situation the leader is elected; in the second he is appointed. Kimball Young emphasizes this distinction by giving the formal leadership role a different title. He used the term *headship*. In his description it is clear to see the distinction. In the leadership of informal groups the chosen leader has convinced the majority of group members of his legitimacy to be leader. In this sense legitimacy relates to whatever human traits are regarded as the most important in relation to a particular situation. In the formal headship situation the appointed leader has to 'win his spurs', so to speak. Ideally the formal group leader aims to win the support of his group to such an extent that if it were an informal group he would be elected to the leadership role.

From the 1940s onwards many studies have been undertaken focusing on the headship role in formal organizations. Among the foremost of these was the Prudential Life Assurance study carried out in America in the late 1940s. This study concentrated on the role of managers and supervisors and was undertaken at the place of work rather than in an experimental setting as was the case with the Lewin, Lippitt and White study.

The first task in the Prudential study was an analysis of the organization and the type of work performed. This analysis produced an interesting organizational division into high and low producing areas. The levels of output were measured by analysing the time taken to process the various clerical activities involved. Thus departments were classified as relatively high producing and relatively low producing according to the levels of output achieved over a fairly long period of time. The next objective was to try to identify if there was any common factor between output levels in the different departments and the style of management adopted by the various managers and supervisors involved. The managers and supervisors were interviewed and their attitudes assessed in relation to such issues as their role in relation to the company, their subordinates and their colleagues. This part of the study produced the conclusion that there were two different types of attitudes adopted in the company; one was described as employee centred, and the other production centred.

Those managers who were perceived as being employee centred tended to give greater attention to personal relationships within their departments, and the preferences, needs and personal wishes of each individual. The attention of these supervisors was primarily devoted to helping individuals through the work situation. On the other hand, the production centred approach tended to rely on close supervision of subordinates. The emphasis was on output control and greater attention was given to such issues as pace and methods of working.

Having identified the two contrasting styles of leadership the task was to determine if any correlation of factors existed linking the different styles with individual work performance levels. Such a correlation was felt to exist. The evidence tended to suggest that employee centred leadership correlated with high production, and that the production centred approach was linked with low production. The conclusion was that the efforts of the production centred approach to be continually 'purging' for output were self-defeating. Such a conclusion leads to the belief that concern for people is likely to be the most rewarding leadership approach. It is interesting to compare this conclusion with the belief in theory Y by McGregor.

Several studies have confirmed the conclusions drawn from the Prudential study, although it must be emphasized that others have done the opposite. Perhaps one of the best known studies was performed by Blake and Mouton, authors of *Managerial Grid*. The Blake and Mouton study came to the conclusion that managers in general adopted a leadership approach which had some degree of concern for production coupled with some degree of concern for people. These degrees of concern could be viewed as measures along different axes; thus one manager might have less concern for production and more concern for people and another quite the opposite, while a third might display equal concern for both. The study also came to the conclusion that an individual manager very often displays different characteristics in relation to different organizational issues. Thus in relation to, say, the planning activity a manager might display dominant concern for production when drawing up plans, but dominant concern for people when executing them.

This study is useful in many ways. First it supports other research which indicates that there is a connection between leadership style, the tasks to be undertaken and the people who will perform the tasks. Secondly, it indicates that individuals placed in formal management roles will have a tendency to adopt an almost instinctive approach to leadership depending on their beliefs and perceptions of different situations. Thirdly, the approach adopted can be measured in terms of effectiveness.

Blake and Mouton produced a self-assessment questionnaire consisting of a series of different organization situations with a description of five different leadership styles relating to each situation. The person completing the questionnaire is required to choose the leadership style he feels would best fit his instinctive leadership approach in each situation. The five leadership styles relate to the five fundamental combinations which are possible, that is:

1.   low concern for people and low concern for production,
2.   low concern for people and high concern for production,
3.   high concern for people and low concern for production,
4.   moderate concern for people and moderate concern for production,
5.   high concern for people and high concern for production.

These five combinations are shown graphically in Fig. 4.3. The results obtained from the questionnaire enable individual managers to plot their own results, the scatter thus

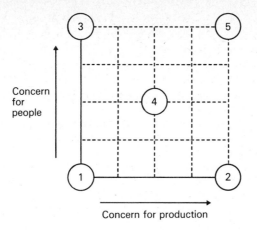

Figure 4.3 *Blake and Mouton's grid*

obtained being an indicator of the dominant leadership style likely to be adopted by that person. Of course an individual can deceive himself by associating himself with the descriptions which sound best in the light of the knowledge gained through reading about leadership theory.

We should now refer to Chapter 2 and remind ourselves of Weber's views when developing his theoretical organization structure (ideal bureaucracy) regarding the essential ingredient of leadership, the acceptance by the group of the leader's authority. In the formal headship situation the individual appointed to a role in an organizational hierarchy is also accepting a post which confers what Weber describes as rational-legal authority. Rational-legal authority describes a situation in which individuals will, in theory, grant others the legitimacy to use power over them, providing the reasons for the use of the power are both logical and conform to the framework of values which they hold. This means that people will tend to obey instructions and rules if they view them as being reasonable and necessary in relation to a specific situation. Since situations vary, the nature of accepted authority also varies. We have already discussed in Chapter 2 the belief that people will obey orders if the consequences of not obeying them are sufficiently unacceptable. This is, of course, coercion, not leadership. Nevertheless, this component of the power conferred on an individual by his job role is a factor which cannot be ignored when examining leadership in the formal situation.

The formula we are seeking is that identified by Weber:

Power + Legitimacy = Authority

The legitimacy component is that which is earned; power is conferred in the formal situation. The two must come together for effective leadership to be the outcome. Remember, leadership is concerned with achieving results through people. The important goal here is to provide the reader with sufficient background knowledge to be able to diagnose situations, and from this diagnosis predict a leadership approach which is likely to be viewed as both legitimate and effective. John Adair suggests that in performing this diagnosis we should give consideration to three interlocking variables: the task, the group and the individuals comprising the group. This is shown diagrammatically in Fig. 4.4.

The task refers to the work objectives to be attained by the group. It also encompasses the manner in which the leader approaches the task in terms of planning and preparation, covering information needs and resource utilization, initiation (in terms of

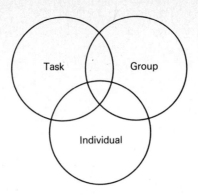

Figure 4.4   *The three interlocking variables associated with effective leadership*

communication, delegation and explanation) and control. In this sense control is not necessarily a negative term, but embraces such issues as giving advice, guidance and help, and clarifying or defining policy, whilst keeping discussions and actions relevant to the task in hand.

Group maintenance refers to the process of developing and maintaining group standards. This involves both support and evaluation: support in terms of job role allocation and assisting in performance achievement and the release of tension, and evaluation by helping the group to an evaluation of its own performance.

Individual needs refers to an attempt at understanding the needs and complex nature of all the different individuals of which the group is comprised.

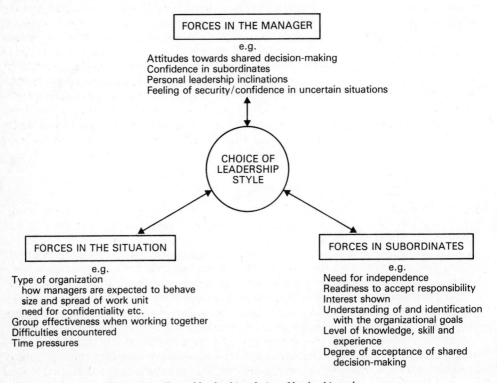

Figure 4.5   *Formal leadership: choice of leadership style*

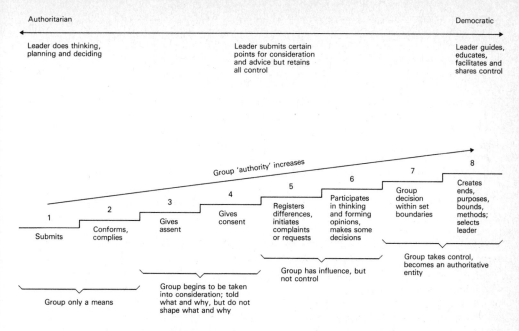

Figure 4.6 *Types of response to leadership*

Since these three variables change there can never be an ideal, clearly defined approach to leadership. Some tasks will rarely be willingly undertaken by people. In such cases it is perhaps better that we try to automate them rather than resort to the coercion which is otherwise almost inevitable. Since individuals vary, so group characteristics are always in a state of flux. In short, leadership style in formal organizations should take into account the nature of the task to be accomplished and its associated technology, social relationships, individual differences and needs, and the prevailing needs of the situation, such as time and urgency. (See Fig. 4.5.) The leadership style adopted will therefore change from situation to situation depending on the interplay of all the circumstances and factors. There exists a spectrum of styles ranging from authoritarian to democratic. The response of people subjected to these differing styles can also be expected to be different according to each style, as indicated by Fig. 4.6.

4.8 SUMMARY

This chapter has concentrated on examining the behaviour of people in the formal work setting. The primary task was to identify how individual differences and the work situations were related to behaviour, both of the individual and of groups.

The first issue to be examined was the question of motivation. Two questions were asked relating to why people attend and become members of a formal work organization and what behaviour characteristics they exhibit whilst at work. Maslow's needs-based theory of motivation was recommended as perhaps one of the best explanations to date of why people perform mental and physical activity. The fundamental basis of Maslow's theory is that motivation requires the existence of a range of implicit human needs, objectives or goals which will satisfy these needs, and a pattern of behaviour which the individual has adopted to achieve the goal. We soon came to the realization that the theory gives a generalized explanation only of the phenomenon of motivated behaviour. It does not explain what specific issues motivate a particular individual. Thus we went on to examine various views relating to the characteristics of individuality.

It was suggested that no two individuals will react in the same way to an identical work situation. There are several reasons for this. First, individual needs at any particular time are likely to be unique to that individual. Secondly, each one of us is the product of our own unique journey from childhood, through adolescence to adulthood. This path exposes the individual to a whole range of influences, each influence being a factor contributing to his values, beliefs, wants and needs. Thirdly, the environmental health and social factors which result in our behavioural characteristics at any particular point in time are in a constant state of flux. As a result the same individual is unlikely to react to an identical work situation in exactly the same way on any two occasions.

Even though we came to the conclusion that it would be impossible to predict individual needs and wants for specific individuals, or even groups of individuals, we did come to the conclusion that we could generalize, and that such generalizations can be useful in providing insights into an understanding of the behaviour of people at work. Thus we were able to suggest possible causes of frustration and aggression such as repetitive work of a low achievement nature.

This conclusion led us to another area of difficulty, that of observing and understanding the behaviour of people at any point in time. No two observers can be sure that they actually see the same thing at all. In fact we have no way of knowing that we see even the simplest of things in the same way; the only basis of judgement is a person's description in words of what he is seeing. What we see is a function of what our experiences in a sense allow us to see. Perception is governed by a frame of references which tends to limit the field of vision. Thus two observers can form totally different views regarding the behaviour of the same individuals. This fact alone can have serious repercussions for the formal work organization. It will result in different styles of management being adopted by different managers in relation to the same working group. At the extremes such differences in perception can result in violently divergent interpretations regarding the nature of different individuals and groups of individuals. Thus one manager will be authoritarian and attempt to control the work group through coercion, whilst another will be totally democratic and will approach the same group with openness and allow full participation in decision making.

These differences in perception have been noted by many writers but perhaps the best known in relation to the business situation is Douglas McGregor. McGregor gives us a clear picture of the two extreme perceptions, or sets of assumptions, that are held by managers working in business organizations; one he calls theory X and the other theory Y.

This chapter also stresses the importance of the work group and draws attention to the differences between the formal and the informal groups. The reader was reminded of the theoretical approaches to the design of formal work organization discussed in Chapter 2. Above all the possible differences in terms of goals and leadership between the formal and informal groups were emphasized and the implications stressed. It was suggested that the aim of management of the formal organization was a marriage with the informal groups in the sense that they both work for the same ends; but so often the informal organization is in conflict. The importance of leadership in achieving this group cohesion was stressed.

The importance of group leadership cannot be over-emphasized. Research has indicated that all groups, whether formal or informal, need control and direction if they are to be effective in achieving prescribed goals. We therefore need knowledge of the characteristics of effective leadership behaviour. Groups as we have seen are collections of individuals. Each individual's needs and wants if he is to become an integrated member of the group must be acknowledged. C. Argyris pointed out that the behaviour of people in formal work organizations results from an interplay of individual factors. Leadership of groups in many ways requires a manipulation of these factors. This manipulation involves both physical and behavioural components. The physical components include the tasks to be performed and the membership and role of the formal working groups. The behavioural components include leadership style, ranging from coercive to normative (a style which relies on group members intrinsically valuing the goals of the group and the individual job roles), authority systems and group affinity.

Student Tasks

Having read Chapters 1, 2, 3 and 4 you should now be in a position to perform a meaningful examination of any organization with which you are familiar. This could be the organization by whom you are currently employed, or the educational establishment in which you are studying.

Your task is basically a research activity based largely on observation. It is not true research since you will neither have the time nor the experience to perform the tasks well enough. What we are seeking to do is to illustrate the theories and concepts raised in the first four chapters in as realistic a way as possible. Any inadequacy in your research methodology will not significantly reduce the value of the tasks you perform.

Organizational Design

1. Identify what you think are the corporate organizational objectives for the institutions you are observing.
2. Find out if the organization has any published statement regarding its objectives. Compare this statement with 1 above.
3. In performing task 2, comment on any differences you identify. In particular, identify any situation where there exists a variance between the objectives of different groups within the organization.
4. Suggest or describe the ways in which any goal conflict identified in task 3 might be minimized or resolved.
5. Describe the departmental structure of the organization and comment on it in the light of your readings, particularly of Chapters 2 and 3.
6. Illustrate, explain and assess how the organization structures contribute towards the achievement of corporate objectives.
7. In performing task 6 describe the nature and function of each major department as you perceive it.
8. Choose any one department and identify its major executive objectives and the policy for achieving them.
9. Identify the management structure and compare it with your reading in Chapters 2 and 4.

Organizational Relationships

1. Describe the 'atmosphere' or 'climate' of the organization (i.e. the state of relationships between people). This can simply take the form of a description of your perception of the state of relationships. Remember to look at both the formal and informal groups.
2. You may find it useful to draw up a list of adjectives to describe the organizational climate. This list could then be used as a rough measure against which to compare your observations of people working in the organization you are studying.
3. Identify possible causal factors which have produced the particular state of relationships you have identified in 1 and 2 above.
4. Assess the predominant management style being adopted by the management team. Describe, in general terms, the evidence you have used to form your opinions.
5. Identify the motivation/behavioural assumptions you think the managers have made regarding their subordinates (remember the McGregor study).
6. Identify and assess the organizational consequences of the conclusions you have drawn in 4 and 5 above.
7. Present a case either for or against the predominant management style you feel you have observed being adopted in the organization.
8. Compare the extremes of management style you have observed and assess the degree to which they resemble theory X and theory Y.

Table 4.3   *Organization evaluation matrix*

Feature	Your Organization	Ideal Bureaucracy	Scientific Management	Human Relations	Systems
Authority hierarchy					
System of rules					
High definition of job roles					
Specialization					
Division of labour					
Clear definition of career structures					
Communication processes					
Predominant motivational assumptions ↓					
Continue as you think appropriate					

Organizational Evaluation

Here we want you to attempt to evaluate the form and structure of the organization you are observing in terms of the theoretical models described in Chapter 2. You will remember that the various approaches concentrated on different aspects of organization structure, for example, the classical model concentrated on division of labour, hierarchy of authority, specialization, and so on.

You may find that the institution you are observing in fact demonstrates some aspects of all the different theoretical models. Some areas may exhibit bureaucratic features, whilst others may clearly resemble 'scientific management' characteristics. In performing this evaluation task try to assess the organization as a whole as well as the component departments.

It might be helpful in performing this task to draw up a comparatively simple matrix with a list of organization features on the vertical axis and the organizations on the horizontal axis. The matrix could look something like that shown in Table 4.3. In using this matrix you can devise your own system of recording/measuring. For example if you use a numerical scale, say 1–9 where 9 equates with high positive correlation with the feature being measured, and 1 low correlation, you simply enter the value you think represents the extent to which your organization and each of the theoretical models focuses or concentrates on each of the features listed. In this way you should be able to perform an interesting evaluation of your own organization while at the same time reinforcing the theoretical concepts raised in Chapter 2.

4.9   H. HURLEY ENTERPRISES LIMITED: A CASE STUDY

This case study is based on the ideas contained in J. King and Co. Ltd and is used with kind permission of Mr Davies, Head of Business and Management Studies, Stockport College of Technology.

Introduction

The Board of Hurleys, during their meeting of 25 May 1981, expressed grave concern about the apparent high labour turnover of restaurant staff, and have minuted that the directors of the restaurant division be requested to initiate an investigation, and make a report recommending action or otherwise to deal with the situation. If the recommendations are adequate, they will be used to form part of the employment policy for the future good of the company.

Objectives

This case has been included here to provide the reader with a situation which will help reinforce many points raised in Chapters 2 and 4. In particular the reader should: consider organizational factors which have a bearing on individual behaviour and relate these to the issues cited here; examine management and leadership aspects raised in the case; and examine the remuneration issues and in particular their relationship to labour turnover (that is, establish how significant pay factors might be in relation to labour stability).

The Task

The Director, Mr Patrick Greenhoff, has appointed you, a consultant, to investigate the problem, analyse the situation regarding labour turnover, and report, making recommendations designed to bring about an improvement. He wishes to know 'something' about the morale of the various restaurant staff, and what factors motivate such people to stay with one particular firm for a lengthy period.

Your specific tasks are:

1. Study the case carefully and note the general and specific points, which will be best discussed in a group.
2. Draw up objectives for the investigation, together with appropriate statistical approaches.
3. Consider and design your method for the collection of information.
4. Seek information from further reading in textbooks, pamphlets, professional journals, government statistics and your own research, that is talk to people in the catering industry about their labour problems.
5. If you can, talk to people engaged as waiters and waitresses about their job roles. Try to establish their reasons for doing the job, and their main problems and criticisms.
6. Write a report making recommendations which you consider may be acceptable to the Board.

H. Hurley Enterprises Limited

The high rate of turnover among food service staff is a major source of concern for the management of H. Hurley Enterprises Limited, Catering Division. On average, a newly appointed male waiter will stay with the company for only four months (slightly longer in the case of female staff).

Company History

H. Hurley Enterprises was founded in 1954 and is now one of the largest and best known catering organizations in the country. At first a catering firm, Hurleys rapidly expanded into allied fields, opening teashops and restaurants, mainly in the London and Yorkshire areas, and developing its own bakery for bread and cakes to supply both its own outlets and private retailers.

By 1969 Hurleys had over 300 teashops throughout the country, besides a number of restaurants which ranged from those offering expensive *haute cuisine* to the well-known

'Hurlikin' restaurants. These were buildings mainly housing several floors of restaurants which provided a variety of service, widely known for excellent value for money.

Hurleys recognized the social change which has taken place during the last decade where more and more people are eating out, and one of the measures they adopted to meet the new demand was to do away with the large floors and expensive image so long associated with them. Special catering was introduced in the form of various restaurants based on different customer spending power, each restaurant offering a distinctive tariff, style and type of service. The first was the 'Grill', which offered a rapid grill-bar service at popular prices. The company developed a number of distinctive restaurants over the period, so that, by the end of 1981, it contained seven different restaurant types catering for customer expenditure ranging from £1.00 to £26.00. (See Table 4.4.)

Table 4.4   *Types of Hurlikin restaurants, summer 1981*

Restaurant (service hours)	Situation	Average expenditure/ customer (£)	Types of service
The Normandy 7.00 p.m.–1.30 a.m.	Basement	10.00	Restaurant with dancing and cabaret, all-in price. Licensed. Service by waiters only.
The Quick Bar 8.30 a.m.–11.00 p.m.	Ground floor	1.50	Rapid (counter) service. Drinks (non-licensed): tea, coffee, etc. Sandwiches, cakes, hamburgers, etc.
The Family Room 11.30 a.m.–10.00 p.m.		2.25	Moderate-priced restaurant. Licensed. Bar and waiter service.
The York Room 11.30 a.m.–2.30 p.m. 7.00 p.m.–11.00 p.m.	First floor	5.50	Steak bar atmosphere. Licensed bar. Waiter service.
The Carvery 11.30 a.m.–2.30 p.m. 7.00 p.m.–11.00 p.m.		4.75	Help yourself from the joint. Licensed. Waiter service.
The Scarborough 11.30 a.m.–2.30 p.m. 7.00 p.m.–11.00 p.m.	Second floor	6.00	Seafood restaurant with appropriate décor. Licensed (no bar). French cuisine only.
The Grill 11.30 a.m.–11.00 p.m.		3.00	Quick grill bar service. Grill in sight of customer. Licensed bar. Waiter service.

Staff

The distinctive restaurants developed by Hurleys, now having the common name 'Hurl Houses', all have a common structure. There is a central kitchen which prepares food in bulk for all restaurants, and attached to each speciality restaurant is its own sub-kitchen where items are cooked to order.

The highly-skilled staff, the chefs, are concerned with the running of the central kitchen where they supervise the preparation of soups, salads, vegetables, meats, fish, sauces and sweets, by cooks and kitchen hands. Each restaurant kitchen has its own small staff who only need be capable of preparing or finishing the particular specialities of their restaurant, for example meat grillers in the Steak Room, fried food cooks in the Grill.

Similarly, the waiting staff in each restaurant are trained in the methods necessary for that restaurant, for example in the Grill less skilled but rapid 'plate service' is required. The customer's order is cooked and placed directly onto a platter, which the waiter takes on a tray to the customer. The waiter's job is essentially one of taking the customer's order and delivering his meal to him, then clearing and laying the table again afterwards. Rapid customer turnover calls for fast work by both waiters and cooks, especially at mid-day and in the early evening.

In the 'Scarborough Restaurant' on the other hand, the pace of operations is a little more sedate; many customers take their time over their meals, speciality dishes take longer to prepare, and the waiters need a fairly high level of skill in 'Silver Service' where dishes are either prepared in the presence of the customer or served from salvers. Even so, there are a limited number of dishes served, and plate service is the rule throughout, with 'The Normandy' being the exception in providing a high degree of French cuisine.

Mr Patrick Greenhoff, director of the restaurant division, is rather proud of the fact that the specialization of the restaurants means that there is no need in every restaurant to have a high level of waiting skill such as that required in a luxury hotel.

Mr Waite, training officer and an ex-waiter, sees the situation from a different point of view. He comments on the fact that: 'We do not get the same standard of labour that we did five to ten years ago. We even have to take on unskilled people and train them in specialist work. They're just not comparable with the old-style waiter, and when we do get people with any form of experience we send them straight to the prestige restaurants.'

Waiters work a 40-hour week, with occasional opportunities for overtime. They are engaged to work in one restaurant, based on their experience and training. A rota system is in operation, so that they sometimes start early, sometimes late. The rota is made out for 26 weeks at a time so that the staff have every opportunity for planning their own time. (The staff and numbers are given in Table 4.5.)

Each waiter has a station consisting of twelve places. The table areas are changed with the rota so that no one has to work for long on a less lucrative table area. Waiting staff look upon gratuities as part of their earnings.

Waiters receive a wage of £60.00 per 40-hour week on the prestige floors, and £65.00 per 40-hour week in the lower spending power restaurants. A service bonus payment is made to the long service waiting staff. The feeling amongst the management is that the basic rate and gratuities make the wages comparable with competitive organizations.

Table 4.5   *Management/staff organization, summer 1981*

| *Resident Director* | Mr Patrick Greenhoff | | | |
| *General Manager* | Mr George Moore | | | |

	Basement	*Ground Floor*	*First Floor*	*Second Floor*
Manager	R. Clague	D. Freak	A. Eastcrabbe	J. Daymond
Deputy manager	2	4	2	3
Restaurant managers	2	4	2	3
Assistant restaurant managers	4	4	2	3

Waiting staff and cooks		
	Basement	75 (inclusive of main kitchen staff)
	The Quick Bar	16
	The Family Room	28
	The York Room	32
	The Carvery	22
	The Scarborough	16
	The Grill	18
		207

There is one distinction between the waiting staff. On the one hand there are the restaurant waiting staff, whose role has been described, and the 'Burger-bar' staff who are known as 'Retail Assistants'. The distinction is marked not only by title, but by their wage of £70.00 per 40-hour week. This extra wage is due to the fact that they do not have the opportunity to receive gratuities.

However, there is an unofficial and far more distinct division within the group of waiting staff: that between long service and new people. The first impression is one of a scattering of elderly British staff nearing retirement age among a variety of younger faces from Spain, Greece, Italy, Pakistan and many other countries confirmed by scrutiny of the staff records (see Table 4.6), but this appears to be typical of many hotels and restaurants throughout the country.

Table 4.6 *Length of service of staff*

	Male		Female		Total	
	No.	(%)	No.	(%)	No.	(%)
Up to five years' service						
British	20	(15.2)	10	(25)	30	(17.4)
Foreign	112	(84.8)	30	(75)	142	(82.6)
Total	132	(100)	40	(100)	172	(100)
Average age	28		24		26	
Five years' service and over						
British	18	(85.7)	22	(91.7)	40	(88.9)
Foreign	3	(14.3)	2	(8.3)	5	(11.1)
Total	21	(100)	24	(100)	45	(100)
Average age	52		50		51	

While the older and new staff appeared to work well together, helping each other out when any of them are particularly rushed, there does seem to be a basic difference in outlook and attitude between them. The older staff consider themselves craftsmen, proud of their experience and training even though some of it was out of place in rapid turnover, speciality catering. The company was clearly identified in their minds and they provided a loyal and able body of workers well-known to the management for long service and catering background.

New staff are predominantly foreign. Their sometimes imperfect command of English makes for additional problems in management/staff communication. A number of them had previously worked in different industries before joining Hurleys; for them the job is only a way of making a living. For others, it is a career, but unlike the older British staff they have no deep-seated loyalty. Therefore this casual attitude is attributed by Hurley's management to a general shortage of trained staff in the industry and the fact that foreign workers are temporary immigrants, working in this country to amass as much money as they can before returning to their own country. Furthermore, Hurley's management believes that the seasonal trade at holiday resorts is a major attraction to the new/younger staff, since it offers comparatively good earnings, opportunity for more interesting use of free time, and often free board; the degree of instability in this type of work was something that younger people and especially immigrants appeared more willing to accept. Management felt that waiting staff tended to drift from job to job. They were individualists: a high gratuity pay structure provided a means for those who desired it to have a high degree of control over their earnings. Since the catering industry relies on this type of labour, they had to accept the turnover problem as inevitable.

An examination of the staff records for the restaurant division shows that waiting staff leavers in 1980 amounted to 180 per cent of the average number of staff employed, of whom 25 per cent left of their own accord within the first two weeks of their employment, and on average it is likely that a new waiter will stay less than four months. (Details of staff and leavers are given in Table 4.7.)

Some of the managers felt they could do nothing about the staff turnover, even though it was a time-consuming problem. They believed that they could never reduce staff turnover to a level which might be considered normal in other industries. All they could do was try to lessen the effect of staff wastage and keep the problem under control by trying to keep staff recruitment in line with staff wastage.

Table 4.7 *Leavers by restaurant: 12 months to June 1981*

	Normandy	Quick Bar	Family Room	York Room	Carvery	Scarborough Grill	Total
Average number employed	75	16	28	32	22	16	18	217
Leavers	85	30	75	75	40	32	24	361
Leavers as average percentage of number employed (rounded off)	(113)	(188)	(268)	(234)	(182)	(200)	(133)	(166)
Number leaving of own accord within two weeks	20	10	19	27	10	10	4	100
As percentage of leavers (rounded off)	(24)	(33)	(25)	(36)	(25)	(31)	(17)	(28)
Number dismissed	8	4	10	10	6	4	3	45
Percentage of total leavers (rounded off)	(9)	(13)	(13)	(13)	(15)	(13)	(13)	(12)

Further Reading

1.   Argyris, C. (1964) *Integrating the Individual and the Organization*. Chichester: Wiley.
2.   Brown, J. A. C. (1967) *The Social Psychology of Industry*. Harmondsworth: Pelican.
3.   Fielder, F. E. (1967) *A Theory of Leadership Effectiveness*. Maidenhead: McGraw-Hill.
4.   Herzberg, F. (1968) *Work and the Nature of Man*. St Albans: Staples.
5.   Likert, R. (1961) *New Patterns of Management*. Maidenhead: McGraw-Hill.
6.   Maslow, A. (1964) *Motivation and Personality*. London: Harper & Row.
7.   McGregor, D. (1960) *The Human Side of the Enterprise*. Maidenhead: McGraw-Hill.
8.   Schein, E. H. (1965) *Organisation Psychology*. Hemel Hempstead: Prentice-Hall.
9.   Tilley, K. W. (ed.) (1974) *Leadership and Management Appraisal*. Sevenoaks: English Universities Press.
10. Wainwright, D. & Smith, N. A. (1978) *Management in the Police Service*. Chichester: Barry Rose.
11. Woodward, J. (1965) *Industrial Organisation – Theory and Practice*. Oxford: Oxford University Press.

5

People: Management
of the Human Resource

GENERAL OBJECTIVES

After reading this chapter the reader should be able to identify and examine ways
in which management may attempt to obviate or minimize problems resulting from
individual and group needs, attitudes and behaviour.

LEARNING OBJECTIVES

The reader should be able to:

1. Examine the relationship between the management of people and the
   problems of change.
2. Survey any organization with which he is familiar and describe how the
   management structure relates to process of managing people.
3. Examine the relationship between welfare provision and employee satisfaction.
4. Contrast views in relation to the management of conflict.
5. Discuss some of the objectives which may be attained by measures taken to
   increase employee participation.
6. Discuss and evaluate some of the ways currently being adopted to change
   employee attitudes.
7. Examine the social responsibility of business.

5.1 INTRODUCTION

There is an enormous literature on many aspects of labour management. It deals with
questions like manpower planning and recruitment at the firm or company level, the
constructions and effects of alternative payment systems, wage and salary hierarchies,
the tactics and process of negotiating with unions, or consulting with workers' representatives, with welfare and safety arrangements, and a multitude of subsidiary issues of
labour management or labour relations, from selection systems to retirement arrangements.

This literature is principally concerned to offer advice to managers on how to deal with employees and is usually about doctrine, as for example the numerous books on work study or job evaluation. Occasionally it is an attempt to persuade managements to adopt a novel incentive pay scheme or method of work arrangement, which it is suggested will in some way improve labour's productivity, performance, or its response and relation to management in general.

5.2   UNDERSTANDING PEOPLE'S NEEDS

This chapter is about the management of human resources. It is about the many variations in the needs of both individuals and groups of workers. We have looked at the relationship between needs, attitudes and behaviour. We are now going to examine the significance of these needs to the process of management of human resources. The work place, whether factory, office, school or hospital, is one of business and society's great inventions. We spend a large part of our life there, and its effect upon us is significant. In it we experience a variety of environmental influences, some beneficial, promoting our success in life, but others harmful, diminishing our vitality and effectiveness as workers; they may even damage our health.

Our attitude to the work place is mixed. We go to work expecting to be involved in an activity of some consequence, be able to participate and make a worthwhile contribution, and be known and valued for what we have done. All of this is a major source of human satisfaction. On the other hand, the work place tends to suffer from being too close and familiar, and often too much is taken for granted. It has become formal and standardized over the years, lacking variety or stimulus, and attendance there has been a dull routine which can dim the worker's sense of the importance of the environment and its activities.

This is unfortunate, because the work place is important for many reasons other than the obvious one of providing a living. It groups people together – they spend many hours of every day together, working in teams, and may even eat together. They do not move away, except briefly, during work hours. They cannot opt out of the operational and social obligations imposed by the environment. They exist, as it were, under continuous scrutiny. From the individual and the organization's point of view, the work place can be stimulating or dreary, productive or inefficient, but it cannot be ignored. People have to learn to live with it, and, for their own and everyone else's sake, make it a success.

In the past few decades we have been trying to understand employee reactions to situations in a work organization. In Chapter 4 we examined some of the current thinking regarding the nature of people. In forming those views research and observation have had to consider the ongoing process of change which has overtaken the whole of industrialized society, particularly in the last decade, as never before. What is significant is that management reaction to the views and theories has been, in many instances, leisurely and cautious. Long-held beliefs die hard; frames of reference are slow to change. It it is therefore perhaps understandable that the response has been leisurely and cautious. The danger is that the rate of change may now have increased so much that the 'honeymoon' period, so to speak, is over.

That leisurely attitude to change is no longer possible today without a risk of a decline in our economy. Change is now occurring as never before at an exponential rate, and we have to adjust to an unprecedented growth rate. Such growth cannot be achieved by piecemeal additions, but must be an organic process involving a revolution in our attitude to work and in the measures employed. To some the new demands may be startling. They should in fact be regarded as a stimulus and a challenge. Vital to any measure of work place reform is, of course, the effect on the individual, who should not be treated like a component to be thrust in measured numbers into a package, though that is what some work places are like. Long periods are spent at work and it must be made liveable.

We occupy the work place with others, and the kind of relations we need to have with them must be taken into account in the layout. Many questions have to be answered. How much space does the particular case require? How many people should the space hold for social and working comfort? What are their communication responsibilities with each other, and with people outside the unit? What kind of access and traffic facilities should the place have? Where are the by-ways where people can meet and talk?

Any good organization manager understands to some degree the enormous potential in the chemistry of human relationships. Organizations are constructed along lines intended to make combinations of people effective. There is a growing awareness of, and interest in, the influence that our direct physical surroundings have on this chemistry. We are, more than we suspect, the products of our surroundings; we act and communicate as our environment directs. Since many of the ideas and recommendations discussed in this chapter are comparatively new, or not yet that widely applied, their implementation does involve change, and in some cases significant change. We have to recognize that change, especially in the material aids to work, is the bane of the decision maker's life. It causes confusion and dislocation, mess and argument, to say nothing of expense, and unless the pressures build up the temptation is to leave well alone. In fact the trouble/cost consideration is so ingrained in management thinking, that ordering or re-ordering of facilities almost invariably lags seriously behind the point at which the change becomes urgent. People and services may pay the penalty of neglect of months, and even years. The fault has been in top management, who have in many ways shown too little interest in the changing needs of employees, too little awareness of increasing importance of the work place in working life, and understanding people's needs in the interest of the national economy. Yet it is from leadership that change must come. The community has a right to expect from its business leaders an ability to appraise and use the proven concepts of the new generation of planners.

5.3 WELFARE PROVISION AND EMPLOYEE SATISFACTION

We have started to sketch out a framework for understanding and improving work organizations. The theme has been that while many of the problems facing firms will not respond to easy solutions, this should not divert us from what are often simple answers. We have touched on the subject of change, and to deal with it so that human values are satisfied will require attention to the topics we shall now examine.

What do we mean by welfare? Welfare used to mean that the work place had to be clean, reasonably comfortable, and adequately heated and lit; but in recent years good employers have realized that welfare means more than good surroundings and house-keeping. Welfare is people and policies as well as bricks, carpets and soap. Workers can be well paid and housed and still be unhappy and unproductive, not necessarily through awkwardness, but because of a lack of imagination, initiative and tolerance on the part of management.

That is the work environment. Let us agree, for the purpose of this discussion, that the initiative rests with management to discover what motivates employees. Many believe that money is the only motive, and the term 'job satisfaction' is in danger of becoming abused, but it does express what an employee wants in addition to his pay packet; indeed many industrialists now hold that non-material satisfactions are becoming *more* important. In the car industry, for example, workers are weary of the monotony of many jobs for which high wages do not compensate, and a good deal of labour conflict in this and other industries can be attributed to the boredom of the assembly line. Thus management in the mass-production industries are seeking ways to put satisfaction back into work.

People also want protection against unemployment, especially at an age when there may be little chance of further employment. This need is not simply material: employees have a need to enter into a sense of belonging.

As motivation means more than cash, and security has a deeper significance than 'holding down a job', so the need for good working conditions is more than adequate lighting. We now know that atmosphere, social environment and attitudes are at least as important as physical conditions. Many industrialists condemn the attitude of treating workers as items of utility, and employees demand the right to be seen as people. They are not prepared to be placed in a set environment, but want to be consulted, to make their contribution. The responsibility for managing will always need to rest with management, but decision making and implementation are no longer exclusively management prerogatives.

The image of the trade unions as initiators of change in the working environment has been distorted. The public is aware of the importance of wage claim negotiations to the neglect of the activities of the union movement in the fields of welfare education, health, planning and industrial democracy, which have led to improvements in the working life and wellbeing of men and women throughout industry and commerce. The priorities look very different when viewed in a more objective way, as we shall see when they are discussed in Chapter 7.

All managers will have to adjust to new attitudes and new knowledge about managing people and examples are shown in Fig. 5.1. Peter Drucker has stated that the principal

Figure 5.1   *How managers create working opportunities*

developments in the future will be in the non-technical field, and will include: new kinds of marketing; new work methods; innovations in the measurement of competence, and imagination of managers; and developments in managing people. These attitudes to people and work, secured in the recognition of the needs of people, are a necessary start to the study of the working environment. A worthwhile part of this study is the interaction of people and the environment in which they work. Good work conditions release latent abilities and performance improves.

We may not realize it, but fewer than 50 per cent of people at work need control by management. Most can rely on their interdependence within their group, and on the pressure of a community of equals. Thus work can be pleasant or frustrating, a source of satisfaction or discontent. It rests with management to decide which of the two choices will prevail.

How Does Management Choose?

Management can choose by putting themselves in the employee's place, viewing the problems and the necessary changes from the position of those most affected.

What then is the work environment? It is buildings, but also, more importantly, the spirit that exists in the organization, the relationships among people at all levels, the understanding of the management, the efficiency of those who manage, the satisfaction of the job, the assurance of reward, and job security.

Many UK firms have studied the problems, but some symptoms have gone unnoticed, for example the relationship between the arrangement of working space and the mental health and morale of its occupants. Very little is known about stress and its consequences, but further study and interest are now centred on the social responsibility of industry, and the time is approaching when it will be a part of business practice.

The simple starting point is the problem that we have in our society, using a range of resources which we must bring together in an effective way. How can we define our own attitudes to people so that we can make them more effective? Here are a few points worth consideration. Take each statement as a discussion issue and record all the points raised.

1. *People are often better than we think they are.* We are remiss in underestimating the ability of people, and thus appear surprised at the quality of their performance. Human potentiality is the richest of all society's resources and also the most under-used.
2. *People have a creative quality.* There is a latent creativity in most people, and good management can develop it.
3. *There is a need for participation.* People want to participate. It is everybody's right to participate; people get satisfaction from performance. We all welcome the opportunity to exert influence, not simply to play a useful part, but to be seen to be playing our part. Self-respect results in a higher performance.
4. *People have integrity and dignity.* Mistrust drives out loyalty. It is right to encourage self-respect in employees, and it makes good business sense.
5. *People respond to fair treatment.* Fair dealing supports leadership and it encourages team effort, and in an advanced society where people are aware of their rights and needs, heavy-handed treatment proves unproductive.
6. *People feel the need to make changes to improve their effectiveness.* All people have a desire and need to improve the quality of their lives.

7. *Most people enjoy some measure of responsibility.* An obligation placed on management is to discover what motivates their employees. Some believe that money is the only positive motive. Money is, of course, important, but job satisfaction, perhaps an overworked term, does express what an employee wants besides cash. In other words, the non-material satisfactions are becoming more important.

So far there has been little in the way of direct analysis of the effects of the internal organization and practice of management on industrial relations in general. It is only very recently, in Britain at least, that an interest has developed in the relationship in the character of management organization and that of industrial or labour relations as a general issue. The question that is raised is 'Why study work organizations?'. Most managers will probably agree on the need to study the way we organize work if it leads to more productive co-operation and a more satisfied work force. On the other hand, the notion that easy 'cook book' type answers will be forthcoming must be dismissed. There is also an awareness that the problems facing individual companies are unique, certainly unstructured, and furthermore only solvable by the managers involved taking a hard, analytical look at each situation as it arises. This is not to suggest that theoretical knowledge is not important – it is – but it needs to be applied as problems arise and not as from universal prescription. This is not to say that there is no need for forward thinking; indeed, a fast-changing society needs a management to plan now for the kind of organization it will need in the next three to five years, always realizing that at the end of the period the whole procedure will probably require changing again. Such changes could involve the manufacturing organization in new layouts, modified control systems, alterations in the pay structure, and – a matter of great significance – some change in everyone's job. If companies are to survive and provide a combination of economic viability and job satisfaction, then managers must be very much concerned with determining if the existing set-up is right for the tasks it faces.

Any survey, such as the one undertaken by the Donovan Commission, would show that there are considerable differences in the management organization of establishments and firms, in the structures of their managerial, executive and supervisory grades, and in formal and informal relationships within and between these groups. In particular, a survey would show considerable differences in the way they were organized to deal with labour and labour questions. The range of variation in this type of specialized organization extends from one extreme, in which the only provision might be a single wage clerk, to another, where there are large and distinct departments, each with a number of formally qualified experts dealing with separate aspects of labour management (recruitment and training, employees' welfare, trade union negotiations, and so on), and where the company's executive board includes one or two full-time directors appointed to deal with industrial relations or other labour questions.

This variation would be found to be connected with the size of the firm or establishment concerned, but by no means entirely. Thus we may find one or two small firms, say, with less than 1000 employees, with specialist departments, not just for personnel matters at large, but for industrial relations. On the other hand, in certain large companies we may find it is still normal practice for all labour disputes and negotiations to be handled by the successive layers of supervision and executive management, perhaps with a resource to an outside employers' federation for assistance if all else fails.

5.4 THE ENVIRONMENT

We have briefly examined the role of specialist industrial relations personnel, and we have looked at this specialist role as an indicator of the modernity of a management's attitude to labour relations. However, there are other indicators which we might equally consider. For instance, there is the more old-fashioned belief that firms which are good employers, in the sense of having a higher concern for their workers' material and social welfare, are likely also to have better employee relations, and hence a lower liability to labour conflict. Many surveys have found little evidence to support this when inter-industry comparisons in earnings and strike incidences are made. However, it could still be true that this is due to the dominating circumstances of specific industries, and that a more positive relationship between welfare and industrial peace might be found in comparison between organizations.

It is interesting to note that other research has shown that what we might call the openness of management to external communications and associations is connected both with the state of its labour relationship and with its activity in internal consultation. The general heading of communication raises, of course, yet another aspect of management policies towards labour. Indeed communication is still a concept which is part of the conventional wisdom of personnel management.

One point which emerged from a recent study (Bland, M. (1980) *Employee Communications in the 1980s (a personnel manager's guide)*. London: Kogan Page) was that the general level of actual consultation is distinctly higher within management than between management and workers. It is notable, however, that the level of consultation within management appears inversely related to that obtaining between management and workers. The effect of size on the level of actual consultation differs between management/worker and within management. The size effects are important not only in themselves, but because they would again lead (other things being equal) to an expectation of a similar pattern in the relationships between consultation and the plant's incidences of working days lost from disputes.

One argument for increased employee participation in management which has often been put forward in the past has been that it would help to improve efficiency. Studies show that this would be weakened if the price of such an increase were a decline in communication and co-ordination between the members of management themselves. As regards what some might call the morale effects of management/worker consultation, however, we now have a paradox. As we have learned from other readings, particularly in Chapters 7 and 8 in this book, the introduction of formal joint consultative machinery does reduce the liability of plants to labour unrest, but the extent to which such machinery is actually used, and the effective level of management/worker consultation in general, depend on the demonstrated level of employee militancy. How can this be explained?

One explanation might link the effect of the existence of formal joint consultative machinery with the similar effect of various other communication devices, and of fringe benefits; to the extent that these are volunteered by employers, they constitute a recognition of employee status; most of them, indeed, were historically part (formally or informally) of the employment conditions which distinguished staff from workers. Thus, the suggestion is that the concession of such status symbols to workers, irrespective of whether or not they also have a material content, will reduce the liability of plants to labour unrest, but on the other hand, genuine worker participation (unless one includes in that term the effective transference of some functions of the management of labour itself to shop stewards' committees, which does happen in some larger establishments) makes demands that could imply a reduction of effective contact or communication between the members of management themselves, and is therefore likely to be resisted unless it is imposed on managers from board level, perhaps as a consequence of active union negotiation.

Summary

To summarize, we have so far looked at a number of issues with regard to the management provision and organization for industrial relations and labour management. The rest of the chapter will attempt to discover how far, and in what ways, these are effective.

The inquiry we are undertaking involves a number of propositions that labour management and industrial relations will be improved by action at the level of the individual firm or establishment, including:

1. More expenditure on specialists in labour management and relations.
2. Orderly collective bargaining, and formal consultation procedures within the enterprise.
3. Improved facilities for work place union representation.

To these we have added, in the light of some of our readings, a number of other hypotheses which represent part of the traditional conventional wisdom of labour management, and in particular:

4. That good pay and employee benefits make for good industrial relations.
5. That provisions for management/worker communication reduce the liability of enterprises to labour conflict.
6. That management/employee consultation is a good thing.

5.5 IMPROVING THE ORGANIZATION

There are many people in various walks of industrial life who believe that the major challenge is how to manage change. This implies that we can either react positively by seeking information about the factors that will affect our particular organization (see Fig. 5.2) and then deal with the problems revealed – taking the bull by the horns – or alternatively we can wait for events to bring about change – the bush-fire philosophy. Survival in modern industrial circumstances demands the first approach: managing the situation. Furthermore, the forces of change need steering so that the organization is reinforced, which in turn should lead to a more productive operation both economically and socially.

The following points must be recognized:

1. Any organization is composed of conflicting economic, technical, social and political beliefs. It is a coalition of those differing interests which somehow needs managing.
2. Conflict is an inherent part of organizational life, but can be dealt with constructively. Furthermore, there needs to be a system that permits the effective airing of conflicting interests.
3. Organizations are living in a constant state of inadequate information.
4. Apart from accelerating technological change, there are deeper social changes at work, which require a reassessment of value systems and attitudes, both on the part of management and workers. If this does not happen in periods of profound social upheaval, this may manifest itself in destructive industrial conflicts, the harmful effects of which can affect large sections of the community. If, however, one takes an objective, detached view, the situation proves not to be quite so unbearable as might appear. Solutions will not come easily, but then all real human progress has been on a hard road.

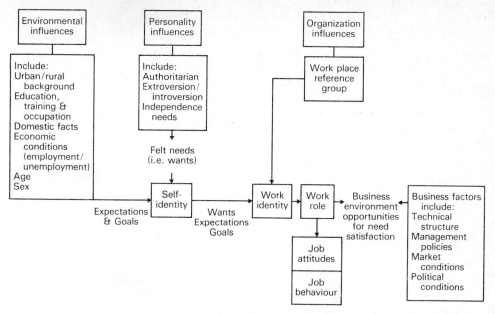

Figure 5.2 *A number of possible influences that shape attitudes and behaviour within a firm*

To effect the right kind of social change and be aware of the social forces that we have to contend with, information is required on the following aspects of the social climate:

1. Trends in labour turnover and absenteeism.
2. Future manpower needs.
3. Changes in job demands relative to existing wage differentials.
4. Increases or decreases in restrictions on overtime, piecework, speed of work and general opposition, all of which affect the organization.
5. Measurement of the movement in the value of the human assets as proposed by writers like Likert. (See Chapters 2, 4 and 6.)

5.6 MANAGERIAL EFFECTIVENESS

An important part of bringing about change is the attitude and effectiveness of industrial managers. Indeed, if they do not feel positive and optimistic about their own future, this is likely to be reflected in their job and in the attitudes of the people who work both for and with them. There are mixed opinions about the effects of managerial efficiency, but research carried out has made use of the following factors: the nature of the organization; the kind of subordinates and peers a manager has; his personality and experience; the nature of the change in an organization; the management education available; the Boss; and the manager's numeracy.

It can be seen from this list that the manager's job depends on a number of inter-related aspects in the complexity of a works organization. If management is truly committed to change, but does not deal with it in a sincere and professional way, we can expect opposition; but of more importance is the fact that no change will occur.

Let us now consider what might be the case for the future. Since the information on the future cannot be gathered and analysed there is nothing that can be proved or disproved, but if we think about it the task is not as easy as it first appears. If we are to undertake our study with some scientific responsibility we cannot give an entirely free range to our imaginations. Instead, we must extrapolate from trends we can see developing, or we outline organizational systems that are even now possible, that exist at present only on a small scale, if at all, but that promise to be sufficiently effective in meeting the problems of the present in that they promise to be more widely developed in the future.

We cannot try to anticipate all aspects of organizational change and development, nor even claim that we are singling out the most important ones. We shall simply seek to present those aspects which seem to us to be of some importance and on which we have at least some evidence to support our predictions. Let us look at some possible predictions.

5.7 THE DECLINE OF AUTHORITY

We shall assume that the organizations of the future will depend less on formal authority than those of the past. The classical theories of scientific management were based upon the vertical dimension of organizations, the authority relations between employee and his boss. Those who propose participation management have for years sought to undermine what they call authoritarian leadership, and have argued for the advantages of democratic leadership in which the superior (the boss) at least consorts with his subordinates and seeks to be responsive to their thoughts and feelings. But the participation management theorists have been stuck with the same problem of the vertical as have the writers on scientific management. While arguing for a different sort of relationship between superior and subordinates, they still see the organization primarily in this vertical dimension.

Modern organizations, and especially those that are based on a higher level of development of science or technology, are made up of very separate parts. If the organization is to be efficient, it must depend upon the co-ordination of activities of people who stand in horizontal or diagonal relationship to each other. What do we mean by these terms? A horizontal relationship links individuals at the same status level in the organization, and a diagonal relationship is one which links two individuals at different status levels, but where the higher status person has no real control over the lower status person.

When differences arise between individuals in horizontal or diagonal relationships, they can be resolved through the exercise of authority, that is appealing about the dispute through the organization until it reaches an official who is of a higher status than those in disagreement. In any organization, and especially in large organizations, the resolution in such disputes through an appeal to authority is counter-productive. We think there are at least three reasons for making this statement. First, the appeal might slow down decision making, and also waste the time of higher level executives, who should rather be investing their time on the larger and more general problems of the organization. Secondly, the further removed in organizational position is the ultimate decision maker from the point of the problem, the less likely his decision is to be fully relevant to the problem. The executive is not likely to have an intimate picture of the problem, and he is likely to make his decision in terms that will make life easier for as many as possible, rather than in terms which will prevent the problem from arising in the future. Thirdly, the appeal to authority in disputes creates a series of win or lose cases. The foreman, supervisor or manager who loses today's case will feel upset, and will try to prepare himself more effectively to win tomorrow's. This kind of conflict and competition undermines the possibility of developing smoothly co-ordinated relations between departments that may depend on each other.

If such differences among people in responsible positions, whether horizontally or diagonally related to each other, can be resolved by direct dealings among these individuals, co-ordination can be improved, friction reduced, and the productivity of the organization greatly increased.

If this can be shown to be possible then it will not be found in the textbooks of management principles, for these teach business students that the standard management principle focuses predominantly on vertical relations, since the classical writers draw their inspiration from military organizations and from large manufacturing firms where, several generations ago, relations were organized primarily along the vertical dimensions.

There is no doubt that companies in the USA show a greater facility in handling non-authoritative relations, and the reason for this is the difference in orientation and behaviour which is an attribute to the American culture and social structure, which tend to play down the reliance upon authority and favours egalitarian ideals. The Americans have a belief and strong feelings that if a problem arises with a person on the same organizational level as another, or in any case not subject to each other's direct control, it is better to try to work it out directly with each other than to appeal to the boss. They recognize that if it proves impossible to work out the problems directly, they will have to appeal to a superior, but to Americans that would be considered a failure.

It is only very recently that behavioural scientists have started to look at horizontal and diagonal relations in organizations. As the studies catch up with the most effective management practices, training programmes for young entrants to management will eventually shift away from classical management theory to a new concept of organizational behaviour, and we can expect organizations of the future to be developed with greater emphasis on horizontal and diagonal relations, and even with some systematic planning as to how these relations may be best shaped.

In the future, the successful manager will depend much less on giving orders and more upon negotiating skills, upon ability to listen and to adapt to the other's point of view, and upon an ability to present his own views persuasively. Does this mean that the exercise of authority will be abandoned? Of course not. There will always be a possibility of resort to authority when everything else fails, but we shall see the use of formal authority reduced, and if top managers find themselves having to give many orders and arbitrating many disputes among subordinates, they will increasingly come to see this as a malfunction in the business system.

The effective executive will think and act in terms of a social system rather than in terms of discrete orders and decisions. Top managers will see their role as that of building and maintaining a co-ordinated system of activities and human interaction.

5.8   HUMANIZATION OF WORK

When early work into human relations was undertaken in management studies there was much criticism of those who studied problems of job satisfaction and dissatisfaction. What was disliked was that those undertaking the study were attempting to show management how to adjust the workers to the jobs and so make them satisfied, but not allow managers to exploit them. Regretfully, management has given scant attention to the studies of job satisfaction over the years, but many trade unions have taken this work very seriously and have started to make demands that management negotiate with them regarding the human aspects of work, as well as those topics more traditionally covered by collective bargaining.

Some time ago, when the first studies were made of worker reactions to the mass production assembly lines, behavioural scientists discovered, perhaps not too surprisingly, that it was indeed an exceedingly oppressive work situation from which most workers sought to escape whenever they could find wages roughly equivalent to those earned on the assembly line. During these early years management offered little in the way of practical recommendations to the job satisfaction problem because assembly line technology seemed so efficient and management could not imagine why they should abandon it, and of course they were supported by many union leaders. The problem was one of looking at ways of production which would involve much higher costs, and therefore would not support the current level of wages. More recently, in America, Europe and Britain, absenteeism among assembly line workers in many industries has been so high and workers willing to suffer assembly line conditions have become so scarce as to force management to consider radical changes in technology. The well-known experiment at Volvo in Sweden took a lead in this search. Here Volvo introduced major changes in jobs and work-flow patterns, and in facilities, and indeed built a new plant to house the new technology that it was hoped would provide jobs that were less oppressive and more meaningful to workers.

In the 1980s, and certainly to the end of the century, pressures from workers towards the humanization of work will increase, at least in the industrialized countries. We must therefore understand what are the forces behind these pressures. Increased education opportunities bring with them rising expectations about the kinds of job that are in accord with human dignity. Rising standards of living also produce a decline in the strength of material incentives, and an increase in concern for social meaning in the factory.

While the immediate practical problem of recruiting and obtaining workers under bad job conditions has been prodding management towards exploration of new technology more in accord with human values, there have even been cases where union leaders have joined with management to explore the development of new forms of work. Again in Sweden the continuing search for new work methods is due in part to serious outbreaks of wild-cat strikes, which have all been directed as much against top union leaders as against management. The workers appear to be saying that it is not enough for union and management to provide them with adequate wages and fringe benefits.

The exploration of new jobs to meet human needs has been carried on rather tentatively and cautiously so far in the United Kingdom with some of the more adventurous companies beginning on only a small scale with projects involved job rotation for jobs that are especially dull, but ranging to more fundamental changes, such as those involving worker self-management on the shop floor. So far many firms have attempted to keep these innovations separate from the broader question of worker control and the sharing of economic rewards; for example, Philips, a large electronics manufacturer in Holland, has found that management is hesitating to make any real jump from experimentation to policy. There have been no radical changes in the basic production system, and it is questionable whether there ever will be. In that factory successful, autonomous work groups assemble television sets, for example, and they could be assembling between 26 and 30 a day. However, those involved in production have not been invited to discuss with management whether they would like to consider reaching a higher production level and be rewarded for example by a reduction in their hours, or a higher bonus. These are the kind of questions that management in this company, as in many others, have not even contemplated asking and discussing with their workers. This sort of observation leads to a prediction that future efforts towards the humanization of work are bound to lead to the breakdown of the separation of collective bargaining from managerial prerogatives.

Let us take an example. We shall assume that the management of the ABC Electronics Company has been successful with a small-scale experiment in worker self-management in one of its departments. When the workers discover that when they manage and inspect the job themselves they are producing as large a volume and as high a quality as when they were directed by the foreman, sooner or later it is bound to occur to them that they are saving the firm the salary of the foreman, and that this saving, or at least a part of it, should be shared with them. Furthermore, as workers discover that self-management works pretty well in a small department, they are bound to think it may be more broadly extended on the shop floor, and even into the management of the firm.

It is not unreasonable to project that a large expansion in worker participation in management, ranging from worker self-management at the department level to broader schemes, will lead to worker representatives participating in decision making at higher management level in the future. In the past, there have been some experiments in this direction, but they have tended to be confined to schemes such as the co-determination scheme in West Germany where, in certain industries, union leaders sit on the board of directors. So far it would seem that experience demonstrates that such participation at director level has little effect on the lives of the workers on the shop floor.

5.9   INTRODUCING CHANGE

Until recently, there have been two general approaches to improving organizations. From the early beginnings of the industrial system right up to the present time, industrialists and observers of the industrial scene were preoccupied, as some still are, with the technical aspects of the organization. This approach was almost solely concerned with such things as the layout of the plant, methods of working, lighting and so on. Then, with the advent of the so-called human relations school during the 1920s, attention was switched to the social aspects. This thinking gained ground during the 1950s and 1960s. The former and latter schools have been termed by Professor Lupton as either hard-nosed or soft-nosed. Clearly, as some now appreciate, it is neither one nor the other, but elements of both that play a part in organization difficulties. Hertzberg sees the problem of designing jobs to suit people rather than the other way round, that is, what the hard-nosed people support. The Tavistock approach, which really complements the Hertzberg philosophy, is outlined in the company development programme carried out at Shell (UK) Limited. In essence, this is an attempt to develop the technological and social systems as an integrated whole, a philosophy which is also reconciled to a policy of joint optimization of resources. This objective recognizes that the aim should be 'the best' in the prevailing circumstances as distinct from the maximum use of resources. The message which we can glean from this is to be wary of easy answers, and to remember that what we do in one part of the organization could affect another part in a negative way.

The vital point is how to introduce effective change, that is, change that leads to some improvement in the socio-technical system. Perhaps we ought first to start with the premise that we are going to manage the change and not let events take over from us. Next is the need to clear our objectives in the light of where the organization is now *vis-à-vis* its external environment. Third is the assumption that both through the formal and informal systems we have all the relevant information, or as much as can be economically justified. Fourth is the need to recognize that conflict is a natural and inherent part of any change process. (This aspect is further developed in Chapter 7.) Indeed, it is only possible when conflict emerges that any real understanding of the issues can be revealed. Much of the industrial relations difficulties in the United Kingdom are no doubt due to each side having different perceptions of the problem. The fifth requirement is the process of developing understanding about the facts and information being presented. Finally, there is the change agent, which is the current piece of jargon for a person, a group of people or a procedure, which aims to bring about some change in a system. Although Argyris, in his *Intervention, Theory and Method,* considers that change agents become too involved with the situation and adopt biased attitudes without realizing it, anyone who wants to bring about change smoothly must avoid fixed positions. Instead, Argyris suggests the idea of the interventionist as someone who helps groups of people to understand and deal with problems in a way that suits them.

Improving organizations, which by implication involves changes, requires attention to communication. Really effective communication is going to involve much patience and some investment in time. If we do not appreciate this, we can expect hostility, suspicion, and indifference.

Many UK companies have been undertaking a process of organizational development for some time, although they probably call it different names. Some have done it well, while others have struggled or failed. Whatever it is called, when seen against the varied changes taking place, the problem will not go away. Therefore, we shall need to give more formal attention to developing our organizations to meet the demands of a changing internal and external environment.

5.10 A STRATEGY FOR MANAGING CHANGE

We must be concerned with the application of behavioural science to our study of the organization. Therefore organization development provides valuable insight into the organization for today and tomorrow. Is this something new of which we must be aware, or is it an old activity? The answer is yes, in part, to both questions. To understand what organization development is today, and where it may be going tomorrow, we need to begin with a brief look at the past. The origins of organization development can be traced back to 1930. The start was the T-Group, in which the members sat in a circle, loosely led by a trainer, to examine their relations with each other, and the problems they had in communication and interpersonal understanding. By the late 1950s increasing numbers of industrial executives were becoming involved in T-Groups, or variants called sensitivity training. The idea is that, through this training, the executive will develop greater understanding of the impact he has on other people and greater sensitivity to their thoughts and feelings. With these new found skills, he is expected to manage them more effectively.

Other experts have argued that a strategy of changing organizations through individuals offers little promise and they advocate changing behaviour through changing formal organization structure, technology, work-flow and the design of jobs. It has been accepted that T-Group involvement often does not carry over into solid organizational changes when the trainee returns to his organization. In other words, personality changes seem to get lost within the culture and structure of the organization. On the other hand, proponents of the structural strategy have come to recognize that interpersonal interventions might be necessary in persuading key figures to recognize the need for structural changes, and since the new structures require new patterns of behaviour it might also be necessary to devise training strategies to help members to adjust to these structural changes.

Today, those concerned with interpersonal strategies are working on a new range of techniques. The trend now is away from discussion groups which focus strongly on personalities and immediate interpersonal relations, towards a more task-oriented, problem solving approach. The classical T-Group is loosely structured so that it can be shaped by its members; other strategies call for group experiences simulating the types of problems that commonly arise in organizations.

In the future, most large European firms will have an organization development policy with its own organization development unit linked with the line organization at a high level, working in co-operation with managers and supervisors on improving organizational performance. While each company will have at least a small continuing unit of its own, to avoid the parochialism of a strictly in-house operation, that organization development unit will bring in outside consultants and researchers to participate in the process of diagnosis, selection of intervention strategies, and development of impact information to provide for feedback and evaluation. We can expect in the future that management will not be content with information limited to costs of production, waste of scrap, rejection in inspection, absenteeism and labour turnover. The aim of management will be to develop a comprehensive and continuous feedback system, providing information on how the organization is functioning.

Organization development specialists will involve line management in evaluating this feedback information, in diagnosing problems, and in determining strategies and techniques for intervention. Choices will be made among three general alternatives.

Research

The organization development worker of the future will recognize that problems described to him will be in terms of their symptoms, and that the first step must be to probe beneath the symptoms to arrive at a diagnosis of the underlying problem. Then management, perhaps with outsiders, will have to determine whether, if further research is needed, a brief study will suffice, or whether a more intensive project is advisable. Management will then be advised on the research methods to be reached, from surveys, to more intensive interview and observational studies. Where the organization is large enough to allow for perhaps two studies this may show different treatment, or they may recommend an experimental approach.

Structural Change

Those specializing in organizational development in the future will not assume that there must be a training programme appropriate for every organizational need. Formal organization will be examined as will the technology involved, the work-flow, and the nature of the jobs involved, searching for structural sources of organizational difficulties, and then, maybe, a training programme might be prescribed.

In this field, the organization development manager of the future will occupy a position very different from the one we recognize today. Up to the present time there has been a separation between the planners of organization structure, technology, work-flow, and job design on the one hand, and those concerned with 'people problems' on the other. This has meant, in effect, that engineers have designed and installed new technologies, work-flow systems and new job designs, with little, if any, attention to the impact on workers of such plans. Only when the engineering plans fail to work smoothly and give rise to people problems would the human relations 'specialist' be called in to try to patch up the situation.

In the organization of the future, top management will recognize that the design of technologies, work-flow systems and jobs must be integrated with the design of social systems necessary to support the technological and work-flow structure. The organization development specialist will work closely with the engineers in the design of new technologies, work-flows and jobs, and when existing structures appear to be giving rise to human problems he will invite the engineer to collaborate with him in re-examining those structures.

Training

The organizational development specialist will not only be able to prescribe among a wide range of training interventions with increasing confidence as to what particular type of intervention is most appropriate for each type of problem that is amenable to a training approach, he will also be concerned with evaluating the effectiveness of each training intervention so that he and his colleagues can continue to improve their ability to man training programmes that are responsive to organizational needs.

In the future, organization development will not be carried out in terms of sporadic intervention. It will be an on-going process in which the feedback of information upon organizational problems and upon past effectiveness of various types of interventions will be utilized to plan and carry out future development efforts.

We have been looking at organizational development as solely a management activity, which indeed it has tended to be up to this point. In the future we may very well see organization development extend beyond management and involve union leaders and representatives of the rank and file. As managements in Great Britain become increasingly concerned over the high cost of worker alienation from jobs, and therefore pay increasing attention to the restructuring of blue-collar as well as white-collar jobs, union leaders will naturally resist any such restructuring which appears to them designed to make the workers into 'contented cows', but there is no clear-cut opposition of interest between workers and management on this front. Both have a concern with making jobs more meaningful, though the reasons for this concern are different at different organizational levels. Workers will not readily go along with a programme to reduce alienation if they see this as just another example of management manipulation. They will go along with, and even make contributions to, the restructuring process, providing that they and their representatives play a role in the definition of the problems to be solved, and the strategy to be brought to bear. The organizational manager of the future should seek to develop this kind of work, and union participation in the restructuring of jobs.

What are the obstacles to change? Perfect harmony in industry is almost impossible because, even if a person works in a small team, harmony involves being aware of people's pride, and keeping them happy and informed. Only in a perfect world are these things done properly. Even managers who are usually efficient can, on occasions, fail to communicate and consult until something suddenly erupts.

5.11 INDUSTRIAL DEMOCRACY

The European Community first tackled the question of industrial democracy in the apparently dry context of company law reform. This is because the EEC Treaty establishes a common market not only for goods, services and capital, but also for persons. In European law (and expressly declared in the EEC Treaty), the word 'person' includes incorporated bodies. For the common market to be a reality, shareholders, workers and creditors must have equivalent (but not necessarily the same) legal protection in all member states. For this reason the Treaty (Article 220) envisages at least some harmonization (but not standardization) of company law.

It must also be possible for companies in different countries to be able to merge. Only in this way, for example, can computer firms be created that are large enough to compete effectively with the American giant IBM. It was in connection with the need to facilitate company mergers that the question of worker participation first arose at Community level in 1966.

Supervisory Board

At that time large German companies were already required by law to give workers' representatives one-third of the seats on a 'supervisory board' which had responsibilities for the overall strategy of the company as opposed to the board of management responsible for day-to-day decisions. The German pattern had been the result of a long fight by the German trade unions, and they were (and still are) adamant in their refusal to give up what they have won. When the Commission began work on a proposed international convention on mergers, the Germans insisted that it should not become a means whereby certain companies could evade the existing German law. Discussions on this and other questions have been continuing ever since. In the meantime, the Commission's feeling that something like the German pattern would be eventually accepted inspired both the Commission's proposed European Company statute and the fifth draft directive on company law harmonization put forward in 1972.

The Commission has always emphasized that its proposals in the field of company law harmonization are a basis for discussion, not an impractical attempt to impose solutions from outside which are not fully acceptable to those concerned. This is even more true today with three new member countries settling in. What the Commission does point out, however, is that worker participation seems to be the coming trend, that the Germans have a pattern that has proved itself in practice, and that national governments are likely to want to introduce their own legislation where they have not already done so.

5.12   RESISTANCE TO CHANGE

Check List of Factors

Kinds of Change

Methods of work
Policies and procedures
Standards of work
Economic changes (salaries, etc.)
Equipment changes
Organizational changes
Transfer of personnel
Status and social changes
Location
Environmental

Resistance by Management

Negative view
Unconscious dissension
Apathy and indifference
Free translation
Pet project attitude
Authoritarian approach

Conditions Contributing to Resistance to Change

Shortage of personnel/equipment during implementation
Failure to justify reason for change
Top management pressure for fast installation of change
Lack of participation
Poor planning for redeployment of people
Insufficient guidance of people affected
Lack of enthusiasm by management
Lack of advance information

Why People Resist Change

Economic reasons:
   Fear of unemployment
   Fear of reduced hours
   Fear of demotion and reduced pay
Personal reasons:
   Resentment of implied criticism that present methods are inadequate
   Fear that skill, knowledge and pride will be reduced
   Fear that job will be less interesting or challenging
   Fear that harder work will be involved
   Resistance because of lack of understanding
Social reasons:
   Dislike of making new social adjustments
   Dislike of breaking present social ties
   Fear that new social situation will bring reduced satisfaction
   Dislike of outside interference
   Resentment of lack of involvement
   Change seen as benefiting only the organization

Conditions for Reducing Resistance to Change

Management support and belief in change
Evidence of how workers have been well treated in the past when changes have been
   made
Commitment through understanding, involvement, and communication
Information given on:
   What is to be done
   Why it is to be done (advantages and disadvantages)
   How it is to be done
   When it is to be done
   Who is involved

The Need for Change

Attitude to the job is the key. If British industry could get a different attitude then it would become a great deal more efficient. This is as true of management as anyone.

Change does not come easily to management, where there are deep-rooted problems of accepting the need for change. Some managers think that if only the operative would work twice as hard and produce twice as much the problem would be solved.

Workers' changed attitudes to the job in general are now more noticeable in the new generation, who do not feel the same sense of loyalty to a company that their parents did. Companies must learn to accept that old allegiances have disappeared with the changes that have come about in society itself, and with the advent of new technology, managerial techniques, and associated redundancies. Nevertheless, for British industry there is a real need to encourage people to be conscious of the fact that their future and that of all society is tied up with profitable employment. The moral problem for management is unemployment, though it could be argued that the problem is not one-sided, and it does not help if the worker does not recognize that job security and profit earning go hand in hand.

Undoubtedly many jobs are dull and repetitive. The answer is to try to enrich them by added responsibility, and to try to make people participate in decision-making where their skills and experience can be more fully employed. Management should strive for less autocratic attitudes and try to break down the barriers that prevent co-operative discussion of whatever is important.

ICI have made many attempts to change attitudes within the organization. They have provided meaningful information to the staff to help them and make them want 'to do their job better', creating, in other words, 'job interest'. ICI accepts that behavioural scientists can teach industry a lot if only industry will listen.

One of the things that ICI learnt from their first investigations was that whereas industrial unrest might appear at face value to be related to money, it was invariably the way of expressing a more general frustration. Contented workers put more into the job, and of course they are not going to work for a pittance: they must have the feeling that they are getting a fair crack of the whip. But the fundamental point made by ICI is that you cannot buy someone's goodwill.

Again, unless there are, in the future, some farsighted attitudes on behalf of the unions, more workers are going to be put out of work. The problem is to make union officials aware of what is going on, and really understand the events. People have to be persuaded to listen to and think about the problems of the company or industry they work in. A common attitude is that there is too much communication about economics, when the real interest lies in ready money and more money; the rest is somebody else's problem.

People in all areas have to take a greater interest in the profitability of the firms with which they are associated; and not only just be interested, but to care about the results, otherwise we may find a situation where people develop a sort of death wish.

This attitude can be intensified in some retail companies which suffer from a casual labour syndrome. A large supermarket chain, for example, can have 600 people leave every week, and the same number join. Not surprisingly, there is little opportunity to build up a tradition of loyalty among the bulk of the ever-increasing number of employees, and there is a corresponding lack of involvement with, and feeling of responsibility for, the employee on the part of the lower levels of management, which sometimes leads to high-handed and arbitrary behaviour. But a more fundamental problem, particularly in the retail trade, is to bring about a change of attitude on the part of management towards union activity, persuading them to pay more than lip-service to the idea that unionism is respectable and that unions have a constructive role to play.

We are fortunate in this country that the trade union movement as a whole remains reformist rather than revolutionary, and is more stable than many of its counterparts elsewhere. We may look for better union leadership and acknowledge the spur to managerial efficiency which more forward-looking unions could provide, yet we must accept that improved managerial performance can still secure greater union co-operation than is offered at present. Firms seeking to adapt corporate attitudes to changes in the social climate can acknowledge that there exists a situation on which they can still build.

5.13   THE SOCIAL RESPONSIBILITY OF BUSINESS

Industry is the economic, wealth-producing institution of our society. As such, some leaders of industry have argued that its main social responsibility is to make a profit for the sake of everyone concerned: shareholders, employees and the community as a whole. Behind this point of view there is a basic truth which is recognized in all circles. What industry decides to do with its surplus is another story, but it can do nothing, if there is nothing to divide.

We may agree that profitability and responsibility are inseparable. There are, however, deeper obligations of responsibility than are implied in profit. The term enlightened self-interest expresses the two-way benefit derived from the social activities of business. We are entitled to the view that social responsibility is an integral part of, and not an optional extra to, the function of providing goods and services at a profit.

Social responsibility is certainly one of the key areas of business, but it is not the only one. Managers have the task of balancing a number of objectives, of taking into account the changing requirements of stockholders, employees and customers, as well as society in general (see Fig. 5.3). That involves making a judgement about what is an acceptable level of risk. A business that fails as a business is a social failure too.

There are examples of enlightened business policies within the profit motive: this is not entirely new. Business has always had to adapt to the changing expectations of the community. For example, child labour in factories, acceptable 150 years ago, would be unthinkable today.

Intense pressure is, however, being applied by the acceleration of change and its implications. It is essential for management to understand the new demands made on people by these changes. Inevitably, the compulsion to adapt to change sets up stresses. Some stress is necessary; it is part of the price of challenge by which we can develop our full potential; but change today is exponential and therefore vastly more exacting than at any time in the past, and likely to become increasingly so in the near future.

Figure 5.3   *Pressures on a manager in the 1980s*

For example, computers have added a new dimension to business. There are in the world today an estimated 1 million computer specialists. By the end of the century, according to experts, 80 per cent of all public companies in Britain will either own or be making full use of a computer. The impact of computers on our lives is already considerable, yet there is widespread misunderstanding about the true nature of the computer and its influence on job control, information systems, organization structure and, not least, on personal privacy. We are in the midst of a revolution in the whole field of information. Unfortunately, the improvements in the technology of communication via computers, satellites and other media have not been matched by discipline in the use of the data obtained. In many British companies one-third of the paperwork produced could be scrapped without anyone noticing or suffering from the loss. In fact, the organization might be all the better for the pruning. People at work are overwhelmed by data, much of it meaningless and unhelpful. It is important to distinguish between data and information. We have never had so much data or so little information. (See Chapter 8.)

The confusion increases with the growth of the organization. The merger mania of the last 20 years or so has concentrated power in enormous companies. In Britain by 1990 the 100 largest manufacturing enterprises will produce over half of net output. Experts forecast that a few hundred giant multinational companies will dominate the free world economy before the century ends.

The economies of size have been discussed elsewhere, but the human implications have been insufficiently studied. Obviously, those who make the decisions in organizations depend on reports proceeding up the line, but the system tends to filter out everything that cannot be expressed in words and figures, that is, the emotions and moods of the human situation (see Fig. 5.4). It also filters out the intuitive sensing of the situation, which is the reality of management. In a giant business the picture received at the top of the organization may bear little relation to the reality of what is happening below. The breakdown of traditional paternalism and the remoteness of the decision-making in big companies have deprived management of the means of measuring the human conflict of business.

Impatience with conditions in the business and external environment is expressed most forceably by younger people. Those of the older generation, brought up in, and conditioned by, the years of depression in the 1930s, have remained security-minded and obedient, but the younger people in business have grown up in a forward-looking, technologically advised society. Whereas in the recent past the business pattern comprised a few educated people managing a mass of unskilled labour, most of the British work force today is knowledge-based at all levels. The questioning of current values, and the demands for direct action and quick solutions, take no account of the costs of the complexity of society. Behind the impulsiveness there is a genuine preference for meaningful work rather than security, and a profound concern with social ill.

The public as a whole expect business to take a more active part in solving the problems of society, even though at times profit might suffer. Prominent among these problems are pollution, consumer protection, conciliation for minority groups, and the use of land for better social purpose. There is sometimes a direct appeal to shareholders and the community, notably by pressure groups, at annual general meetings. The conflicting responsibilities produced are a major source of tension amongst senior management.

These are a few of the social facts that confront business today. The outlook may seem bleak, but we must remember that most of the threats also present opportunities. In an exponential situation, however, the opportunities do not stand indefinitely. They have dwindled at an accelerating rate. In other words, time is not on our side.

Another limiting factor is that we may be very near the limit of our ability to adapt to change. The evidence of history has led us to believe that we can always adapt, but there is no historical precedence for the rate of change we are experiencing now. In his book

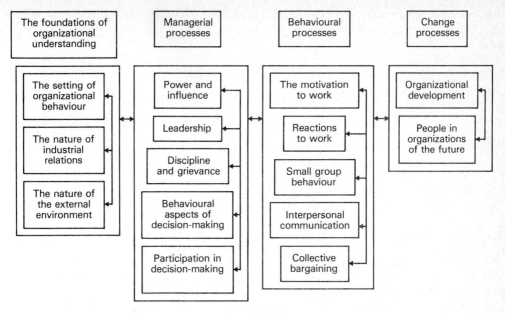

Figure 5.4 *Understanding the foundations of the study of organizations*

Future Shock Alvin Toffler defines the shock as 'the shattering stress and disorientation that we induce in individuals by subjecting them to too much change in too short a time'. Large numbers of people are already suffering from the effects of that persistent over-stimulation. A great deal of production time is lost through stress ailments, more than through influenza and common colds combined; perhaps more, indeed, than through strikes and other industrial action. Stress at work is more widespread yet more difficult to deal with than the direct bad effects of poor physical environment. To make matters worse, business convention requires us to repress our emotions and assume a calm and assured exterior, often turning the harmful effects inwards.

Successful management of change requires an understanding of human motivation. Perhaps, contrary to what many managers may believe, material progress is not the over-riding motive of society, nor are workers motivated by money only. Progressive British companies have done a good deal to meet the safety and psychological needs of their employees, but few have accepted the real challenge to provide self-fulfilment for those who care about achievement. People need self-esteem, a sense of belonging and self-expression at work. They want an opportunity to stretch their abilities and enlarge their skills and responsibility. Business organization and human goals are often in conflict, and this is one of the basic sources of stress. The organization requires order and discipline, while people want much more autonomy, flexibility and involvement with other people in a satisfying team effort.

Considerations of adaptability and motivation are not, as some leaders of industry believe, merely of academic interest, but are of practical importance to business. The economic costs of accidents, absenteeism, pollution, and so on, are visible and measurable, but they are still only the tip of the iceberg. Underneath is the massive hidden problem of talent and enthusiasm lying dormant and unused, and the great mass of workers who have become demotivated and insist aggressively on being treated like human beings. This is not peculiar to one group of workers. Every employee, however inarticulate, has some hope and expectation of being recognized as a person and valued for his or her contribution.

The problem is universal and action must take place on the broadest possible front. Unfortunately, few organizations make a total, systematic audit of the whole field of social responsibility. Any detailed examination of a company's social responsibility should be preceded by some management self-questioning about existing general policies. Is the business making the best use of its financial, physical and human resources? Is it clearly understood that long-term profitability is in the best interest of all concerned – employees, shareholders, government and society at large? Where would further study appear to be most worth while? Who should be appointed to conduct the inquiry? In each area chosen for social study the team could attempt to identify the strengths, weaknesses, opportunities and threats in the organization, and then suggest what action might be taken.

Let us look at some of these areas in the light of social responsibility beginning with the internal environment. The social responsibility audit would study work place and working conditions, as they affect the mental and physical health of the worker, and creditability. For example, are ventilation, heating, lighting and sound insulation adequate? Surveys of British factories over the last 10 years have revealed that 25 per cent had inadequate ventilation, 20 per cent unsatisfactory heating, and 80 per cent lighting levels below the recommendations made by the Illuminating Engineering Society. Is the office designed for efficient working? Are equipment and processes designed on sound ergonomic principles to prevent physical and mental strain? Safety is often given a very low level of consideration. Witness the fact that each year in Great Britain about 1000 people are killed at work and over 500 000 injured.

How often does business make a critical and professional appraisal of its methods of recruitment, selection and placement, promotion policies, the handling of redundancies, the possibility of introducing flexible working hours? Flexi-time is making slow progress in Britain, but in Europe it is in operation in well over 2000 companies. The value of a place to eat from both a nutritional and cost point of view should receive professional investigation as part of the general concern for the physical and mental well-being of people at work.

Very few British companies have a specific policy on the recruitment, selection and placement of ethnic and other minority groups. Racial discrimination is still widespread in spite of legislation. The mentally and physically handicapped are another neglected minority, capable of making a useful contribution, but often not included in company plans. The social audit must also take account of discrimination against women in pay and promotion, and examine what initiative the company has taken or could take in the light of the legislation that now exists.

The organization's structure can be inhibitive or expansive, encouraging original thought and initiative, or preferring the 'company man'. The bureaucratic structure is a breeding ground for frustration and stress. In such organizations authority and individual responsibility may not be clearly understood because they have not been adequately defined. Changes in industrial relations over the last two decades have made a company's attitude to trade unions a more sensitive issue than ever before. The social responsibility audit could look at the company's consultation and bargaining procedures, its policy and method in handling grievances and dealing with such comparatively new phenomena as the 'sit-in', its ability to forecast five years ahead the basic developments in industrial relations, and assess the probable effects of changes in the values and expectations of society at large upon the spirit and practice of the company's internal industrial relations.

Training is a complex object for analysis concerned not only with the current needs at all levels, but also with its relevance to its future requirements of knowledge and skill as far as these can be foreseen. Workers resist technical change if it makes traditional skills obsolete and does not make provision for new ones to be acquired. The social auditors will investigate whether the training budget is adequate, whether the company evaluates its training programme systematically, and whether the workers are given a hearing on their training wants and career ambitions.

Finally, business in the long run must mirror the ideals and values of the society of which it is an integral part. A comprehensive approach to any audit of a firm's social responsibility will start the learning process and hopefully provoke constructive action.

5.14   CONCLUSIONS

The Social Responsibility of Business

The present concern about the social responsibility of business rests on the unease about business policy today. However, this unease has so far had very little impact on the formulation of business policy. Academics and managers both advocate that business policies should attempt to reconcile the interests of the stake holder groups in the firm, such as shareholders, management, workers, consumers and the government (representing the community). On the other hand some people may say that by pursuing the firm's traditional objectives of profit and growth the firm will best fulfil its social responsibilities. There is very little evidence that resources are being diverted to any significant extent from the orthodox profit or growth goals to other purposes, despite numerous examples of the opinion which seems to accept the case for a more socially conscious approach to business practice.

There is an organic view of responsibilities among management that sees no incompatibility between the firm's obligations to its employees, customers and the wider community, and orthodox policies of profits and growth. Such an outlook is not far removed from the spirit of Charles Wilson's reputed remarks when President of General Motors: 'What is good for General Motors is good for America.' However, many believe that it is not the responsibility of business to *initiate* the widespread social changes that would be brought about by a radical reorientation from orthodox objectives.

Concern about pollution, low wages of overseas workers, or exaggerated advertising claims are the expressions of anxiety about *means* rather than the *ends* of business activity. The appeals for greater professionalization in management and for codes of ethics are, in essence, appeals for collective support for transgressions from normal profit centred behaviour that may be thought socially desirable, but threaten survival if other managers do not follow suit. Of course there are examples of firms initiating new standards of practice without such support, but their position seems to be somewhat insulated from other firms by virtue of their size of profitability.

A final reason why the alternative policies for radical revision of business policy have had so little impact is that the advocates of these policies are not usually top executives. Many of the critics wish to do more than change the attitudes and behaviour of productive organizations. Their aims, to the extent that they can be identified, are for a very radical change in the organization of society itself, encompassing the public ownership of production and distribution. Some have very different notions about human society, equality and the use of power. Others approach world problems from a conservationist's standpoint, fear the destruction of the earth, the pollution and/or exhaustion of resources and, therefore, desire an end to economic growth. Such views are, of course, quite opposed to those prevailing in business. This lack of basic empathy inhibits constructive debate and serves to maintain the boundaries of present subjective perspectives.

Finally, it has become obvious in recent years that a crisis between business and society is developing over policy anomalies, and many people are suggesting that the continued existence of such social problems as unemployment, war, racism, income inequalities, pollution and worker alienation represents the failure of policy rules, at least based on the theoretical findings of the work that has been done so far. Since it is fair to assume that the present policies in business are derived from much the same sources as many of the policies that rule our society, it is therefore sensible to conclude that the present concern about the social responsibility of business is, to a large extent, derived from criticisms of our own society. We can therefore conclude by arguing that business policy as it is at present interpreted by management and society at large has its shortcomings in two main respects: first, in that insufficient attention is paid to the interactive relationship of business and society, as only the management's prospective is emphasized; secondly, as the subject prospective of too limited a business policy cannot answer the current radical criticisms of conventional economic objectives of both business and society as a whole.

There is a severe limit to what can be done to remove people from their environment, but a lot can be done to create an environment in which people can realize their potential. Far too many work places inhibit rather than liberate what is best in the worker. That liberating ideal has been the motive for most of the innovations introduced into the changes required in the work place over the last decade. Management has been acutely aware of the deadening atmosphere of the typical work place, and has become convinced that it could and should be given new life. They have observed what bad conditions and poor environments were doing to the people who worked there, and have decided to infuse some human quality into the work place to make it compatible with and sufficiently malleable to people's character and needs, instead of resistant and extracting a price in mental and physical distress for every grudging adjustment that was conceded.

Management's most disturbing conclusion about the work place in general is that it has virtually ceased to evolve. Most work places reflect standards and practices that have been outdated for years. They are static in character and in the facilities used, and have acquired a reputation for employing equally static people. In the past these characteristics may have conveyed a sense of cosiness, stability and permanence to people who were suspicious of change. Such changes that were made were no more than modifications and improvements of existing conditions, a gradual straight line development that provided no surprise, but yielded no dynamic progress.

5.15   CHECKLIST OF CONDITIONS AFFECTING MORALE

Extent to which members have common goals
Extent to which goals are regarded as worthwhile
Extent to which members think goals are attainable

Other Important Factors

A fair hearing and square deal on grievances
Prospects of a satisfactory future

Organization's knowledge of individual's qualification, experience and progress
Recognition of, and credit for constructive suggestions offered
Friendly and helpful criticisms of work or correction of mistakes
Pay increases when deserved
Pay comparable with jobs elsewhere
Promotion on merit
Amount of work required not unreasonable
Freedom to seek help when problems arise
Freedom from unjust reprimand
Organization's holiday policy
Satisfactory working hours

For a group to have creative ambition and realistic aspirations, the following must exist:

Job achievement: that is real creativity, changing goals, controlling method, etc.
After achievement: recognition from peers, subordinates and superiors must be deserved.
Personal growth by own standards, derived from:

1. Meeting challenge in the work itself
2. Increased responsibility or stature
3. Advancement or promotion.

5.16 CONFLICT

We recognize that this chapter has been discussing the positive approach to management of human resources. If everything worked according to plan there would be little or no conflict in organizations. Individuals would co-operate, and work would proceed smoothly, but, as most of us can testify, organizational life is one conflict after another. Most human interactions are characterized by disagreement, and those that occur on the industrial scene are no exception.

Some conflict is inevitable in organizations, as for example, inspection departments that are set up to check on production. Accordingly, we need to consider how such conflicts originate, and what strategies individuals can use to cope with them. We believe conflict can occur in five areas of the organization: individual differences; jobs that may conflict; competition; status differentials; work-flow difficulties. We can deal, briefly, with each of the five areas of conflict.

Individual Differences and Jobs that Conflict

People who are required to work together may be unable to co-operate because of differences in attitudes or behaviour. We make the assumption that others share our values and interests; unfortunately, this is often not the case. However, we believe that conflicts caused by individual differences are not as common as generally believed. Many conflicts assigned to individual differences are caused by something in the formal organization. For example, we have previously suggested that many conflicts are caused by built-in checks and balances. In addition, it often happens that some duties in an organization are shared between one or more individuals. In this sharing are the seeds of the problem. In many cases the conflict is in the job, not in the people.

Competition

Another common condition in organizations is inadequate resources – people, materials, money and time – to meet all of the needs. If you were to examine many organizations' budgets they would add up to more than the organizations can afford. So both departments and individuals are rationed, and there are inevitably winners and losers. In short, because the organization has insufficient resources conflicts emerge over the division of those limited resources.

Status Differentials

All organizations are based on status differentials. Sometimes the job an individual does is under-valued. For example, many secretaries in offices are in conflict with personal secretaries. Supposedly, the personal secretaries are of higher status, but in the work situation they may have to work to directions given to them by lower status individuals, and the result is conflict.

Work Flow

We would argue that an enormous amount of conflict is generated in an organization by the way the work flows. An example would be the conflict that evolves when individuals in separate units must depend on each other to complete their work.

A further cause of conflict is when the work flows unevenly. Thus, there are heavy demands at times and light demands at others. When work comes in spurts, resentment and conflict will result.

We have mentioned in Chapters 5, 6 and 7 that resentment occurs when individuals cannot get the information they need to do their jobs. In summary, work-flows that create interdependence and uncertainty, and insufficient information, can cause conflict.

5.17 MANAGING CONFLICT

There are a number of possible ways of managing conflict. These include:

1. Avoidance (sweeping the conflict under the carpet),
2. Dominance (a settlement is ordered),
3. Smoothing (pouring oil on the troubled waters),
4. Appeal to higher authority (let the boss decide),
5. Establish policies and rules,
6. Appeal to neutrals (personnel departments),
7. Changing the work-flow,
8. Inter-group confrontation,

9. Selection and training (change the people),
10. Bargaining, and
11. Consensus problem solving.

Much management thought, however, accepts conflict as an inevitable part of work organizations. We do not regard it as an evil, but rather as a fact of life that must be handled.

Our first proposition, *avoidance*, is the course that pretends the conflict does not exist, and is a common way of responding to conflict. The problem is eventually dealt with either indirectly or through intermediaries. If, however, the issue remains unresolved it will create further problems. This is the weakness of avoidance. However, this form of management is useful when the issues are not important. Avoidance allows the situation to cool down, and thus may lead to a later resolution.

Perhaps the next most popular way of handling conflict is by *dominance*. The manager simply orders a settlement. It requires power, and the problem is there are clear winners and losers, so settlements are often short-term only, and impose long-term costs. This win-or-lose situation often results in poor co-operation, but it is valuable in resolving situations that require decisive action, for example, budget reductions in times of financial constraints.

Smoothing. We would argue that playing down differences and avoiding known problems is useful. For example, smoothing is useful when the parties involved in a conflict are about equal in status and their goals are mutually exclusive. This tactic also achieves a temporary solution to complex issues, particularly when there is time pressure. However, smoothing only postpones the frustration which is often the long-term by-product of dominance.

When individuals cannot agree, the easiest solution is to *appeal to a higher authority*. Sometimes someone higher up has a broader perspective and can see the conflict objectively. However, as in a resolution by dominance, it suffers in that someone wins and someone loses.

The establishment of rules and policies can reduce conflicts. They achieve this by increasing the amount of certainty in the relationships between people and groups. This reduces the conflict. Regretfully rules cannot be made for every situation.

Appeals to third parties are helpful. They investigate the situation and make recommendations for solutions. This technique has been used with considerable success in union-management conflict, and this is the accepted role of ACAS.

Because of the need for individuals to work together, *changing the work-flow* is one way to reduce conflict. Making jobs 'whole' and defining jobs more completely can reduce conflict. Most conflicts arise because the duties of various jobs are not precisely defined. As individuals seek to complete their own work they inevitably step on other individuals' organizational toes. In short, by changing the flow of work, either by separating, unifying or defining the job with more precision, it is possible to reduce the amount of conflict.

We have already suggested that conflicts between groups in an organization can become tough. There are ways of resolving these conflicts by *inter-group confrontation*. In this approach, each group meets and drafts two lists. One lists how they see the other group, and the other how they feel the other group sees them, and so on until the groups meet finally to list what the other group can do to reduce the conflict, and what they believe the other group will want them to do. Usually by this stage much of the emotion has gone out of the situation. The strategy can work, but it does have the risk of escalating the conflict.

Selection and training deals with conflict by changing the individuals. Selection reduces conflict by changing the cast of characters. Training, on the other hand, seeks to change the characters who are present on the stage.

Bargaining, we have argued, requires confrontation, and involves give and take. The original demand isn't imposed when true bargaining occurs. Some compromises are involved so that the final agreement meets only some of the first preferences. This is the mode by which union-management agreements are negotiated. The principal weakness in bargaining as a means of conflict resolution is that it may lead to mutually unsatisfactory outcomes.

We have detailed many means of resolving conflict, but the essence of this book is about *consensus problem solving*. This is the method of managing conflict that is most enthusiastically received today. It has a number of steps:

1. Both parties present their own position;
2. Both parties listen to the other;
3. Both parties accept there is a disagreement, and do not avoid the fact;
4. Neither party quickly appeals for arbitration;
5. Both parties search for the best solution.

We have argued throughout the book for a positive approach, that is for consensus which is creative and results in an unresented solution. The possible responses to conflict are several, and part of becoming effective at work is learning both how to use and control conflict so that it aids effective performance and development.

5.18 LEADERSHIP AND AUTHORITY

You have been learning about leadership all your life. We suggest that the ideas we shall next discuss will be more meaningful if you try to recall the various instances in your own life, from early childhood to the present time, that involved your leading or being led. A leader is one who influences his followers to achieve an objective in a given situation. What makes a good leader? This question has been debated for centuries. Unfortunately, no clear answers have been found, and it is apparent that, so far, leadership remains a rather illusive art practised more on the basis of 'feel' than cognitive knowledge. Because the terms authority and power are central in understanding leadership, we need to explore them. Formal authority can be thought of as the right to command another person to perform a certain act. Power is the ability to influence or to cause a person to perform an act. Most managers believe they must have authority to accomplish their jobs. Where people live or work together in a community there must be agreed rules of behaviour. One of the required activities of a leader is to get people to co-operate with these rules. This is the meaning of discipline. However, only in a few cases, and as a last resort, is some form of sanction needed. For the most part, discipline involves getting individuals to come in on time, work safely, pay attention to quality and good house-keeping, to work a full day and carry out the procedures. A primary objective is to make sure that people know what the rules are.

When people break the rules, they should be seen by their immediate boss. If more serious action is needed, then the case should be referred to a higher level. Where sanctions are necessary, then a clear process should be laid down, which usually starts with an interview. In any organization the great majority of interviews are about problems. Such interviews may concern an individual, a group of people, or involve thousands. Problems encompass two main areas: grievance and discipline.

Grievances are mainly the complaints made against the system or other individuals. They create problems for work harmony and affect co-operative effort; the sooner they are dealt with the better. Even the most minor grievance can get out of proportion and can lead to disputes.

As the name suggests, disciplinary interviews deal mainly with offences of an employee who has breached a rule or code of behaviour, such as exceeding authority, disobeying instructions, dishonesty, absenteeism, careless workmanship or laziness.

The disciplinary interview is about conflict, and thus the interviewer must be neutral; he must discriminate between truth and distortion, fact and fiction, before proposing a resolution. You will recognize that the purpose of the interview is to resolve the difficulty not aggravate it. If a reprimand is considered it should be just and must be seen by all the parties to be so. Thus the interviewer needs to be calm, precise, reasonable and direct, and consequently the interviewee knows that while his failure has been highlighted, he will also be encouraged to improve performance.

Following the interview there should be some method of enforcement, that is, any required improvement in performance should be checked, and the individual should be told if improvement has been achieved or not. If there has been no improvement, the individual may be demoted, transferred, lose privileges, suspended or recommended for dismissal. Dismissal should only be a last resort. Depriving an individual of his livelihood is an enormous step, not to be taken lightly. We would argue that dismissal is an indication of failure, often a failure to select the right person for the job to be undertaken.

Finally, we return to the positive approach of the book, and pose the following challenge. If an individual is recommended for dismissal the ten questions outlined below have to be faced before any dismissal is contemplated:

1. Was the individual unsuitable for the job?
2. Did the individual have a clear job description?
3. Did that individual have sufficient training for the job?
4. Was that individual treated fairly?
5. Was sufficient allowance made for his deficiencies?
6. Were his skills put to the best use?
7. Did the individual have any personal problems affecting his performance?
8. Did anyone else fail him?
9. What should the organization do to avoid this kind of failure in the future?
10. What must others do to avoid this kind of failure in the future?

Interviewing is only one part of the skill of a manager in an organization in controlling and influencing individuals. If undertaken properly it should produce the desired results.

5.19 SUMMARY

This chapter has examined the management of human resources and the needs of individuals in the formal work setting. The chapter started by discussing the varied attitudes to our place of work, and raised the many questions that need to be answered if we are to understand the chemistry of human relationships.

You will remember that we warned that many of the ideas and concepts discussed are comparatively new, and that their implementation involves change. It was suggested that the trouble/cost consideration is so ingrained in all our thinking that change almost invariably lags seriously behind the point at which it is needed. Secondly, we argued that it is from leaders that change must come. Thirdly, if human values are to be satisfied, the process of change must take into account the ideas and concepts discussed throughout this chapter.

The notions of environment and welfare were examined in the light of some of the scientific forecasting by Peter Drucker, specifically that it is now recognized that fewer than 50 per cent of people at work need control by management. This recognition led us to examine how managers can create good working opportunities by developing relationships between people, job satisfaction and the coherence of reward and security.

The chapter challenges you to consider seven issues that relate to the important concept of motivation, and to developing a satisfactory work force. The need for a forward-thinking approach to work relations was argued, and it has been suggested that a 'modern' attitude on behalf of management was increasingly essential. We briefly looked at a number of propositions, such as creating more open management, and increased employee participation in management, improving the organization through a better understanding of the social forces with which we all have to contend.

You have been advised that we cannot anticipate all aspects of organizational change, but we have highlighted some of the more significant ones such as the decline of authority, the humanization of work and introducing change, the vital point being how to introduce effective change, that is, change that leads to some improvement in the socio-technical system. We have suggested that a starting point is to manage change and not to let events take over.

The chapter discusses the three parts to an organization development policy for coping with change, research, structural change and training, which leads to the social responsibility of business. Industry is recognized as the wealth-producing institution of our society, and as such, it is argued, it is man's social responsibility to make a profit. There are, it is stated, deeper obligations of responsibility that are implied in profit. We have suggested that you examine the view that social responsibility is an integral part of, and not an optional extra to, the function of providing goods and services at a profit.

The chapter concludes with a brief examination of the problem and management of conflict in organizations.

5.20   CASE STUDIES IN INDUSTRIAL RELATIONS

The purpose of the three case studies is, first, to attempt to analyse the variations in the needs of individuals and groups at work; and secondly, to trace the relationship between needs, attitudes and behaviour, with particular reference to an identified situation. And in the course of study the following objectives are attainable: the identification of ways in which management may minimize problems resulting from individual and group needs, attitudes and behaviour, in respect of a particular organization and situations; the examination of a variety of work-related situations requiring inter-personal skills; and the recognition of a relationship between inter-personal perceptions to attitude formation and change.

1. A Complaint Against a Supervisor

Arthur White & Co. Ltd is engaged in general engineering. The company was founded in the latter part of the nineteenth century by Mr Arthur White who had been a skilled tool-maker by trade. The company flourished.

In the 1920s it was converted into a limited liability company which remained substantially in family control and continued to develop. In 1970 the company decided to open a new factory in the North West. This was undertaken by Mr John White, grandson of the founder, who was then Chairman and Managing Director.

The old employees of the company agreed to accept transfer to the new works, expansion continued, and in 1980 the company employed approximately 200 men, all of them skilled engineers. Of these 75 per cent were members of the AUEW, but there was no pressure to create a closed shop. Arthur White & Co. is not a member of an employers' association, but observes general engineering terms and conditions, and pays rates above the local level.

The company has no recognized apprenticeship scheme or management training arrangements. If they require additions to their labour or supervisory force they enter the open market and advertise in the usual way. This means that they recruit skilled labour which has had the traditional apprenticeship training elsewhere, but the position is less certain in the recruitment of supervisors. If an appointed supervisor has any training in management techniques this is very much a question of luck.

In January 1980 the company appointed Mr S. Homes to an advertised supervisory position. Mr Homes was a skilled engineer who had spent all his life in heavy engineering. His only period out of the industry had been during his army service, in which he had risen to the rank of sergeant-major.

The company prides itself on being a well-disciplined organization. It is particularly severe on the use of bad language, and six months before Mr Homes' appointment a workman had been dismissed for swearing. Mr Homes is a disciplinarian, and his approach to people sometimes causes resentment, but no official complaints had been made to higher management until in April three of the shop stewards approached Mr White and informed him that all their members had ceased work. They alleged that Mr Homes had used a number of swearwords when reprimanding one of their members. They indicated that there would not be a resumption of work until Mr Homes had been dismissed.

Student Activity

Advise Mr White on how to handle this situation, and on the nature of the problems to be considered in weighing the alternatives.

2. Tom Firth

You are the manager of a local TV rental shop. You employ two receptionists, 12 engineers, one apprentice, and three aerial riggers.

The engineers service 500 subscribers, 60 per cent of whom have colour televisions. Each morning they come in to pick up their service calls. They usually repair about 10 sets per day, which may be located anywhere in the district.

The apprentice works with Sid Button, an engineer who started work with the company in 1938. Sid and the apprentice work on the difficult repairs.

You are basically a salesperson so you tend to spend most of your time selling. You often go out and try to sell by cold canvassing. You are particularly concerned when customers complain about bad service, so you usually call the relevant engineer to your room and give him a long talk.

Recently you have been getting a lot of complaints about Tom Firth, a skilled engineer, aged about 50. You do not know Tom very well, but you do know that he is usually a good worker. You investigate the complaints and find that Tom avoids talking to the customers and is generally rather grumpy.

Student Activity

You could give Tom a long, hard talk, but what else could you do?

3. 'Sweetness and Light'

Denise Loft caught her usual bus and travelled the ten miles from her village to Ambridge, the largest town in the area.

She then walked along the High Street, passing both Dents and Tates. 'They are such attractive television shops,' she thought as she went down a side street to Grumps, the other television shop in the town, where she worked.

As she unlocked the door she smiled at Mr Downs, who owned the other shop in the road, a florist.

Denise turned on the light, checked her till money and began to open the mail. There was some window display promotion material for 'Japo', the new Japanese television they had just had delivered. She began pasting these on the window. 'For after all,' she thought, 'there is little else to do.'

The first customer came in at about ten o'clock, just before Mr Green, the manager. The lady only wanted change for a pound note, but Denise did try to interest her in a portable radio.

A scowling Mr Green turned to Denise as the lady was leaving.

'What the hell did you give her change for?' he snapped. 'You know how difficult it is to get to the bank.'

At that moment a young woman entered the shop, somewhat hesitantly. Mr Green continued mockingly, 'Well, and how many TVs have you sold today – ten, a hundred, a thousand, maybe?'

Denise admitted that she had sold nothing.

'I don't know why I employ you,' he said. 'You never get any business. In future I'll get trained salesgirls.'

Denise replied, 'But nobody ever comes in. Can't we advertise our existence some-how? That would solve our problem.'

Mr Green's face darkened. 'You know full well that we've tried that. We advertised those French mixers, remember?'

Denise remembered. She also remembered that those French mixers fell apart after a little use. Still, she stayed silent.

Mr Green looked up and saw the 'Japo' display stickers.

'What's all that junk on the window?' he shouted. 'You really are the limit. I'm not allowing my shop window to be messed up like that. I really can't leave you for a moment. Take those stickers off at once.'

The young woman who had hesitantly entered the shop some time earlier made as to leave. Mr Green rushed up to her and asked what she wanted.

'I'd heard that there was a sales job going here, but I wouldn't take it, even if you offered all the tea in China.'

Student Activity

Why do you think Green acted as he did? What advice would you give to Green?

Further Reading

1. Argyris, C. (1970) *Intervention, Theory and Method*. London: Addison-Wesley.
2. Bell, D. (1974) *The Coming of Post-Industrial Society*. London: Heinemann.
3. Blumberg, P. (1968) *Industrial Democracy: The Sociology of Participation*. London: Constable.
4. Bright, J. R. (1958) *Automation and Management*. Boston: Pergamon.
5. Burns, T. (ed.) (1969) *Industrial Man*. Harmondsworth: Penguin.
6. Child, J. (ed.) (1973) *Man and Organisation*. London: George Allen & Unwin.
7. Gershuny, J. (1978) *After Industrial Society?* London: Macmillan.
8. Hirsch, F. (1977) *Social Limits to Growth*. London: Routledge & Kegan Paul.
9. Kumar, K. (1978) *Prophecy and Progress: The Sociology of Industrial and Post-Industrial Society*. Harmondsworth: Penguin.
10. Nichols, T. (ed.) (1980) *Capital and Labour*. London: Fontana.
11. Salaman, G. (1974) *Community and Occupation*. Cambridge: Cambridge University Press.
12. Salaman, G. (1979) *Work Organisations: Resistance and Control*. Harlow: Longman.
13. Scase, R. (ed.) (1977) *Industrial Society: Class, Cleavage and Control*. London: George Allen & Unwin.
14. Tivey, L. (1978) *The Politics of the Firm*. Oxford: Martin Robertson.
15. Vanek, J. (1975) *Self-Management: Economic Liberation of Man*. Harmondsworth: Penguin.
16. Watson, T. J. (1980) *Sociology, Work and Industry*. London: Routledge & Kegan Paul.

6

Recruitment, Selection and Training of the Work Force

GENERAL OBJECTIVES

Analyse personnel policies relating to the manpower needs of organizations with particular reference to recruitment, selection and training.

LEARNING OBJECTIVES

The reader should be able to:

1. Explain the concept of manpower planning and relate the concept to actual organizational practices with which he is familiar.
2. Compare methods of personnel selection used in different types of organization.
3. Relate organizational training to an appraisal of need.
4. Carry out a simple job analysis exercise and prepare a job description and personnel specification.
5. Discuss the major problems associated with manpower planning and performance appraisal.
6. Identify the key issues in relation to training.
7. Discuss some of the possible personnel issues of the future.

6.1 INTRODUCTION

Many readers will have already come face to face with some aspects of personnel activities. Those who have applied for a job will have probably witnessed, and taken part in, the process of searching through job advertisements in newspapers and journals, or visited employment agencies and job centres. This search usually results in a letter of application for the post the individual has decided he would like, and for which he is qualified. In many instances the organizations concerned ask for a detailed application form to be completed. These forms have been designed to provide sufficient and relevant information from which a long list of people can be selected for interview. 'Long list' refers to the first list of applicants who seem, in the opinion of those making the selection, to match the requirements of the job position. These candidates are subjected to further selection techniques, invariably including a face-to-face interview, which are designed to select the best applicant for the vacant post.

This is probably the first exposure to the personnel function for most of us, and many young people perceive it as a glamorous activity. This perception is usually formed on the following bases. First, it is obvious that the personnel function deals with people. Secondly, the authority to hire labour is perceived as being very important and vested solely in the hands of personnel officers, and the like. Thirdly, the working environment is usually most attractive, particularly in larger organizations.

In fact, this initial impression often turns out to be a distortion of reality. In many cases we find that the personnel activity is not given the same degree of status in the organization as, say, finance, marketing or production. The authority to hire is often vested in people outside the personnel function, the final selection being made by managers occupying line management roles. This, however, does not detract from the importance of the personnel function.

We have already provided an overview in Chapter 3 of the role that the specialized department plays in relation to the operation of the whole organization. The aim of this chapter is a more detailed look at issues relating to the recruitment, selection and training of an organization's manpower. The essential focus is a development of the concept of management of the human resource which we began in Chapters 4 and 5. Many writers now argue that the role and importance of personnel management have developed into a more embracing function in relation to the management of people, and that a more appropriate title for the role is the management of the human resources. The role has three basic responsibilities: the utilization, motivation and protection of people employed by work organizations. The utilization responsibility embraces the activities associated with the recruitment, selection, transfer, promotion, appraisal, training and development of employees. The motivation responsibility is related to the ways in which management attempts to develop working environments which lead to employee satisfaction in work. The protection responsibility is concerned with working conditions, and employment protection and legislation. In reality these three components merge into an integrated whole. The essential feature is that people are recruited, selected and trained for the right job in the first place. If this essential feature is attained the odds of the employee being satisfied and motivated by the job role are considerably enhanced.

6.2 DEVELOPMENT OF APPROACHES TO HUMAN RESOURCE MANAGEMENT

Historical Background

In recent years, many personnel specialists and writers on personnel management and human resources have strived to get away from the historical image of the personnel officer as the company welfare officer. This derived from the belief that welfare is synonymous with paternalistic investment for its own sake, without any thought of economic return. In the past, it was probably true that personnel policies were viewed by management simply as making people happy in their jobs, as an end in itself. But now there has been a shift of emphasis in personnel management from the sole pre-occupation with human relations and welfare problems to giving greater weight to economic effectiveness. This move towards a more professional approach to human resources management has been influenced by a number of factors, including changes in legal responsibilities of management, social expectations of employees, economic costs of employing people, educational and technological demands, and ideological and social science developments. Although all these changes are inter-related, we shall give particular emphasis to the changes and developments in management ideology, for commercial competitiveness has forced companies to exploit human resources potential more than improvements in technical efficiency.

6.3   CHANGING APPROACHES TO HUMAN RESOURCE MANAGEMENT

Scientific Management Approach

In the scientific management approach, whose main advocate was F. W. Taylor, labour is treated the same as other factors of production, and not in any pre-eminent position. Taylor adopted the view of 'economic man', attributing to the worker the wish to work only as much as necessary (McGregor's theory X) and to be responsive to economic motivation, that is, to be prepared to do more for money.

This movement, which probably reached its peak between the two world wars, was generally an adequate basis for personnel management. Thus, it was partly the abuses of scientific management, together with the growing scale and bureaucratization of enterprise, that influenced the development of the human relations school. For it was during this period that the organization itself was viewed as a formal 'mechanistic' system (classical management school) together with the theories of bureaucracy.

Human Relations Approach

This approach was essentially an extension of Taylor's theories, tending to broaden the details and looking at only the general characteristics. In this mainly industrial psychological approach, developed from the Hawthorne study, people were treated as humans and not just another factor of production. Furthermore, human relations stressed the importance of the informal group and the organization as a social system, and the fact that employees were largely motivated and controlled by the human relationships within the system. Thus emphasis shifted from the purely economic view of employees (scientific management approach) in which the object was to maximize the profits of the firm, to one of organizing human relationships so that employees receive greater personal satisfaction from their working environment.

Personnel as human resources management turned to the human relations approach in the hope of creating a better understanding between management and employees, thus reducing frustration and conflict. But there were abuses in the human relations approach to personnel management as there were in the scientific mangement movement. Personnel management was seen as synonymous with human relations specialists, that is, was only practised by personnel managers. Welfare work and keeping workers 'happy' were seen as the major function of the personnel manager. Because of these misconceptions, the human relations approach failed when forced to meet the criteria of economic efficiency and effectiveness.

Apart from these misconceptions, however, the human relations approach is criticized in particular on the inadequacy of its theoretical foundations, particularly its treatment of the bases of conflict and the ideological basis which is seen as explosive.

Nevertheless, since managers have become concerned with the best use of human resources, various approaches to human relations training have developed. Most of these approaches, however, reflect the thinking that stems from the Hawthorne study, when it became clear that concentration on human relations provided for improvements in the work situation and performance. Ever since, efforts at training in this area have been considered in terms of the 'Hawthorne effect'.

On the whole, however, training of this type has generally been disappointing. This may be related to the fact that a realization of what should be done is very different from a desire to ensure that something is done, and a commitment to improve. Knowledge of the rules of good human relationships is only a first step. Results were reflected mainly in the adoption of an assumed friendliness towards staff and a move towards democratic structures.

In many cases, the true style was rather more paternal than democratic. Emphasis was on fringe benefits and employee activities which were mainly recreational. The approach has been accused of producing a manipulative, insincere style, as well as ignoring harsh economic realities.

'Socio-Technical System' Approach

The 1950s marked a broadening of the human relations approach. 'Interest shifted from the group to the organization and the links between its social, economic and technical system' (*Industrial Society* (1968) Pym, D. (ed.) Pelican, p. 23). Amongst the chief contributors to the development of theories about the relation between the organization and the individual are the Americans Rensis Likert and Douglas McGregor.

The socio-technical approach, however, provides for the economic aspect of personnel management, where both social and technical factors can interact to produce both high productivity and human satisfaction. Moreover, employees are considered as important individuals whose dignity needs to be respected, while at the same time they are important economic resources to the organization. The essence of the socio-technical approach is that behaviour and management policies are largely structurally determined by the social organization and the technical means of production. A number of British researchers have made an important contribution to the study of organization and technology, notably Burns and Stalker, Woodward, Scott, Banks, Halsey and Lipton. The organization in this approach was viewed as an 'organismic', as opposed to a 'mechanistic' structure, which was considered to be more appropriate and flexible in an environment of rapidly changing conditions.

Finally, managers should not, therefore, be guided solely by the achievements of maximum profits, but they should also be concerned with the social goals of employees.

Personnel Management Approach: A Change of Emphasis

This change of emphasis in personnel management has been reflected in the various Institute of Personnel Management statements on the aims and functions of personnel management.

In 1945, Moxon wrote of personnel 'the reasonable satisfaction of human needs is an inescapable function of management and a necessary prelude to productive efficiency' (in Kelly, J. (1967) 'The Changing Role of the Personnel Manager', *Technical Education*, March, p. 98) whereas the current 'official' definition, in the IPM's 1963 statement, is 'personnel management to achieve both efficiency and justice neither of which can be pursued successfully without the other'. Thus, personnel management has now come to be considered in terms of efficiency and justice, profitability and job satisfaction, and in its contribution to productivity.

Perhaps the major influence on personnel management, however, has been the social sciences, for the interaction with social climates and ideologies has paved the way for changes in personnel practice. Moreover, these changes in practice have demanded the development of analytical tools for providing concepts for use in management. Training itself has become a prominent technique, reflecting the new technologies to meet the need for the modernization of British industry. More important, however, new technologies require a new organization: the framework and people to run them to the best advantage.

Developments in psychology have provided the personnel specialist with new techniques. Social psychology has contributed to the field of career planning and managerial assessment, whereas manpower planning has been viewed from an inter-disciplinary approach. Finally, sociology has provided the main contribution towards developing the 'organizational development' approach to human resources.

Organizational Development Approach

Organizational development is concerned with all aspects of organizational life which affect the working lives and relationships of its members: structures, systems, procedures, work patterns, supervision, delegation, control, management style and values. It is not concerned solely with the development of staff as an end in itself, rather with the optimum use of their skills and potential in the achievement of the organization's goals. For, in addition to the areas of shared learning needs brought about by common problems, there are other approaches to management training, also involving shared learning needs, which are now beginning to supplement more traditional approaches. These are team development and organization development, both of which stem from research into the ways in which organizations work and into the real barriers to effective performance.

Team Learning Needs

Managers work in groups in many situations and in many cases the quality of work produced is limited by the ability of the group to function as a team. It is possible, however, to design activities which focus attention on such important aspects of group performance as competition, trust between members, candour and communication, working relationships and problem-solving skills. Training at this level is frequently able to prove the real issues in team performance and is, therefore, capable of making a substantial impression on effectiveness.

Organization Learning Needs

It is the overall quality of an organization (especially the management team) more than any other factor which determines company effectiveness and profitability. The ideas of organization development are intended to enable organizations to improve the quality of their performance by use of social-science based methods.

Organizations, as all social groups, acquire a climate or culture of their own which can itself inhibit effectiveness and necessary change. Such a situation requires an extensive programme of planned change, that is, of organizational development.

This approach is relevant when the efficiency of the system as a whole is the logical unit for investigation. Where managers' values, perceptions and behaviour are out of place with the organization's goals, an organization development framework is relevant. It is particularly important to discern how authority is being exercised. Authority can be used to inspire and integrate; wrongly handled the outcome is sullen resentment.

An organizational development approach begins by looking at the organization as a system. It may look at management styles, efficiency of groups, and the communication and decision systems. Of particular interest is the way in which groups are organized in relation to tasks undertaken arising from this, and a planned programme for change is developed.

The responsibility for organizational development, as with all training, rests firmly with line management. They will, of course, need specialist help and support, so long as the specialists don't take over line management's basic responsibility. The view expressed in the USA was that organizational development support should be part of the personnel function. It was, therefore, thought necessary to re-staff the personnel function with people with a much wider perspective of the personnel function and people skills.

Organizational Development and Management by Objectives

Since organizational development is a total approach to constructive change and development within an organization, part of this process may be concerned with the re-definition of objectives. For a scheme of management by objectives could be examined from two aspects: that of system and that of style requirements. Within the system requirement, goals and objectives are defined both at company level and individual manager level. Results are reviewed and controlled. If the style element is to be effective, however, then management style within the company must be conducive. This implies the joint definition of objectives and a joint review of results and progress, incorporating high subordinate involvement, for, to be effective, there must be a supportive environment, and the coaching role must be practised.

Furthermore, it is normally important to introduce some collaborative, objective framework within departments and locations. This can provide a clear basis for planning and work improvement and enables individuals and groups to progress in line with agreed criteria. Group targets are normally developed in consultation with staff, and reflect the organization's overall business strategy.

Although there are many ways of tackling objective setting, in view of the need for integration and group learning, there is an increasing awareness of the need to approach any objective setting programme within the context of broader change and learning within the organization. Effective learning stimulated by a widespread organization development programme can produce a wider understanding of, and a commitment to, an objective setting system. In this way, organizational training can provide staff with a better opportunity of really understanding the processes of collaborative effort and improving team work.

Through the organization development approach it will be more possible to ensure that a sound management by objectives system really takes root in an organization rather than becoming an administrative formality.

6.4 MANPOWER PLANNING

An essential feature of the management objective approach is that all functional areas of an organization should have defined attainment objectives which contribute in a controlled and specified way towards corporate policy objectives (see Chapter 3). For the personnel function the manpower planning activity is concerned with forecasting the quantity and quality of employees required to reach the performance objectives of the other functional areas. This planning process attempts to forecast the need, on both a short- and long-term basis, in order to attempt to achieve the following:

1. recruitment needs,
2. training needs and objectives; staff development,
3. a planned approach to redundancies and redeployment,
4. management development,
5. labour cost planning including payment systems and levels and productivity planning,
6. space requirements: buildings, rooms, etc.

Manpower planning must form part of the organization's corporate planning process if it is to perform any useful function at all. Thus it will need to be a continuous process of adjustment and readjustment as the marketing, production, finance and technological objectives change. In addition the process is bedevilled by a number of important independent variables such as population change, skill changes and availabilities, competition, and so on. Nevertheless, it is on the basis of a manpower plan that many organizations develop their policy and objectives in relation to recruitment, selection and training. Such a policy and objectives will include statements concerning:

1. the approach to internal promotion and existing staff development,
2. the number of appointments to be made from outside the organization,
3. long- and short-term alterations to the organizational structure of job roles,
4. the training policy, including an identification of budget and resource needs,
5. policies and programmes relating to redundancy, retirement and redeployment,
6. negotiation objectives, e.g., agreements with trade unions regarding manning levels, payment systems and levels, productivity and redundancy agreements. In fact, in modern times, nearly all the issues contained in a manpower plan are discussed with employee representatives, and in many instances the detailed implementation plans are negotiated.

Determining Specific Recruitment and Selection Goals

In order to determine precisely what the recruitment and selection needs are, many organizations recognize the requirement to analyse what the various job roles actually embrace and what skills, knowledge and experience are essential for the job function to be performed effectively. This process, not unnaturally, is called *job analysis*. This process will vary in relation to the complexity of the different jobs. The techniques usually adopted include observation of employees performing the same or similar roles, the completion of questionnaires and log books and interviews with supervisors and managers. In some cases a detailed knowledge of the machinery and the technology involved is essential, together with a knowledge of the application of the technology before a meaningful understanding of the demands and requirements of the job roles can be assessed. The use of specialist techniques such as method study and work measurement is often invaluable.

The information obtained through job analysis is collated and presented in a specific form, called a *job description* (see Fig. 6.1). The form and basic purpose of the job description are described in Chapter 3. This description is essential to the recruitment and selection process. An analysis of the job description will enable the organization to

Job title _____ *Location* _____	*Size of job* 1. number of subordinates _____ 2. budget responsibility _____ 3. production responsibility _____
Position in organization Responsible to _____ Responsible for _____	*Limits of authority* Without the permission of a senior the job holder cannot: _____ _____ _____

Specific responsibilities

75 per cent of time

  1. _____

  2. _____

  3. _____

  4. _____

10 per cent of time

  5. _____

  6. _____

  7. _____

15 per cent of time

  8. _____

  9. _____

10. _____

Working conditions

1. Physical: sitting, standing, working, driving, etc.
2. Environmental: noise, heat, cold, dirt, wet, etc.
3. Hours: shifts, holiday work, emergencies, etc.
4. Health risks

Figure 6.1 *Example job description proforma (management and supervisory post)*

describe the attributes of the person it is felt will most effectively perform the job role (the *personnel specification*). This forms an important analysis in relation to the specification of the job advertisements, and as a set of bench marks for the selection process.

The job descriptions and personnel specifications have an important, perhaps essential, relationship with decisions taken regarding selection, promotion, staff appraisal, training and development, job evaluation and the setting of performance standards. They provide a yardstick against which individuals can be compared. Thus the objectives of recruitment and selection should be to attract sufficient suitably qualified and experienced people to apply for vacant posts, and to select the most suitable applicant by isolating appropriate behavioural characteristics and choosing the person who most nearly matches them, deficiencies forming the basic objectives for an early training programme.

Student Tasks

1. Take several examples of job vacancy advertisements from the reputable national newspapers and/or professional journals and identify what you think each organization is searching for in terms of skills, knowledge, experience and, if possible, personal characteristics.
2. Evaluate the advertisements in terms of:
    (a) Attractiveness. Do they encourage people to want to read them?
    (b) Quality of specification. Is it clear what qualities the organization is seeking?
    (c) Selectivity. Does it discourage unqualified and unsuitable people from making an application (i.e., does it itself perform a selection activity)?
    (d) Information. Is sufficient information about the job and organization provided?
3. Choose a fairly uncomplicated job role, either at your place of work or your college, and try a job analysis exercise (remember to ask permission first). From the information you obtain write a job description, remembering the various items which might be included in a job description (see Chapter 3). Translate the job description you have written into a personnel specification. Remember here that you are describing the person's ability and personal characteristics which are likely to fit the job requirements best (e.g. age qualifications, specific experience, physique, health, etc.).

6.5   RECRUITMENT AND SELECTION

The first task all organizations have to perform when a vacancy occurs is to decide quite clearly why it exists and the nature of the job role. The second task is to examine the existing work force to see if the vacancy provides a promotion opportunity for an employee. Only if no internal movement is possible, either because existing employees are not suitable or because 'new blood' is felt necessary, should external recruitment be considered.

Recruitment refers to the first stage of the process of filling a vacancy. This stage includes all the preparatory work, including writing the job description, personnel specification and recruitment advertisements. It also involves identifying all the possible sources from which a suitable applicant might be found, such as employment agencies and exchanges, job centres, lists of previous employees, school leavers, college and university leavers, professional associations, etc. It is also concerned with identifying ways of attracting suitable people to apply for the vacant job role.

Selection is the process of selecting from amongst the people who have applied to the organization for a job position. The process involves developing techniques of information-gathering which enable the selectors to measure each candidate against the predetermined requirements of the job. This involves carefully constructed application forms, selection tests designed to measure such attributes as intelligence, aptitudes, attitudes and mental and verbal reasoning, stress situations to measure control and stability, leadership testing, and face-to-face interviewing.

One issue which is always difficult to assess is that of references. The first problem is when to ask for them for, in many cases, applicants do not wish their existing employers to know they are seeking other employment. In such cases many references are not asked for until after a person has actually been offered a post. The second problem relates to the objective value of references. If applicants can choose their own referees it is highly unlikely they will select anyone who will say anything detrimental about them.

During the process of selection it is most important that the organization explains clearly the nature of the job role and the conditions appertaining to it. Any special conditions such as unsocial hours or a trial period must be clearly explained to all applicants. In addition, applicants should be given every opportunity of asking for information themselves since the selection process is essentially a two-way activity.

An essential feature of recruitment and selection is follow-up. The only real way of evaluating whether or not the selection process is succeeding in selecting people who effectively perform the requirements of the job role is to appraise the performance of the people selected some time after they have taken up the post. (This can mean one or two years later in the case of the more complex job positions.) It is crucial to try to determine why the process failed in those cases where the performance fails to measure up with expectations. In performing this process it is equally important to remember the perceptual difficulties discussed in Chapter 4.

The Selection Interview

The universally used method of final selection is the face-to-face interview. As many readers will know there comes a moment in the recruitment and selection procedure when the prospective employees and representatives of the organization meet. This first meeting is usually planned in detail, certainly on the part of the organization, and in many cases on the part of the applicant as well. The organization carries out detailed preparation for a number of reasons. These can include the objective of presenting the organization in the very best possible way, a public relations activity aimed at creating a very positive perception in the eyes of all applicants. Then the interview must perform a measurement function: the procedure, questioning and discussion are designed to both obtain information and test achievement. Finally, it is the most commonly used method of assessing personality. To achieve these objectives the interviewing process needs careful preparation and skilful application.

The physical resources needed will vary from situation to situation; some will be designed to create stress, others a relaxed and convivial atmosphere in which every candidate has an opportunity of 'being himself'. In all cases the physical resources (rooms, waiting areas, desks, etc.) need to be identified and organized to match the various objectives of the interviewing process. Similarly, the number of organization people engaged in the process will vary according to the nature of the job, and complexity of the measurement being attempted.

There are many pitfalls in the process and it is essential that all students of business, as well as those who specialize in recruitment and selection, are aware of them. The first basic problem is that most of us form clear and specific first impressions. Once these have been formed we tend to be conditioned and constrained by them in the same way as the concept of frame of reference and perception which we discussed in Chapter 4. Many of these first impressions can often prove false in the light of longer acquaintance. Nevertheless, in many cases, applicants are not given the chance of a longer acquaintance since the conduct of the interview focuses on evidence which tends to confirm the profile of the individual which resulted from first impressions.

The second problem is the frame of reference which all interviewers will inevitably have. Some may, for example, be convinced that physical stature and apparent strength correlate with good job performance in any situation. Hence the person of small stature and physique has a difficult task in such instances. Similarly, many other physical characteristics have behavioural connotations for most of us. We ascribe talents to people on the basis of personally held beliefs. For example, some people believe that intellectuals usually wear glasses, have a pale complexion and actually look studious. This is a little exaggerated of course merely to illustrate the point being made. The third problem is the behaviour of the individual applying for a job vacancy. It is rare for any individual, under the stress of a job interview, to act normally. He will initially be tense and nervous. Then he is attempting to make the very best impression, and to do this gives the answers and behavioural responses he thinks the interviewer wants to hear and see. He will therefore consciously, or sub-consciously, distort and exaggerate some points, and minimize or hide others. The fourth problem is that the interview usually lasts for only a very short period of time and many individuals can successfully sustain an unnatural behavioural style throughout.

Interviewers will develop their own way of grading each of the attributes listed in each surement. Several systems to aid the assessment process have been developed and perhaps the two best known are the National Institute of Industrial Psychology's seven point plan, and John Munro Fraser's fivefold grading system (see Tables 6.1 and 6.2). Each of these systems relies on the technique of identifying a series of factors against which candidates can be assessed during the interviews.

Interviews will develop their own way of grading each of the attributes listed in each system. Remember, whatever approach is adopted the process is subjective and variable. No two interviews are conducted in precisely the same way, and therefore the method of comparing one candidate with another is difficult and imprecise, particularly when several good candidates are being assessed.

Table 6.1   *Interview assessment processes*

NIIP Seven Point Plan	John Munro Fraser Fivefold grading classification
1. Physical make-up	1. First impressions and physical make-up
2. Attainments	2. Qualifications
3. General intelligence	3. Brains and abilities
4. Special aptitudes	4. Motivation
5. Interests	5. Adjustment
6. Disposition	
7. Circumstances	

Table 6.2 *Personnel specification based on the NIIP seven point plan*

Job title: Safety and security manager
Department: Personnel
Division: Personnel services

No. employed in
this position ...
Date of completion
....

	Essential	Desirable
Physique, health and appearance		
Height	Minimum 5 ft 8 in.	Minimum 6 ft
Build	—	Proportionate to height
Hearing	Normal	
Eyesight	Normal colour vision	Perfect eyesight
General health	No serious complaints	
Grooming	Well turned out	
Dress	No eccentricities of dress	
Voice	Clear speech	
Sex	Male	
Attainments		
General education	Sufficient for reading and writing reports and preparing budgets, and for mixing easily at management level. Sufficient understanding of employment and health and safety legislation	BEC National or Higher National Award in Business Studies with employment law options, or equivalent
Job training	Interpretation and enforcement of criminal and civil law. Protection and security of property, etc.	First aid certificates. Report-writing. Budget preparation. Insurance practice, as relevant to the company and its employees
Job experience	Police Inspector or above or commissioned rank in armed services, police or provost branches, or senior security officer	3 years' experience 3 years' experience 3 years' experience
General intelligence Tests		
Top 10 per cent		
Upper 20 per cent		Upper 20 per cent
Middle 20 per cent	Upper middle 40 per cent	
Next 20 per cent		
Bottom 10 per cent		
General reasoning ability	Ability to relate the security function to other organizational operations	Ability to reason in the abstract
Special aptitudes Manual dexterity	—	Understanding of mechanical devices
Skill with words	Sufficient for written and verbal reports	Fluency in interpersonal relationships backed up by sufficient business knowledge to be able to form meaningful relationships with other managers
Skill with figures	Sufficient for budget preparation	

Table 6.2 *(Contd)*

	Essential	Desirable
Artistic ability	—	
Musical ability	—	
Interests		
Intellectual	Sufficient interest in the topic to keep up to date with legislation and practices	
Practical constructional	Sufficient knowledge of processes and machinery to be able to identify unsafe practice	
Physically active	Must be mobile	Participation in physically active pursuits
Social	Must be capable of maintaining positive attitudes to health, safety and security	Evidence of wider contacts than work alone
Aesthetic	—	
Disposition		
Acceptability	Must be acceptable to employees at all levels	
Leadership	Must be able to influence and persuade others	
Stability	High degree	
Self-reliance	High degree	
Circumstances		
Age	40–50	45–50
Marital status	—	Married
Dependants	—	
Mobility	—	
Domicile	Must live near enough to work irregular hours and to be called out in emergencies	
Other points	A car or some other vehicle is essential if he is not within walking distance of work	

6.6 SOME EARLY CONCLUSIONS

The climate of human relations in an organization is no better than the employees selected to work in it. Therefore, considerable attention should be paid to the recruitment and selection process. This implies a need for a central policy and specialized knowledge and expertise. Errors in selection can be very costly. Poor operatives usually equate with poor products; poor management with weakly-run and ineffective organizations. To some extent certain employee deficiencies can be made good through well-planned and operated training schemes, but these cannot make up for people who do not basically possess the knowledge, skill and aptitudes required for their job roles.

Indicators of poor recruitment and selection activities are high levels of labour turnover, poor quality of work, work group conflict, customer and client complaints, high levels of administrative errors, and so on. It is important to remember that such symptoms are only indicators. They could just as well relate to other organizational problems and issues, such as responses to management attitudes and styles, or redundancy fears. The danger for the future is that as more technical jobs are created by the micro-chip revolution there will not be the trained people available to match the needs. The dangers here are twofold, first that we shall not set out to train in the right skill areas soon enough, and secondly, because of this, we shall recruit people who are not really equipped to perform the tasks required.

Recruitment and selection effectiveness is a crucial factor in relation to both the stability and development potential of the organization. In many respects the organization's ability to respond to change is a function of the quality and attitudes of the people employed in it. This development potential can be further enhanced by well-planned and resourced training programmes.

6.7 INDUCTION TRAINING

What the organization does with a newly appointed employee during the first few days and weeks of his or her employment is crucial to the formation of a positive perception of the organization in the eyes of that individual. Try to remember your first few days in college or in your first job, and jot down your feelings. In particular list the issues you regarded as being important to you at the time, and which you felt the organization gave scant attention to, or even ignored altogether. Often organizations tend to forget even the most basic issues like the location of the toilets, cloakrooms and canteen. How helpful it would be to a new starter to be allocated to an experienced employee as a guide and mentor during the early days. Many new starters would welcome an explanation of the structure and purpose of the organization, and even a short historical review of its development. Research has shown that this induction stage can have a significant effect on the level of labour turnover; those organizations with a sound and positive approach generally experience lower levels than those who ignore it. The basic aims are to take the tension out of the first few days in a strange job, to make the newly appointed person feel that the organization values him and his intended contribution, and then to provide basic but essential information.

Student Task

Write an induction programme yourself, by imagining you have recently been employed. Identify the type of information you would expect to be given and what activities you might be engaged in during your first week of employment.

6.8 SYSTEMATIC APPROACH TO THE ASSESSMENT AND PLANNING OF TRAINING

In undertaking an assessment of training needs and the subsequent formulation of training plans, it is important to distinguish between two main areas of training needs:

organizational training and individual training. Although these two needs are inter-related, and in some cases may become synonymous, it is nevertheless essential to make this distinction if *real* training needs are to be identified and the maximum contribution from training is to be gained. There are many organizational and management problems which are often not recognized by line management as training problems, and thus real training needs become 'hidden'. A useful individual or group exercise here would be to identify and discuss any examples from your own experience. Try to explain why the need was 'hidden'.

Organization Training Needs

In this context, the term 'organization' refers to the operation as a whole: the head office, specific functional areas, departments and sections within those units. To deter-mine where organizational training needs exist, therefore, requires a thorough examin-ation of these areas in the light of corporate policy and overall executive objectives. (See Fig. 6.2.)

Throughout this approach, the emphasis is centred on the organization and, in par-ticular, the identification of those barriers to efficiency and problem areas which pre-vent the achievement of organizational objectives. It is equally important to identify areas of opportunity which may result in the achievement of more desirable objectives. The implication here is that training needs should be considered in relation to both pre-sent and future organizational goals. A training need exists where training can make some contribution to alleviate these barriers or can assist in the development of new opportunities.

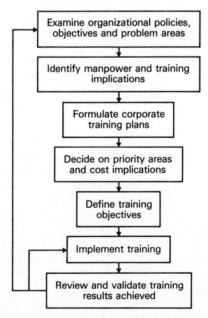

Figure 6.2   *A systematic approach to the assessment of organizational training needs*

From the results of this organization analysis, a *corporate training plan* (see Fig. 6.3) can be produced which will ensure that training is directed at the real needs of the business, which in turn will facilitate the optimum utilization of manpower resources in the achievement of objectives.

Organization policies, objectives and problem areas	Manpower and training implications	Training objectives	Priority	People affected (groups/individual)	Training plans/methods	Estimated cost	Action required (target date)	Action taken and results achieved

Figure 6.3   *Corporate training plan*

Individual Training Needs

On completing an assessment of organizational training needs, the next stage is to determine who needs training; to identify individual problems of knowledge, skill or attitude which either prevent the effective performance of the job, or which are necessary to prepare an employee for some future job (that is, manpower development).

In respect of managerial staff, this process is normally undertaken by annual appraisal and reporting systems, but is undertaken on a less formal basis for other employees. In either case, an individual training need should be determined by an examination of the performance the organization expects from a particular job, as well as actual performance achieved by the holder of that job. (See Fig. 6.4.) The difference which occurs between actual and required performance is a learning need which is subsequently referred to as a training need where it is considered that training can make a contribution in fulfilling this requirement.

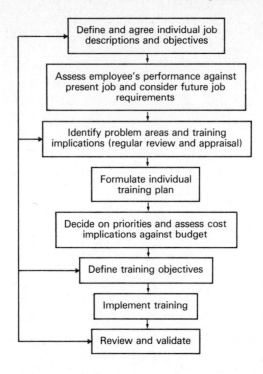

Figure 6.4 *A systematic approach to the assessment of individual training needs*

If the organization is to discharge this responsibility effectively, however, it is important to ensure that:

1. The job itself has been clearly defined, by providing an up-to-date job description.
2. Acceptable standards of performance have been agreed (objectives).
3. Performance is regularly reviewed through frank two-way discussions against objective criteria (boss/subordinates appraisal interview).
4. Opportunities exist and consideration is given to effective training where this will contribute to improving performance in the present job or as preparation for a future job.
5. Organization training needs have been established in terms of objectives and policies and problem areas identified.

In the light of the information derived from this assessment of individual training needs, an overall individual *training plan* can be formulated (see Fig. 6.5). Through this approach, training is more likely to be directed towards ensuring that individuals are developed to their maximum potential within their current jobs or adequately prepared for some future job which will be of benefit to the individuals and the organization.

The planning process is not a once-and-for-all activity, but a continuing programme of assessment, implementation and review. If training plans are to remain viable and training objectives are to be met, the process should be sensitive in highlighting new problem areas and be able to react quickly to changes in economic circumstances, market, financial resources, employee climate, and so on.

Individual job description/ objectives	Name of job holder	Problem areas/ training implications	Training objectives	Priority	Training plans/methods	Estimated cost	Action required (target date)	Action taken and results achieved

Figure 6.5 *Individual training plan*

This process is a dynamic activity where employees' performance is assessed against current and meaningful objectives. In identifying training needs, this should be seen in terms of improving and alleviating problem areas and performance in the present job or preparing for a future job. The appraisal interview is a culmination of previous discussions and not a one-off exercise.

To identify an individual's training need, consideration should be given to the following questions. Does each individual have a clear understanding of his or her role, together with an up-to-date job description? Are work objectives, targets and standards of performance clearly defined and agreed? Is individual performance reviewed on a regular basis against agreed standards of performance? Does an individual achieve or exceed targets and objectives? If he or she *exceeds*, agree new targets. Consider whether he or she is ready for promotion or more responsibility. If so, can *training* assist in preparing him or her for promotion or new responsibilities? If he or she *fails* to achieve, discuss reasons. Can *training* help to overcome the problems which prevent achievement of objectives? Training is concerned with creating those learning conditions in which the necessary knowledge, skill or attitude can most effectively be acquired by the learner.

The essential aim is to develop an approach to both organizational and individual training which is systematic and focused on meeting needs. It is through manpower recruitment, training and development that organizations develop the flexibility to accommodate change (see Fig. 6.6).

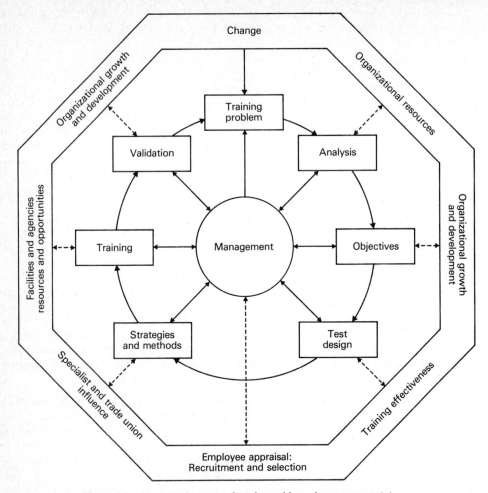

Figure 6.6 *A systematic approach to the problem of manpower training*

6.9 HOW PEOPLE LEARN

Considerable attention has been given to the process of learning over the years and many books have been written on the subject. Controlled research has been possible with animals, and the findings have been extrapolated to fit the human situation. These extrapolations have been further enhanced by detailed observations of human behaviour in learning situations. All the research and observation point to the importance of four factors each of which is fundamental to the achievement of successful learning. These are drive, stimulus, response and reinforcement.

Drive refers to the readiness to learn, in a sense a motivated behavioural response directed towards the satisfaction of a need (remember the Maslow motivation theory discussed in Chapter 4).

Stimulus implies a force which triggers off the drive. The force in question can be initiated by visual, sound, taste, smell or touch impulses. Thus in training people to perform new tasks or understand new concepts we need to identify the type of stimulus which is mostly likely to trigger an interest and commitment. *Response* refers to the behavioural pattern which results from stimulus. In a sense we are searching for predictive relationships between stimulus and response so that in a training situation we can programme an individual to behave in a certain way when confronted with a given set of circumstances. Thus in a specific job situation we try to identify and describe the behavioural characteristics desired, and then develop a programme of activities which attempts to develop these characteristics in the trainee. Finally, *reinforcement* refers to the mechanisms used to encourage the progress of an individual to develop the behavioural response which is aimed for. Praise, approval, and even rewards are associated with this process. Thus if a trainee is making progress in the attainment of a new skill, encouragement and praise are the type of reinforcement factors which encourage him to continue striving for higher levels of accuracy, reliability and output. In some cases the reinforcement factor is provided in the pay packet, but there are inherent dangers and weaknesses with such a method, for example, employees may come to expect financial reward from even the most minor variation in working patterns, perhaps even when the new job task is less demanding than the old.

In looking at these four factors, and remembering the complexity of human behaviour discussed in Chapter 4, it will probably come as no surprise that the design of training programmes is a skilful activity. No two individuals will have the same drive characteristics, will respond to the same stimuli, or react in the same way to methods of reinforcement. The learning process therefore needs to be designed to incorporate a variety of techniques and learning situations. Experience has shown that all programmes of training should be developed with the following points in mind:

1. Trainees must be selected on the basis of suitability and willingness. Suitability means an assessment of skills, knowledge and aptitude already possessed by the employee. Willingness refers to the individual's apparent wish to undertake the training. In many instances people will not undertake a programme of training unless they can see tangible benefits at the end, for example, the guarantee of a new job role or a pay rise.
2. The design of the programme should be sufficiently varied to maintain motivation. This implies careful planning of the time available. No individual training programme should be too long. Individuals quickly attain a saturation point beyond which continued activity fails to add further to the learning process. This is called the learning curve, which may be long-term or short-term. In this sense individual training periods can be too long and total training programmes can be too long. What is needed is a fragmented or staged programme which optimizes the learning curve potential of individuals. Relate this concept to your own experience of training programmes or college lectures. Notice how your attention and retention facility reduce in relation to the length of the various sessions.
3. Each training session should be carefully designed to give balanced and varied presentations and practical activities. Too much tutor lecturing can be disastrous. The use of visual aids can prove immensely valuable. Demonstration followed by trainee practice is essential to many programmes, particularly in job instruction.
4. Trainee progress should be monitored at regular intervals. This monitoring process is essential for two reasons: it gives a feedback control technique to the trainers regarding the progress of the training programme, and it lets the trainee know how he is getting on.
5. The training programme will be designed with specific training objectives in mind.

Thus, for example, operator training will usually have high levels of job instruction and on-the-job training units; management training will have a high level of theoretical content and off-the-job training. (The terms 'off-the-job' and 'on-the-job' relate to the place in which the actual training takes place. Off-the-job training usually refers to the activities which take place in a training school or college. These are generalizations since some operator training might have high levels of off-the-job training, while some management training will take place *in situ*.)

6.10   TRAINING AND ORGANIZATIONAL CHANGE

Most theories of change accept the idea that change does not occur unless individuals are both motivated and ready to change. Such an idea implies three things: first, that an individual must perceive some need for change; second, the individual concerned must be able to change; and third, he or she must perceive and accept that the people initiating the change can lead it in a direction acceptable to him or her. The importance of this view to the training activity is significant in that any training activities designed to accomplish change must take into account both the development of a motivation to change as well as the detailed development of the changed skills, procedures or practices.

In many cases employee appraisal, often known as performance appraisal, which indicates the apparent deficiencies in an individual's performance is sufficient to satisfy the motivation component to accept change. This is particularly so when the deficiency identified relates to skills or practices. On the other hand, a lower level of willingness to accept that deficiencies are present is likely to be the case when the issue concerns an individual's attitude. In such cases any suggestion to change implies, or can be perceived to imply, a threat to both an individual's sense of identity and his position or status in relation to others employed by the organization. The suggestion of a need to change attitudes not only implies a criticism of the individual's own self-image, but also threatens his relationships with others. Hence any training programme designed with attitude change as an objective must be developed and applied with great care.

6.11   APPRAISAL

If we accept these views, we must also accept a change in the purpose of performance appraisal. The development of the systems views of work organizations, discussed in Chapter 2, demonstrates the change of emphasis since the early 1960s, which basically reflects the view that organizations cannot view their employees in isolation from the jobs to be done and the processes involved. The needs of the organization result from an interplay of a whole variety of factors including people, machinery, processes, customers and competitors. Any attempt to appraise individual employee performance and contribution cannot, therefore, be meaningfully undertaken without reference to the needs of the organization. Taking this view, it is difficult to give a prescriptive approach to any particular institution regarding the methods by which people can be appraised. Every organizational situation is inevitably unique and its needs are unique. The criteria for assessment must reflect the individuality of the need.

In order to perform any valuable function, appraisal must satisfy two needs: first, the immediate need to identify strengths and weaknesses in relation to a given job role; second, to predict the likely development potential of individuals. Many organizations still have no formal appraisal system at all, not even of a rudimentary kind. Others, however, operate highly sophisticated but incomplete systems. Many of these are firmly rooted in appraisal of the individual without reference to the systems concept mentioned above, but concentrate on assessing personal qualities irrespective of jobs, tasks, role development and foreseeable change. In a small number of cases experiments are being conducted to develop systems of appraisal which will satisfy both the essential requirements. These experiments concentrate on defining organizational issues in a very open-ended way. Such definitions will attempt to specify the kind of environment organizations are likely to have to face, and the changes that will be required. The crucial factor is an evaluation, no matter if inaccurate, of the change needs. Such evaluations are likely to include managerial skill requirements, cash implications, technological skill developments, and so on. It is apparent that appraisal is moving away from the concept of just measuring people to appraising the organization as a whole.

In the case of attitude appraisal we must not forget the problems of perception raised in Chapter 4. McGregor clearly illustrated the point that our perceptions are fundamentally attitude-based, and that attitudes can vary quite drastically between different individuals. The problem, therefore, is that attitude appraisal is a very emotive and value-based judgement. Objectivity is difficult. In some ways the problems can be overcome if the assessment is performed by a number of appraisers, the belief being that consensus opinion is likely to have an acceptable degree of validity.

The question of raising an attitude assessment with an individual is extremely difficult. Many people strongly resent the implications that their attitude is suspect, and such resentment is natural. Think about the problems yourself by referring to people you know well but who hold different views regarding such issues as politics, religion and morality. Look at the different ways people express their views, and the different reaction patterns when such views are challenged. The essential issue is why one attitude is any more acceptable than another. In relation to a business, the most we can say is that certain attitude patterns seem to correlate with greater success in given situations. For example, it is possible to indicate that certain attitudes are likely to achieve better results than others in a negotiation situation or a leadership relationship. We therefore state again that any training programmes designed with attitude change as an objective must be developed and applied with great care.

6.12 PERSONNEL PLANNING AND CAREER DEVELOPMENT: SOME THOUGHTS OF THE FUTURE

We are now into the 1980s, and a new technological revolution is upon us. This revolution has been triggered by the 'silicon chip' and the possible ramifications of this have already been discussed several times in this book. The important issue in this chapter is how the foreseen developments will affect the manpower of work organizations, and in what ways policies and procedures are likely to change. Predictions include:

1. That there will be a gradual transfer of work in the unskilled, semi-skilled and even some highly skilled categories from people to machines. This movement will include many clerical, administrative and service job roles, as well as those in manufacturing processes. This movement is already in clear evidence, for example, in the British Leyland Mini-Metro production line.

2. The amount of work available for people in traditional occupations will reduce, but other, new occupations will be created in the technological, service, environmental and caring fields.

3. Organizational structures, particularly manpower structures, are likely to incorporate many of the suggestions made in Chapter 5.

4. People will be exposed to the necessity of changing their job roles several times during a working career.

5. There will be an increased requirement for technologically trained people to develop and service the equipment created to do work, for example, computers, word processors, robot-operated machines, and so on.

6. Whilst wealth may be generated by manufacturing organizations, a redistribution will be needed to finance the new organizations in the areas identified in 2 above.

7. There may be many other social changes, for example, changes to the pattern of our working careers such as later entry and earlier retirement, shorter working week and work sharing schemes.

8. That new technology will reduce stress as we know it today, and many 'dirty' jobs will be taken out of the hands of people. Thus a new level of employment health can be expected since people will not be exposed to the dirt and chemicals which have been associated with so many illnesses. Many dangerous situations will also be removed.

9. All these changes will have far reaching implications for the role of trade unions, and will present a challenge to their historical and traditional relationship with management.

10. There are likely to be similar challenges to the role of management and the authority system within organizations, along the lines developed in Chapter 5.

If these predictions even begin to represent the future, the implications for personnel policies are considerable. First, there is the important need to forecast, with some accuracy, the technological skills that will be needed to service the new style manufacturing organizations. Secondly, there is the urgent need to identify how quickly the new social, caring and environmental organizations will be developed. The forecasts here are of particular urgency to educational organizations which must plan for a change in curriculum content and design so that people are prepared for the new job roles and career opportunities. Thirdly, there are important considerations for training and retraining the adult working population. The government in Britain is highly conscious of the problem which this rapidly changing environment is creating. The Manpower Services Commission in 1981 is carrying out a large-scale consultative exercise involving industry, education, government departments (both local and national) and trade unions. The aim is for a corporate planning approach to national manpower training which involves all agencies. In a sense the Manpower Services Commission is attempting an appraisal along the lines of that suggested earlier in this chapter.

Student Activity

Imagine you are employed in the training department of the Yorkshire Insurance Company Limited. You have recently been informed of a senior management decision to introduce word processing and microcomputing facilities in an attempt to improve efficiency and profitability. At the moment the clerical work is organized on fairly traditional lines at head office, the senior management staff having individual secretaries, and the major functions organized on the typing-pool model. Your task is to identify the likely implications for retraining.

Some questions that will probably need answering are:

1. What changes may be anticipated with respect to the traditional roles of office workers?
2. What impact on employee morale will the introduction of this new equipment have? In what ways might it be possible to limit any negative response?
3. In what ways might the training need be identified? What are likely to be the issues which you would want to investigate fully and why?
4. Is the introduction of this equipment likely to have any implications for the design of the work organization? Predict the most likely changes.
5. Identify the changes which are likely to affect the recruitment and selection of any new employees.

6.13 SUMMARY

The first part of this chapter attempted to demonstrate the rather subordinate role that the personnel function has traditionally played in most organizations. The essential point made was that in recent years this subordinate role has changed due to many influences, among the foremost being the effects of employment legislation and the increased influence of trade unions. These two influences will be examined in depth in Chapter 7.

Specifically, we have examined the issues of recruitment selection and training of the work force employed by organizations. To understand the importance and the nature of modern practices in this field a review of the development of personnel viewpoints was given. This review focused on the issues which have ultimately led to personnel management being regarded more as embracing functions more appropriately described as the management of the human resources. The essential focus in the 1980s is the organizational development approach which attempts to relate individual employees to all aspects of organizational life: structure, systems, procedures, work patterns, supervision, delegation, control, management style and values. Such a focus stresses the need to view the management of human resources in relation to the achievement of organizational goals.

Two dimensions are emphasized in the organizational development approach: team learning needs and organizational learning needs. The aim is organizational effectiveness through team performance, which is integrated with identified organizational need, viewed as a total integrated system. Such an approach is viewed as a method by which manpower recruitment, training and development – major contributors to an organization's corporate effectiveness and responsiveness to change – will be improved.

The chapter then emphasized that recruitment and selection processes need to be firmly limited to a manpower planning policy which attempts to forecast and evaluate need. It is from an analysis of the need that specific recruitment and selection goals can be determined. Once we have clearly identified the goals, each job role needs accurate specification before any attempt at attracting applications is initiated.

In looking specifically at the recruitment and selection process the importance of the interview was examined. Interviewing is still the universally-applied selection activity. To be successful it needs careful planning and application. It is an assessment activity without any precise methods of measurement. Nevertheless, by using a structured approach, perhaps involving the National Institute of Industrial Psychology's seven point plan, or the John Munro Fraser fivefold grading system, a reasonable level of objectivity can be introduced.

We came to the conclusion that the climate of human relations in an organization is no better than the employees selected to work in it. Errors in selection can be extremely costly, but some employee deficiencies can be made good through a well-planned and structured training programme. Recruitment and selection effectiveness is important to both the stability and development potential of the organization; in fact the ability to respond to change is a function of the quality and attitudes of the people employed.

Having selected the labour force with care, it is essential to have a systematic approach to their further training and development. We identified that in undertaking an assessment of training needs and the subsequent formulation of training plans it is important to distinguish between organizational training needs and individual training needs. Whilst these two aspects are inter-related it is important to make the distinction in order to identify the true nature of the training need.

In designing training programmes it is important to give consideration to theories relating to how people learn. We identified four factors as being crucial here: drive, stimulus, response and reinforcement. In addition, our knowledge of learning curve patterns should be a guide to the length and timing of activities to be included in any specific programme of training.

We then related the process of training to the issue of organizational change. An important realization is that change does not actually occur unless individuals are both motivated and ready to change. This realization implies three things, that an individual perceives the need to change himself, that he is able to change, and that he accepts true leadership of the people initiating the change. In this respect performance appraisal is a key activity. We took the view that the traditional approach to appraisal, which concentrates on assessing individual qualities with little reference to organizational needs, is of limited value. In order to be valuable appraisal must satisfy two needs: an identification of the strengths and weaknesses of an individual in relation to a given job role, and a prediction of the development potential of the same individual when compared with the foreseeable needs of the organization.

The chapter concluded with a look into the future and a prediction of changes which are likely to have a significant effect on personnel policies and practices.

6.14 STUDENT EXERCISE

This exercise illustrates the practice of personnel management by identifying types of problems, issues and/or conflicts of an organization. It further requires the formulation of decisions to deal with a variety of problems. The objective of the exercise is to encourage effective operation in a simulated situation which involves a varying degree of responsibility in respect of communication, people and money.

Student Activity

You are the personnel manager of the main plant of a sweet company. This plant, which is located in Manchester, employs 2000 people. The staff are mostly semi-skilled, but there are also tool-room workers, electricians, 20 lorry drivers and 40 office workers. There are six supervisors, a works manager, a nurse, a cost accountant, a canteen staff of 10, five maintenance staff, five staff in the payroll department, and eight people in purchasing. The company recognizes five trade unions.

You are responsible for all day-to-day personnel decisions at the plant. You have been off work for a week because of illness. You return to find the following in your in-tray. How would you deal with them? Indicate separately the factors you considered in reaching your decisions.

1. A resignation letter from Daisy Hopkins, an assembly worker. Daisy has worked for the company for six years. She is weekly paid, and has been contributing to the firm's pension scheme.
2. A local headmaster has written inquiring about the possibility of arranging a works visit for his 60 fourth-year pupils.
3. A note from the canteen supervisor complaining that the canteen toilet doesn't work, and that the plumbing is faulty.
4. A letter from a supplier with the information that the packaging used for some of the sweets is going to increase in price.
5. A memo from the works manager complaining about shortages of workers on the night shift. He notes that you have tried press advertising and asks you to suggest alternative methods of recruitment.
6. A letter from a man who has recently moved into the area. He states that he has been an assembly shop foreman in Liverpool for the past 20 years. He wonders if you can offer employment.
7. A memo from the cost accountant about the appointment of a deputy cost accountant. He wants the promotion to be internal and suggests Ralph Peters, a local man, who has worked for the company for five years. The cost accountant thinks that Peters is better than both Dave Baker who has been with you eight years, and Mrs Andrews who is a newcomer.
8. A letter from a local government social worker about May Griddle telling you that May, who is divorced, leaves her four young children unattended at night.
9. A memo from the works manager about safety clothing. He wants to know where to obtain safety footwear, safety helmets, protective goggles, and any information about dangerous chemicals at work.
10. A note from Angus Burns, a storeman. Last year Angus borrowed £200 from the company; since then he has been repaying at the rate of £2 per week. This money is deducted from his weekly wage packet. Angus is in difficulties again. He wants to borrow another £200 or at least stop his repayments for a while.
11. A letter from Pep Co. Ltd asking for a reference on one of your ex-employees, Rose Hart. Pep Co. want to know if Rose was a good worker and whether she was honest. Your records will show that she was sacked for stealing.
12. A memo from one of the supervisors, Gordon Hughes, complaining yet again about the continued lateness of John Crane. You have already issued two official warnings to this worker.
13. A letter from Moss Roberts, TGWU shop steward. Roberts complains about the victimization by Hughes of John Crane. Roberts claims that Crane is a good worker and that his time-keeping is usually good. Roberts hints that the alleged victimization is due to Crane being a Protestant and Hughes a Catholic.
14. A memo from the works manager asking about courses for the supervisors on 'Safety at Work'.

6.15   ALLIED YORKSHIRE BREWERIES LTD: A CASE STUDY

The following case study is a written account of a real company operating in the brewery industry. The facts remain the same, although the names have been changed to preserve anonymity and confidentiality. The study has been included to illustrate the type of traditional organization patterns and problems found in many old, established family concerns. Detail has been excluded since it is felt that this would merely confuse the essential aim which is to indicate the type of personnel organizational weaknesses which are relatively common.

The objectives are to: identify the main organization deficiencies; identify the major factors which impinge on personnel and training practices and suggest courses of action for improvement; develop report writing skills.

Student Activity

You have recently been appointed personnel and training manager for the company with a view to establishing professional, personnel and training practices designed to enable the company to achieve their profitability and growth objectives, by increasing effective use of their manpower.

You are required to write a report, analysing the situation as you see it and giving your recommendations for future action. You have investigated the situation and found many difficulties. (Facts about the company are shown in Fig. 6.7.)

Prepare your presentation from the information available. It is expected that you will concentrate on personnel and training aspects, although other relevant issues could be noted. You may make assumptions, but clearly state the assumptions you have made in your report.

Background

The company was established in 1805. It is an independent brewery, operating at Rothwell. It is a family business, 80 per cent of the shares being owned or controlled by the directors or their families.

It has 60 off-licences and about 120 public houses, mainly in West Yorkshire. All the outlets operate within the 'tied trade system'. Increasing competition, however, is being felt on the wines and spirits retailing side and consideration is being given to new development in the free trade market.

The company employs about 500 people, of which 30 per cent are engaged on the off-licence side.

The directors regard the company as being fairly profitable (60 per cent of profits coming from the off-licences) although lately these are being found to be insufficient to finance the future development of the company, particularly in respect of the need to modernize plant within the brewery.

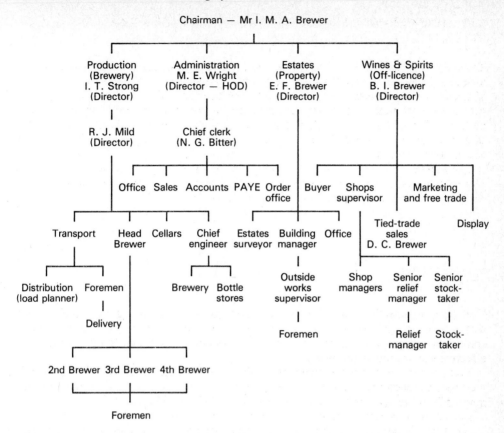

Figure 6.7 *Organization chart for Allied Yorkshire Breweries Ltd*

Observations (Made by personnel and training manager in an initial investigation)

1. *Planning and Organization*

There appears to be no formal planning system operating within the company and there is a tendency for a 'wait-and-see' policy to operate. Departments tend to operate fairly autonomously, with decisions apparently being taken on a vertical basis with little cross-fertilization of ideas taking place with other departments. Important policy decisions appear to be made by the Chairman, Mr I. M. A. Brewer, and the board meetings tend to be used as a rubber-stamping exercise, rather than as a forum for policy making and co-ordination.

In the absence of any formal, central co-ordinating mechanism, communications and the decision-making process appear to operate vertically under the direction of the departmental head, with insufficient lateral and functional communications with other members of the company, either on an individual or group basis. Thus there is apparently

more identification with the department (more often than not the individual head –
highly personalized) rather than with the company as a whole.

At the individual level, many of the jobs have not been adequately defined resulting
in unclear lines of authority and responsibility and frequent overlapping of duties.
Although the need for flexibility is recognized, excessive informality can lead to the
inefficient use of human resources. The value of this process has been recognized at
lower levels within the brewery where a job evaluation scheme has been installed.

2. *Employee Performance*

From directors down, most company employees do not appear to be working to any sort
of targets, standards or objectives. Since little is written or defined, it is difficult to
evaluate and control performance and to identify training needs whether they be at
company or individual level. Where verbal standards operate, they do not seem to be
adequately communicated, at least on a company-wide basis. The extent to which this
poses a serious problem varies from department to department.

Since all the directors are working directors there is a tendency for them to become
too involved in the day-to-day running of their respective departments, with less attention being paid to forward planning and policy making. There seems to be a lack of
awareness of where their responsibilities end, and their subordinates' begin. An apparent reluctance to delegate exists, which is often seen by subordinates as 'interfering'.

In some departments, the director concerned expresses lack of confidence in the
abilities of his own staff, whilst in other departments the director is very dependent on
his staff and perhaps not giving sufficient direction. The concept of the director's role is
unclear within the company, and more often than not the role is determined by the personality of the director, which may or may not contribute to the corporate objectives of
the company. Apart from the commercial implications resulting from lack of delegation, there is also a missed opportunity in developing subordinates both in their present
jobs and in any future positions that may arise.

3. *Recruitment and Labour Turnover*

In general, there are no immediate problems resulting from labour turnover. Since
there are many long-serving employees, turnover of staff is very low indeed. Significant
labour turnover tends to be confined to such areas as the tun room, bottling hall (very
high turnover, thought to be due to monotony of the job and poor working conditions)
and off-licence managers (15 per cent).

Nevertheless, this low turnover now could result in long-term replacement problems, particularly in middle management and first line management, such as foremen
and charge-hands. The precise implications, however, are difficult to determine since
the company has no systematic scheduling of future staff requirements.

More immediately, there is no defined company-wide recruitment policy, for in practice this operates on an *ad hoc* basis in each department. Moreover, selection methods
and standards are highly subjective; a more professional approach would be beneficial.

There is no one person given the responsibility for seeing that new recruits are adequately introduced into the company, and no defined induction procedure exists. This could have adverse effects on maintaining and promoting a company image with which employees (and potential customers) can identify themselves.

4. Careers and Pay

Being a family concern there are very few career opportunities for people with potential who are outside the family. It is felt by most employees that advancement to higher levels is reserved for family members. Nevertheless, employees feel they are 'looked after' and regard their positions with this company as very secure.

In terms of pay, responsibilities and promotion, it is not clear to many employees how the company recognizes talent and ability. Since there is no formal company wages policy, many inconsistencies have developed between departments, which have generated feelings of inequity. This has manifested itself in terms of attitudes of other employees towards the brewery staff, the latter having a more formal wages agreement.

Although the company has frequent verbal communication of its policy, this is not entirely reliable, and often results in grape-vine methods being adopted, with the inevitable distortions of the true facts.

The company's attitude on education and training is not written or defined, and in practice appears not to be effectively communicated to most employees.

5. Sales

It seems that there is no overall company strategy for sales. It tends to be developed on a departmental basis. Related functions, such as marketing and advertising, are pursued on an *ad hoc* basis with little or no central co-ordination. Management's conception of marketing and selling tends to be confused.

Executives and staff involved in these functions appear to have received little professional training to equip them in what is a vital role in meeting company objectives. In terms of role there appear to be many 'grey' areas in this particular function of the company. Where knowledge and experience are available, they are not being fully utilized and channelled for the overall benefit of the company.

In this situation, where there is no defined policy or professional training given in modern marketing and sales techniques, fragmentation results, and the chance of the image of the company being upheld and consistent at all levels is put in jeopardy.

6. Costs and Finance

Overall, there is apparently no *formal* financial control system in terms of budgets, standards or controls.

Apart from the accounting department, top management is not fully aware of the potential contribution that basic management accounting procedures can make to practical problems of the company. There appears to be a reluctance to adopt a more rational and professional approach to business management where decisions can be taken on the best information available.

Many managers and key employees are not fully aware of the cost implications of their job. Other than specialist personnel, none has received basic financial and costing appreciation to show its importance and contribution to their particular job, department and the company as a whole. Without these basic systems, it is difficult to assess the *real* performance of either employees or departments (other than cost centres) in order to maintain controls and decide corrective action or indeed to identify training needs of either individuals or groups.

The traditional 'historical' approach to finance will not provide this information since feedback is often too late to enable corrective action.

7. *Industrial Relations*

The significant aspect of industrial relations is the strong loyalty that is shown by employees towards the company. In common with other areas, however, no company industrial relations policy has been written or defined. Where formal procedures exist, these tend to be confined to the brewery rather than part of a coherent company framework.

The lack of a policy throughout is probably a reflection of the style of management – paternalistic in outlook, and which tends to think and operate in departments rather than on a company-wide basis. This is evidenced by attitudes of some employees and management on the inconsistencies and inequalities that have arisen between departments (see careers and pay), on such aspects as pay structures and disciplinary matters.

Managers, supervisors and employee representatives have not received formal training in industrial relations procedures and practice. The director with special responsibility for industrial relations tends to confine his role to the brewery, rather than on a company basis.

8. *Methods and Plant*

There is talk of probable new plant being introduced into the brewery in the fairly near future, but at the time of the investigation no definite plans appear to have been determined. Employees in the brewery consider the plant and equipment to be fairly antiquated and in need of renewal if the company is to remain competitive.

Improvement in present methods and layout is limited because of the plant and structure of the building. Nevertheless, plant maintenance knowledge was felt to be of a particular need for the charge-hands.

Further Reading

1.   Cuming, M. W. (1975) *The Theory and Practice of Personnel Management*. London: Heinemann.
2.   Flippo, E. B. (1966) *Principles of Personnel Management*. Maidenhead: McGraw-Hill.
3.   Munro, Fraser J. (1978) *Employment Interviewing*. Plymouth: Macdonald & Evans.

7

Management:
Work Place Relations

GENERAL OBJECTIVE

To define the characteristics of industrial relations in the UK, together with a study of recent issues in labour management relations.

LEARNING OBJECTIVES

1. Identify the nature of the UK industrial relations system.
2. Outline the growth, structure and organization of trade unions at all levels.
3. Examine collective bargaining processes, including the TUC and CBI.
4. Assess government influence on industrial relations.

7.1   INTRODUCTION

It is strange that so many people imagine that the only function of a trade union is to negotiate for better wages and conditions of employment. Of course, this remains and will always continue to be an important aspect of its work, but the modern trade union has to undertake many other activities, such as participation in economic planning at all levels, looking after its members' interests in health, safety and welfare, and carrying out a hundred other obligations as well.

Investment in people is an unusual idea. Yet the UK has suffered for a long time the consequences of regarding this idea as odd, in the form of strikes, 'go-slows', restrictive practices, and so on. It should be obvious that man is more important than money and equipment, but many parts of our industry do not appear to believe so. Money is only a means of barter, and materials are worthless unless man transforms them. There is therefore a need to assess our work principles to ensure our industrial future. There are unmistakable signs of malaise all around us. The statement, 'I'm all right Jack', is a clear sign of a lack of responsibility. We must realize, before it is too late, that our most precious asset is the skill, knowledge, loyalty, enthusiasm and goodwill of the work force. We must therefore deal with employees accordingly, giving them the training they need, the security they deserve, the real trust they will not betray, the status and dignity they should have, and safe working conditions and efficient machinery: the negotiation of terms and conditions of employment must exist, and be seen to be working fairly.

Conflict resolution is a joint endeavour. In such an atmosphere the habit of behaving as two sides largely disappears. Where there is a sense of participation by all, militancy and obduracy will be seen as the outmoded weapons they are.

In the competitive world in which we live we cannot afford promotion through influence or nepotism. It is an inefficient system and creates frustration among the able. Injustice may cause a waste of talent and ability.

Joint consultation is an attempt to remove the impersonal aspect of large-scale organizations, as none of us is the repository of all wisdom, the embodiment of all experience, or the possessor of all worthwhile ideas. In other words we can all learn from one another. Furthermore, humans are like steam-boilers: without means of ventilation they are liable to blow up. Joint consultation can provide this means.

7.2 INDUSTRIAL RELATIONS

The trade unions' field of activity is that of industrial relations, but responsibility for the state of industrial relations does not rest with the trade unions alone; employers, too, are responsible.

If industrial relations are to be improved, the first step must be the development of a new, positive attitude on the part of both trade unionists and employers, based on the proposition that the purpose of industrial relations is to promote industrial peace. The objective should therefore be to bring about such reforms of attitude as will lead both employers and trade unionists to accept that the purpose of industrial relations is to resolve quickly, and without coercion on either side, conflicts arising from their differing interests. The media, recently, have spoken much about the need for reform on the part of the trade union movement. We cannot delay that need. The intention here is to stress the need for a change of attitude on the part of all concerned with the future of industrial relations – employers, unions and government.

It is important of course that responsibility for this change of attitude should be accepted by the leadership of the trade unions, but this alone is not sufficient. A responsible relationship at this level does not necessarily mean that the same kind of relationship exists where it is needed most, on the shop floor. It has to be stressed that it is at shop floor level that management must seek close contact.

7.3 LEADERSHIP

It is important for the trade union movement to develop leadership on the shop floor. Trade unionists are aware of this need, and the education and training schemes organized by trade unions make an important contribution towards satisfying it.

Like any other organization a trade union has a number of objectives; some of these change to meet different circumstances, but others are fixed and continuous. The TUC in its evidence to the Donovan Commission (the *Report of the Donovan Commission on Trade Unions and Employers Associations* (1968)) stated what it considered to be the ten fixed objectives of trade unions. The first certainly was to secure a fair share for their members in wealth, but it was clear that not all the TUC's objectives could be met simply by increases in wages. Four of the objectives (improved physical environment at work, full employment, job security and industrial democracy) are concerned essentially with the quality of life for the worker in his work situation. Like most other trade union objectives, the securing of improvements in the quality of working life can bring the union movement into conflict with the interests of other groups, including employers, management and government. There are many sources of such conflicts; for example, questions of power, control and income distribution. There are also different ways in which they manifest themselves, but it is strikes which usually attract the most attention. The source of conflict we are concerned with here is the impact of the industrial system on workers as total human beings, a source of conflict which manifests itself in more repressive and less measurable ways, and is therefore given less attention.

The worker possesses a great variety of interests, attitudes and abilities, which may all be developed or, as often happens, constrained by the way in which industry is organized socially. One writer has put it like this:

> In large reaches of our society, but particularly in the industrial sector, it is not the man that is wanted, it is rather the function he performs, and it is the skill with which he performs it, for which he is paid. If a man's skill is not needed the man is not needed. If a man's function can be performed more economically by a machine, the man is replaced.
>
> This has at least two obvious implications. First, that opportunities for social participation in the industrial sector are contingent on a man's imputed usefulness. Secondly, once admitted to participation in the industrial sector, men are appraised and rewarded in terms of their utility, and are advised or removed in accordance with their utility as compared with that of other men. (Goulder, A., 'The Unemployed Self', in Fraser, R. (ed.) *Work II*)

The problem facing any trade union, therefore, is this whole question of the 'utility value' of man, which is predominantly the way in which the employee's work is evaluated by the employer. Indeed, this utility view is held by many members of society, and it is understood by most workers. In an extreme situation a section of the working population cannot obtain work and is thus termed unemployed; in a general situation, it is a waste of a man's talents, which remain unused. It is, therefore, the function of a trade union to attempt to control the extent to which an employer can use a worker as a utility item, either to be employed or dismissed at will.

In the United Kingdom, which is a mixed economy, what is produced, and the manner in which it is produced, are largely determined by the employer in terms of what is profitable. In this system trade unionists have little say over *what* is produced, but they can have some say in *how* it is produced.

Let us examine this point. It is believed that modern technology can make some work degrading, and that this is a major cause of worker alienation. (We have looked at this point before.) We can also suppose that technology is potentially a liberating force. But whether liberating or alienating, the consequences are not entirely attributable to the machine itself, but to the way the machine is used, and who makes the decision. It is not just in relation to technology, but to the whole area of work allocation, job content, pattern of work, that the decision-making process is so important. The point is that to attribute poor social consequences to machines or to the nature of the job is to ignore the whole area of human actions and decisions, which, either by cause or neglect, cause these consequences.

Thus, within the area of conflict with which we are concerned, there are two possible roles for trade unions: first, to contest the extent to which their members are viewed as utility items to be used or discarded as required; second, to secure a voice in the decision-making process, which, with the machines and objective factors in the working situation, go to make up the employees' job and working environment.

Let us assume that management understands these two roles, and has formed a good personnel and industrial relations policy, and staffed it with experienced people, who are paid to give specific attention to these issues. Could they deal with these questions themselves? The answer to this is probably no, and for one principal reason: industry has to be profit-centred, because it is capital-centred. Work is not intended necessarily to satisfy employees. Although what industry produces is bought by people, industry is not necessarily man-centred; that is where a conflict arises.

It is in the area of trying to secure an advancement in the quality of life for workers that trade unions may come into conflict with employers, because the social organization or the kind of work which would most improve the quality of life, and also reduce fear and tension for the employee, is not necessarily the type of organization which would best meet the productivity, profit goals and efficiency of the enterprise. (See Table 7.1.)

Let us look at a couple of examples. Increased automation can and does reduce the skill content of many jobs. This increased efficiency replaces workers and it may also result in a reduction in the variety of work; this kind of change can make workers insecure and fear redundancies. Even the most benign firms find it difficult to defend these opposing forces. It is for the trade unions to represent their members and safeguard their interests in the best way they can, thus, management must allow areas that they have regarded as their right to become areas for joint consultation and participative decision making. By tradition, we mean issues such as the introduction of change in working arrangements and machinery, the deployment of labour, the dismissal of employees, and greater flexibility and concession over issues such as sickness leave. We have made this point before but it is important to bear it in mind.

While we accept that many trade unions attempt to improve the working environ-

Table 7.1 *Varieties of industrial disputes*

Parties	Example
Management–Government	Anti-monopoly action
Inter-management	Price competition between companies; disputes over payments, patents and fulfilment of contracts
Inter-union	Jurisdictional disputes, as between engineers and millwrights over installation of factory equipment
Union–Government	Prosecution for secondary boycotts; collusion with employers against customers
Intra-management	Factions within management striving for control of company
Intra-union	Factions within union striving for control of union
Union–Management	Union and company debate over division of earnings between wages/profits

ment of employees, and most firms recognize this role, we nevertheless come to the question of the allocation of resources by the trade union movement to implement these requirements. The unions are subject to the demands of their members, and to many and varied external circumstances which often control their freedom to determine priorities. So far as the membership is concerned material well-being and job security are of major importance, and therefore do occupy a large part of union time, but workers have interests and needs outside these two areas, and it is therefore difficult for a trade union to marry collective policies to individual situations. For the external pressure issues such as unemployment, inflation, the problems of the European Economic Community, and government legislation on industrial relations all make demands on the attention and the meagre resources of the trade union movement. In the 1970s, and to a large extent in the 1980s, a large part of these resources have been used, and will continue to be used, to combat the imposition and effect of much legislation on industrial relations. The same resources will have to be deployed against the ever-increasing problems of loss of jobs for many workers. These conflicts have led to some hostility between the trade union movement and individual employers, and have threatened those advances in co-operation between the trade union movement and the employers' federations.

Both internal and external pressures dictate trade union priorities. However, there are other objectives which must not be undervalued. The trade union movement has fought hard for many years to secure for their members the right to be consulted on changes affecting the working situation, and the power of the employers to use workers purely as units of labour, and these have been modified as a consequence of this fight. Also, trade union members now have the right to have their grievances dealt with by properly appointed union representatives. These grievances are not only concerned with disputed overtime payments or a shift premium, but they concern the whole range of human problems, for example, family problems, personal conflict with a supervisor, even clashes with fellow workers. It is here that the system of shop stewards, or fathers/mothers of the chapel, which unions have fought hard to preserve, is so important. It is a myth that workers only go to the shop steward with problems of pay and conditions. A good shop steward is also their counsellor in personal problems, the person who will support them and speak for them, and often the person who combines the common identity of the work group.

Let us remember that it is the trade union movement which has also secured social improvements through negotiation. Through hard bargaining gains have been introduced, such as a shorter working day, increases in annual holidays, and vastly improved shift working conditions. All of these improvements have benefited many millions of workers.

At the national level individual trade unions combine to form the movement known as the TUC which works continually as a pressure group within industry, and with government. We must, though, recognize that there are times when the trade union itself, or the TUC, fails in its responsibility to its members. Often this failure is a consequence of the internal structure of the trade union, and so is a consequence of a failure in commitment to the members themselves. Membership within many trade unions reflects a variety of interests. Effort has therefore to be channelled into several areas, and the consequence of this can often be a restricted amount of personal attention that can be given to employees in any one industry. Those trade unions whose organization is based on few industries are better placed to serve members in the working environment than those who have a wider industrial involvement. (NUPE is an example of one such troubled union.) Thus moves towards increased rationalization, such as the amalgamation of those unions which serve very similar members and purposes, the consolidation of areas of membership recruited by individual unions, and deliberate moves towards industrial unionism where this is feasible, together with improved organization within the wider trade union movement through the TUC, all will directly affect the service which unions can give to their membership.

Of course, workers themselves have their own priorities, and dictate their priorities to their trade unions (see Fig. 7.1). The current assumption in this country that work cannot, or should not, have an intrinsic meaning or creative quality can lead workers to value their jobs largely in terms of earning a living; this means of course that increased satisfaction for some people is linked to higher wages. This understanding of job satisfaction is not peculiar to the trade unions or their members, but can be found in society at large, often promoted by manufacturers through advertising and other forms of 'persuasion' in favour of the conspicuous consumption which is so necessary for a thriving economy. Since workers themselves manifest how highly they rate this emphasis on earnings in the manifestation of 'the strike' or other industrial action, some people assume that this is the workers' sole concern, and that they are not interested in increasing job satisfaction, security and self-fulfilment. When we learn of workers making their demands, this is portrayed in terms of wages, but here we are only seeing workers in the immediate negotiating situation. This is the situation when the utility view of the worker is at its most prominent; they are in the market, they are selling, and management are

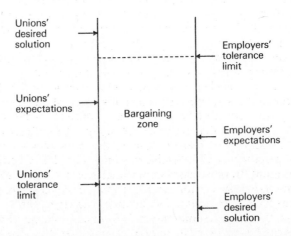

Figure 7.1   *Desires, expectations and tolerance limits that determine the bargaining zone*

buying, labour and co-operation. Nevertheless, we must remember that this is only one context in which you find the worker; the other is the ongoing working situation where the worker becomes interested in other things, and his priorities change. It is wrong to think that because workers are concerned with obtaining the best possible remuneration, they care little for the scope for responsibility and interest in their work. Once they have reached agreement their priorities change, and the day-to-day activities and the opportunity to show interest and ability become more important.

Those other interests, which are not normally shown in the major negotiation situations, need to be dealt with through local and national machinery, and designed for their specific consideration. Trade unions and their officials must have access to management, and to the decision-making process which affects the working situation; they must not be kept at some remote point, but at a level close to the work. This often means setting up some form of plant or local joint consultative machinery, in which discussions should be about a wide range of issues and made regularly, and not on an *ad hoc* basis only when a problem appears. Managements must make sure that what they are talking about are things that workers are anxious to talk about, and not the irrelevancies of the work situation; they must be about the kind of decisions that management wants to take. In this way workers will be immediately involved in all the developments at their own work place, and managements will have the advantage of the feedback on employees' feelings, and thus will be able to identify sources of stress, hostility and dissatisfaction.

In the accepted sense of the word consultation is not enough. What is also required is a proper set of consultative arrangements at local, regional and national level. Many firms, and indeed some industries, try to set up consultative machinery separate from the agreed negotiating machinery, and practice has shown that this is not the way to achieve consultation. Nine times out of ten the people who negotiate also want to consult, and very often the subjects or issues about which they want to consult are also those which they want to bring within the negotiating area. Thus, the need is threefold: first, we should try to structure the machinery so that there are not separate areas of consultation and negotiation; second, the things that are discussed should be things that matter; third, industry and industrialists in the future must be prepared at times to share what they have regarded as their right to make decisions, and recognize the workers' right to be a part of that decision-making process. So within that system employees would feel that they had some control over the arrangements connected with their own working environment. In particular, the doubts that are often aroused by change, especially unexpected change which often brings a threat to job content, control and security, would be met by allowing the workers themselves to have some control over how that change is brought about. It is also important that the union representatives be allowed to play a major part in the design and operation of change.

The success of any machinery set up to bring about an improvement in joint consultation and participation in decision making is heavily dependent on a good communications system. Many firms neglect this, which leaves workers and their trade unions ignorant of development and possible changes; this brings about fear and rumours, with the result that suspicion and often hostility are expressed to management.

Though a trade union can negotiate the setting up of joint machinery, it can only encourage the commitment of management to the principles involved. Many trade unionists know of cases where consultative machinery has failed because management has lacked commitment. In those cases important issues have not been referred to that machinery and thus to employees for consideration, employees have been left in ignorance, and decisions have been unilaterally taken by management.

It is also true that the process sometimes fails from lack of commitment on the part of the workers. This can happen for one of two reasons: first, the issues the management allows the employees to participate in are so basic, so unimportant, that the employees lose interest; second, the employees do not know how to participate effectively in the process, and are consequently led by the management. The result, of course, is that participation in these cases becomes meaningless, because management are still making the decisions. The problem can be met by widespread education for employees and their representatives, and this really amounts to education for shop stewards and for trade union members. The need for such education was recognized by the trade union movement a long time ago, and extensive programmes are now a common feature of many trade unions. The TUC itself has mounted an extensive education programme through many schools, which takes the form of week, day or postal courses, and so on. The bigger unions have their own education programmes, and a good example of this is the one run by NALGO.

During the 1970s there has been a considerable increase in trade union education organized by the union movement itself. This type of education has become increasingly sophisticated, and the range of subjects covered has widened. To take the example of NALGO, the union organizes local government education programmes and public service courses, such as health programmes, and the union operates an internal training programme for stewards employed in many branches of both local and national government services. These developments are only a start to the total workers' education programme which is required, but they do indicate the increasing commitment to the provision of such education. Despite this increased activity, however, only a minority of the total labour force in the UK are receiving training and some form of education, and the unions, with the employers, need to put even more effort into this important function.

7.4   WHAT DO WE MEAN BY NEGOTIATION?

We have from time to time in this chapter used the word negotiation. We have also made an assumption that industrial relations are about relationships between a manager, who may also be an employer, and a union official, who is the representative of organized labour. This assumption may, however, be false.

It is, of course, a fact that it is these relationships which do tend to dominate industrial relations today. Indeed it was an important part of the recommendations of the Bullock Committee (*Report of the Committee of Inquiry on Industrial Democracy* (1977), para. 14, London: HMSO) that some 70 per cent of the employee force in companies in the private sector employing 2000 people and more are members of a trade union.

However, this still does mean that 30 per cent of the work force are not part of the trade union movement, and in some individual companies there are still no union members, and if we consider smaller companies the proportion of non-unionized employees increases quite sharply.

Industrial relations, therefore, is about the relationship between the employee and his employer, whether or not he has a trade union to represent him. From a practical point of view there are, of course, some disadvantages for a manager in having to deal with non-unionized employees, as well as the obvious advantages. For as long as it is feasible to deal with each individual employee as an individual – and of course it is still possible to do so in small companies – it does not matter much, but the reality of individual treatment is difficult to maintain when you are dealing with a large mass of production workers all doing an identical job.

For a firm, and indeed a manager, it is much easier to deal with the terms and conditions of employment in any large group of employees in an undifferentiated way. It may not be better, but it is certainly easier, since making a clear distinction between different contributions is always difficult, and usually gives rise to accusations of unfairness.

It is also difficult for a firm or a manager of a very large group of employees who wish to have their views on a different policy or practice to do so effectively, other than through a representational system. To do it simply by taking an informal sounding generally leads to the influence of a loud-voiced minority. Representatives, on the other hand, have to be able to represent employees' views, and employees have to be able to ensure that they do.

Managing in a situation where there is no formal representational system, and in particular where there is no union, is definitely, in many ways, more difficult for the manager than that in which he is apparently free to do what he wishes. His responsibility to act justly in every respect to every single one of his employees is much greater, since the trust that each employee is obliged to put in him is absolute, and there is no way in which his mistakes, or his misjudgements, can be adequately dealt with.

It follows from what has been said that not all industrial relations are organized between employers and trade unions. These relationships are very varied. Some companies, especially large ones such as ICI and Fords, have individual agreements with the trade unions which represent their employees, and often these agreements operate separately from what may be operating elsewhere in the industry. Other large companies are prepared to accept a wide variety of agreements reached independently by their various constituent companies with the local appropriate trade union. For example, Unilever has something like 120 such agreements.

These agreements vary greatly in their nature according to the size of the industry to which they apply, and the nature of its technology. A good example are those which exist between the Engineering Employers' Federation, and the Confederation of Ship Building and Engineering Unions, and we shall have a brief look at these agreements.

The Engineering Employers' Federation is a large and influential bargaining organization. The federation is made up of 18 regional associations, with some 6000 member companies, employing over two million employees. Basically it has two objectives: first, it negotiates on a national basis a framework of terms and conditions with the Confederation of Ship Building and Engineering Unions, which then applies these terms and conditions to manual workers throughout the industry; second, it provides the basis for an agreed disputes procedure with the unions.

The first of these activities is, in a sense, the one essential activity in industrial relations. The result of the negotiations on terms and conditions of employment affects every manual worker in the industry. Disputes procedures are a different matter. Here the manager may have a feeling of isolation. The issue of a dispute will be dealt with through the federation's disputes procedure, and may be one in which he and his employees are directly affected. The problem is that in the disputes procedure, the individual manager is not mentioned at all: the shop steward is, but not the manager. An explanation for this is that most agreements assume that any particular dispute will have already gone through the 'domestic stages of procedure'. The domestic stages which are referred to in the agreement vary from one company to another, as indeed they should.

There are, nevertheless, some ways of going about this which are better than others, and as a result some model procedures exist as a basis on which individual domestic procedures can be built.

On a national scale, industrial relations often appear to be about the traditional never-ending manoeuvres between employer and employee, but industrial relations all start and finish with the relationship between the two. There are many pressures and temptations to forget this in practice. Some managers believe that their real role is a technical one, and that their responsibility is only to keep the machines running. Some feel uncomfortable when in personal contact with the workers, and the majority prefer the personnel officer to handle face-to-face relationships. Similarly, inexperienced shop stewards often take a grievance away from an individual and 'force it to the top', by-passing the system.

   Both of the examples given are wrong, and both actions require a challenge. Industrial relations are between people before they are between systems, and the correct process is for an employee who wishes to air a grievance (real or not), to first discuss it with his foreman, and then take it up the management line.

   It does, of course, place an extra responsibility on the manager and the foreman, which means that the necessary authority must be vested in the management representative to be able to respond to the employee's approach. It is also important that both know about agreements negotiated and how procedures are supposed to work. Ignorance on the part of both sides is the cause of a lot of industrial relations trouble.

7.5   THE PROCESS OF NEGOTIATION

The process of negotiation is arriving at an agreed solution to a shared problem without recourse to threat. Though it may indeed be required for either party to do some tub-thumping and put on a show of strength, it is difficult to negotiate from a position of weakness.

However, strikes help no one and thus it is the role of both parties to find an appropriate solution, recognizing any legitimate concern which either party may have without sacrificing the essential position either party may hold.

At the first level the foreman dealing with the shop steward is an informal and effective process, but it does depend on the existence of mutual respect between the two parties. It is the human element behind the style which is more important than the style itself. What is it we should look for? Integrity, firmness, an ability to listen are equally important. These qualities are necessary through all the levels of negotiation, but as the process of negotiation proceeds to the top of the company or industry, other qualities become equally necessary.

Finding a Solution

The most common form of negotiation is where both sides are trying to find a solution to the following questions:

1. What is the other party hoping to achieve?
2. What is going to be the least they might settle for?
3. Are there any alternative settlements?
4. What are the things the negotiator himself will not concede?
5. Are there any concessions that can be made?
6. Are there any weaknesses in either argument?

The advantage of this formal structure of industrial relations negotiation is that while it is in operation on a particular dispute work can go on. Sometimes the agreement is broken and a resort to industrial action is used before the disputes procedure is complete, but it is the exception rather than the norm.

Once the procedure has been exhausted then there is nothing to prevent a total withdrawal of labour. It is not all easy. The manager and the firm must attempt to frustrate the effect of a strike, but it has to be borne in mind that when the strike is finally settled, all have to attempt some way of working together again.

7.6   LAW, INDUSTRIAL RELATIONS AND THE WORK PLACE

In the UK most practitioners of industrial relations believe they can manage without the control of the Courts. However, the law is now a part of the industrial relations scene and it is likely to remain so.

Successive governments do not always agree and since the 1963 Contracts of Employment Act was passed it has been amended and revised.

Let us examine this Act, and assess its importance. Its purpose is to ensure that employees know what their principal conditions of employment are. The basis structure of the Act, which is on the whole a practical guide, has remained unchanged since 1963, but some significant changes of detail have been inevitable as other major pieces of industrial relations legislation have been introduced. For example, the Employment Protection Act (1975) and the Employment Protection (Consolidation) Act (1980) require that the written Contract of Employment makes a clear statement of the disciplinary rules which apply to the employee and also of the arrangements for an employee to appeal against disciplinary decisions. The purpose of the Contracts of Employment Act is to ensure that employees know what their principal conditions of employment are. This has to be done by a written statement, which may be held by the employee, and it applies to all employees who work for more than sixteen hours a week.

The written statement provided to the employee must include amongst other details the rate of pay, notice period, holiday and sickness entitlement and pension provision. The statement may, however, refer the employee to a document or documents which he has reasonable opportunities of reading in the course of his employment.

7.7   TRADE UNIONS AND LEGAL STATUS

During the last decade there has been considerable debate about the legal status and rights of trade unions. We may assume two issues. The first centres on the belief that there is a malaise in Britain's system of industrial relations which can be solved by legislative reform. The second is the desire of the trade unions to make firm their industrial support and develop their political influence. Neither of the issues, which may not be inconsistent, has been combined by Statute.

It remains for the future to assess the worth of the role of law in industrial relations. In the end arguments have to be settled by the parties involved, and those who have the responsibility for seeing that any solution provided works. But to the extent that the framework of law provides a rigour for both managers and trade unionists to carry out good practice, it can be seen as useful.

The dominating feature of the legislation and other intervention by government into the industrial relations arena of the last 20 years has been its relationship to the national political debate about the legal status and rights of trade unions. The decision is not a new one and it has been about two issues: a belief that there is something wrong with industrial relations in Britain and it can be put right by law, and concern about the trade unions' ambitions in the political field.

Recent Proposals for the Legal Status and Rights of Trade Unions

On 23 November 1981 Mr Norman Tebbit, the Employment Secretary, proposed a wide-ranging series of sanctions against actions taken by union members which, if his proposals are enacted, will be considered unlawful.

Thus, unions with more than 100 000 members could be sued to a limit of £250 000 for any unlawful action carried out during a trade dispute.

This is the cornerstone of the proposals formulated by the Employment Secretary in a consultative document which eventually will lead to a Bill being introduced into Parliament in 1982.

A union with fewer than 5000 members will be liable for damages of up to £12 500; those with between 5000 and 24 999 members will be liable for up to £62 000 damages; and for those with between 25 000 and 100 000 members the limit of the damages will be £125 000.

The Government does not accept that the breadth of the immunities enjoyed by trade unions is necessary in modern conditions to enable them to represent their members effectively.

The Government, therefore, is proposing that the immunities of unions should be brought into line with those of individuals under section 13 of the 1974 Trade Union and Labour Relations Act.

It is proposed that legislation should provide that, where torts are committed by union officials, the union would be held vicariously liable only if the national executive of the union had specifically authorized or ratified the action, or if a subordinate body or official of the union whose action is the subject of complaint had authority for the action under the rules of the union.

Another major plank of the legislation proposals covers the increased compensation available to closed-shop victims. The Employment Secretary believes that more protection should be given to dismissed employees, particularly low-paid employees whose dismissal involves a serious loss of livelihood. Thus the upper limit on present compensatory awards, subject to a maximum of £6250, would be abolished.

Other points from the consultative document are:

1. On the closed shop itself, the Government argues that there is widespread concern. It goes on to propose a periodic review of existing closed shops. It says that in future dismissal for non-membership of a union should be regarded as unfair if:
   (a) There has been no secret ballot of workers covered by the agreement.
   (b) Where there has been a ballot, it has not shown the support of 85 per cent of the workers for the continuation of the closed shop.
2. The Government is proposing that any clause in a contract requiring the employment only of those who are or who are not members of a union should be void.
3. There are also amendments to the present statutory definition of a trade dispute. They are:
   (a) Unions will not be allowed to support disputes outside Great Britain.
   (b) Employers will be able to sue trade unions for damages resulting from secondary action directed at an employer whose employees are not taking industrial action.
   (c) Disputes between an employer and a trade union, where an employer has no dispute with his own employees, will be made unlawful.
   (d) It will be necessary to ensure that an employer could not avoid being in a legitimate dispute with his own employees simply by sacking those with whom he was in dispute.
4. On selective dismissal in a strike, the Government wants to allow tribunals to have jurisdiction only where an employer discriminates by dismissing some but not all of those employees on strike at the time of the dismissal.

Finally, on ballots, the Government proposes extending the use of public money for union elections to cover votes on wage offers.

Some observers of recent legislation and government intervention into the industrial relations scene have seen it as strengthening the power of organized trade unions. Whether it has helped the individual employee is open to doubt.

7.8 INDUSTRIAL RELATIONS LAW AND BRITISH INDUSTRY

The law is now firmly a part of industrial relations in Britain, and various Acts introduced in the last two decades are shown in Table 7.2, though both trade unions and employers often think there is too much of it. Those that think that way believe the law to be an arid, remote subject, not likely to help those whose concern is about the relationship of people at work.

Table 7.2 *Industrial and social legislation 1963–80*

1963	Contracts of Employment Act
1963	Office, Shops and Railway Premises Act
1964–73	Industrial Training Acts
1965, 1969	Redundancy Payments Act
1965, 1973, 1975	Social Security Acts
1965, 1968, 1976	Race Relations Acts
1966, 1973, 1975	Social Security Acts
1966	Pay Freeze
1967, 1968	Prices and Incomes Acts
1968	Transport Act
1968	Donovan Commission Report
1969	'In Place of Strife'
1969	Employers Liability Act
1970	Equal Pay Act
1971	Industrial Relations Act
1971	Attachment of Earnings Act
1972	Contracts of Employment Act
1972	Employment Medical Advisory Act
1972	Pay Freeze
1973	Pay Limitation (£1 + 4 per cent followed by 7 per cent)
1974, 1976	Trade Union and Labour Relations Acts
1974	Health and Safety at Work Act
1975	Sex Discrimination Act
1975	Industry Act
1975	Employment Protection Act
1975	Remuneration and Charges and Grants Act
1975	Job Creation Programme
1975	Road Traffic Act
1975	Pay Restraint (Social Contract) Phase I
1975	Work Experience Scheme
1976	Pay Restraint (Social Contract) Phase II
1977	Bullock Report
1977	Green Paper Future of Companies
1977	EPA Codes of Practice Disclosure of Information Disciplinary Procedures
1977	Finance Act
1977	Pay Restraint (Social Contract) Phase III
1978	EPA Codes of Practice Time Off (Trade Union Activities)
1978	Employment Protection Act
1979	Banking Act
1979	Sale of Goods Act
1980	Finance Act
1980	Companies Act
1980	Social Security Act
1980	Employment Act
1980	Industry Act

There is a fundamental belief to which both the TUC and the CBI subscribe, that industrial relations are better dealt with by the two parties face to face, rather than by reference to the courts of law.

However, governments do not see it that way. Before 1963 there was very little law which affected the manager in business and the manner in which he operated at work. Since 1963 a number of laws relating to employment have been passed, amended and repealed, and committees, tribunals and other quasi-legal bodies have been established.

This part of Chapter 7 seeks only to draw attention to some of the things that you will need to keep in mind when you enter business life.

7.9 THE TRADE UNIONS AND LABOUR RELATIONS ACT

The aim of this Act (TULRA) was the repeal of the 1971 Industrial Relations Act and it seeks to re-establish the rights of trade unionists within the enterprise, and establish new rights where this was thought appropriate. The Act establishes what is meant by a 'trade union' and it titled them 'independent', so that it 'is not under the domination or control of an employer or a group of employers or of one or more employers' associations [and] is not liable to interference by an employer or any such group or association (arising out of the provision of financial or material support or by any other means whatsoever) tending towards such control'.

The most important rights which rest with independent trade unions and their members under this Act relate to the closed shop and to unfair dismissal.

Unfair Dismissal

The concept of unfair dismissal has a fairly precise meaning in law. This is necessary because the law now lays down procedures by which an employee may appeal to an industrial tribunal against his or her dismissal on the grounds that it was 'unfair'. If the tribunal finds the complaint justified it may then order reinstatement in the employee's former job, re-engagement in a comparable job, the payment of compensation, plus a basic award to rate of pay, length of service and age, up to a maximum.

TULRA makes it *unfair* to dismiss an employee for belonging to, or taking part in the activities of, an 'independent' union, or for refusing to join a non-independent trade union.

In addition, any employee who has 52 weeks' service or more is given wider protection against unfair dismissal. To be *fair*, the dismissal must be because of one or more of the following: incapability or the absence of appropriate qualifications; misconduct; redundancy; contravention of statutory requirements; refusal to join a specified independent union, where a closed shop exists; some other substantial reason to justify the particular dismissal. The Act also introduces the notion of 'constructive dismissal'. If an employee is obliged to resign without giving the requisite notice, because of the conduct of his or her employer which has in some way forced that person to resign, this counts as dismissal within the meaning of the Act.

The Right to Strike and Picket

Peaceful picketing is permitted under the law, but the interpretation of the law is difficult. On the whole trade union officials will usually try to see that their members observe both the letter and spirit of this law, but pickets are easy to exploit.

To make the matter more difficult TULRA affords legal protection to any individual 'Acting in contemplation or in furtherance of a trade dispute', who cannot be sued for inducing another person to break a contract, or for threatening to break a contract, or for causing someone else to do so.

However recent government legislation has affected the legal immunity to cover breaches of any type of contract, thus making unlawful various types of secondary action (when carried out in furtherance of a trade dispute) such as blacking or blockading the goods of companies not involved in the dispute.

The effect of these aspects of industrial legislation is to cause everybody a great deal of difficulty in doing the jobs for which they are paid, but there is little we can do about it, except hope the law is applied justly in the case of picketing, and that all disputes are speedily settled.

Employment Protection Acts

The first legislation was introduced in 1975 as part of the government's obligation to the TUC under the terms of the 'Social Contract'. It is about 'job security', with the regulation of collective bargaining, and with the extension of the role of the advisory, conciliation and arbitration service (ACAS).

Other literature deals with the provisions of these Acts, therefore, let us look at just two aspects here: those concerned with maternity leave, and with time-off for trade union activities.

Maternity Leave

If a firm dismisses an employee because she is pregnant, that is 'unfair dismissal', and that firm is liable to find itself before an industrial tribunal on that count. What is more important from the firm's point of view is that, provided the employee informs her employer before she leaves that she intends to return to work, she has the right to return to her previous job at any time within 29 weeks of the time when the baby is born.

You will readily see the problems this can cause for the firm, which may be tempted to avoid recruiting women of child-bearing age. Firms have learnt to avoid the temptation, for if the firm discriminates against women generally they are in breach of the law, and will, again, find themselves in front of an industrial tribunal.

Time off for Trade Union Activities

This is considered in the Employment Protection Act and ensures that an employer gives reasonable time off to employees who belong to an independent trade union to take part in the activities of that union.

This time off concession has now been translated by ACAS into a code of practice which may be quoted in support of a case brought before an industrial tribunal. The code recommends giving officials of the union, such as shop stewards, time off with pay to perform their recognized duties in a manner which is practised in most companies with long experience of industrial relations.

The Advisory, Conciliation and Arbitration Service (ACAS)

In the implementation of industrial legislation ACAS has a key role. It is a government-sponsored independent body run by a council consisting of a Chairman and nine members: three nominated by the CBI, three by the TUC, and three independent members.

ACAS' terms of reference charge it with 'The general duty of promoting the improvement of industrial relations, and in particular of encouraging the extension of collective bargaining, and the development, and, where necessary, reform of the collective bargaining machinery'.

Serious industrial disputes can be sent to arbitration through ACAS, which has a range of methods available to it for this purpose, but the emphasis of ACAS is on conciliation, and it is this that is of particular importance to the manager because it applies to disputes concerning individuals, as well as to major trade disputes.

The kind of individual dispute in which a manager is most likely to get involved is that concerning unfair dismissal. In such a case a conciliation officer from ACAS will see the individual concerned, the manager and any other persons involved to see if a settlement can be reached. However, if a settlement is not achieved, then the dispute will go to a tribunal. A tribunal consists of a chairman, who is a lawyer, plus two lay members with relevant experience of industry. It is normal practice for one to be an employer and one to be a trade unionist. Beyond the industrial tribunal is the Employment Appeal Tribunal, which consists of judges and lay members from both sides of industry, who hear appeals on questions of law from the decisions of industrial tribunals.

From the point of view of the firm which is on the receiving end of a complaint brought to one of these tribunals, there is no reason to expect biased treatment. As a matter of fact, only approximately one-third of the complaints of unfair dismissal ever succeed, but it can be a harrowing experience.

An individual may bring a complaint of unfair dismissal up to three months after the dismissal, and the tribunal hearing will take some time after that to arrange. Thus, by the time a case is heard, many firms may well have forgotten some of the details on which they are likely to be challenged. It is therefore necessary that the exact circumstances of the dismissal are properly recorded at the time it happens.

There is obviously a need for industrial tribunals as part of the democratization of industrial life. If a dismissed employee wins his case, then the firm may be in all kinds of difficulties over reinstatement, and even if the employee loses his case there will be a considerable loss of time.

As some indication of the way industrial tribunals and unfair dismissal cases have increased over the last decade, in 1972–73 there were approximately 2000 cases; in 1979–80 there were over 17 000. It can be seen that, at this rate of progress, most firms are likely to experience an unfair dismissal case at some time.

Some solutions do rest with the firm. All selection processes and personnel departments ought to be aware that those employees who are not of the required standard should be dismissed before they have completed 52 weeks of service. A second solution is that all firms should have a properly organized and publicized disciplinary procedure, and should follow it. A third solution is that where a dismissal is contemplated, all the steps leading to it, including the warnings, are properly documented, and held at one source.

The most important thing, however, is that all firms should act fairly. This has more to do with good industrial practice than with the law; it is the essence of good industrial relations, and eventually the law will recognize it.

The Health and Safety at Work Act

This Act lays responsibility on firms to provide safe conditions of work, and other litera-ture covers that aspect. However, statutory regulations, together with an approved code of practice, on safety representatives and safety committees are now enforced, and as trade union members and their representatives are likely to be very much involved as safety representatives we might just look at a part of the Act. The Health and Safety at Work Act requires all firms to consult with appointed representatives 'with a view to the making and maintenance of arrangements which will enable him and his employees to co-operate effectively in promoting and developing measures to ensure the health and safety at work of the employees, and in checking the effectiveness of such measures'.

Safety representatives are appointed through the necessary trade union machinery. Where unions are not recognized employers are advised to organize similar procedures, but this is not part of the law. The employer must also establish a safety committee if this is requested by the safety representatives, and it nearly always is.

Safety representatives have a legal right to carry out inspections in the factory or the office and to make written reports to the employer of any unsafe practices which he observes during the course of his inspections. He also has the right to inspect relevant documents. Safety representatives have no legal right to enforce any suggestion on an employer, and indeed, the spirit of the Act emphasizes the need for the safety represen-tative and employer to work together on safety matters, in a spirit of mutual co-opera-tion, but of course safety representatives can take any disputed matter through the negotiating procedure if they wish.

The possible areas of friction have proved to be in the legal requirement that the employer gives safety representatives time off with pay to exercise their functions, and for training. The health and safety commission advise firms to act on the side of generosity, but whatever firms do all arrangements ought to be clearly agreed with the union in advance of any possible dispute arising.

7.10   HARMONIZATION OF BRITISH AND EUROPEAN LAW

It is necessary for us to speculate on the answers to questions on the relationships between Community law and UK law. In the last few years, there have been the negoti-ations to add to the membership of the EEC, the development of the European monet-ary system, and direct elections to the European Parliament. The European Court has, to date, delivered judgement on some 250 cases falling within its scope, and the Courts in this country have begun to make extensive use of their power to apply EEC law and to make reference to the European Court. As a result of all this activity there are now answers to the many questions on the relationship between EEC and UK law. However there is still the question of the sovereignty of Parliament and the EEC.

There is no doubt that the European Court has said the member states have limited sovereign rights, although within certain areas, so that the member states have contrac-tually bound themselves in international law to do certain things and refrain from others. Sovereignty in the sense we wish to use it is 'the ultimate Sovereignty of Parlia-ment' and is the constitutional doctrine that there is nothing that, in the eyes of the law of the United Kingdom, a statute properly enacted cannot do. In the international sphere and in the political sphere there may be a limitation of sovereignty, but there is no reason to believe that there has as yet been any limitation on the sovereignty of the United Kingdom Parliament.

Article 48(1) of the EEC Treaty provides that freedom of movement of workers shall be secured by the end of the transitional period. Freedom of movement implies the right of entry, residence, and exit. Of interest to our study it also means in particular the right to accept offers of employment; move freely within the territory of the host country for this purpose; reside in a member state for the purpose of employment; remain there after the termination of employment in accordance with implementing regulations. Thus member states are bound to eliminate any discriminations based on nationality between their own and fellow member states' citizens as regards employment, remuneration and other conditions of work.

Participation in West Germany

In West Germany there are two levels of control in the firm: the board of supervision and the board of management. (See Fig. 7.2.) The board of management has real executive and managerial control. The other, the board of supervision, is responsible for the dismissal and for the appointment of the members of the board of management, and for the general supervision of the role and their functions.

The board of supervision can also inspect and examine the books and records of the company. In the case of the steel and coal industries, labour and management are equally represented on the board of supervision, and on employees' welfare the director must sit on the management board. However, for the rest of the West German industry only one-third of the members of the board of supervision must be employees' representatives, and there is no provision for their membership on the board of management. The board of supervision normally meets six times a year and requires the board of management to supply it with information. Nevertheless, its presence has had the effect of adding to the unions' strength, and involving their leaders in company administration. Again, workers can, through their representatives, obtain full information as to the finances and future intentions of their employers, and, in wage bargaining, they are well informed as to the likely effect of any pay increases in their company.

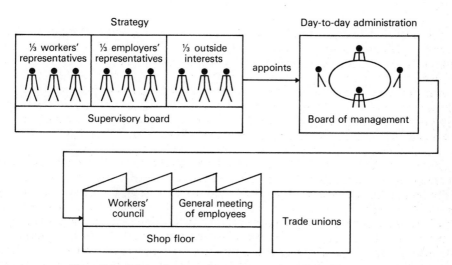

Figure 7.2 *Scheme for a two-tier company with worker participation*

The selection of members to a West German board of supervision is by secret ballot, supervised by a shop council, a body representing and elected by the employees. The shop council exists in most companies. Where there are under 100 employees, it represents employees in personnel and social matters. Where the company employs over 100 people the council can also require information in relation to management and economic matters, for example, plant changes, work methods, production programmes, profits and profitability, and the production and sales position of the company.

The shop council and one-third representation arrangements have worked well and are now largely accepted by German managers. The equal sharing in the coal and steel industries is considered in West Germany to be less successful.

7.11   INDUSTRAL RELATIONS AND THE LAW – SOME CONCLUSIONS

This system of industrial relations in Great Britain is as complex a system as any to be found in the western hemisphere. It is the legacy of a long process of evolution during which time its component parts, that is, its patterns of rules, regulations, institutions, policies and practices, have been structurally determined by a complex interplay of social, economic, political, technological and multi-cultural forces. The essential question today is 'Has this evolutionary process resulted in a system of industrial relations which is over-powerful and disruptive to the general social and economic welfare of the nation?' If the answer to the question is yes, then a second question must be asked: 'What action should be taken to control the system?'

The debate, which has pervaded the last two decades, has fundamentally concerned these questions in one form or another, and has produced conflicting standpoints concerning the method of bringing about reform. Perhaps the arguments have polarized into two predominant camps, one which we shall call the unitary camp, the other the pluralistic camp.

To explain these two standpoints we must first attempt to delineate the industrial relations problems of today. The Donovan Commission saw the problem as being threefold: the strike problem, the restrictive practices problem, and the wages or earnings drift problem. The strike problem refers to the alarming increase, during the last quarter century, in unofficial and unconstitutional strikes in practically every area of industry. The restrictive practices problem refers to the lack of efficiency in the use of manpower in much of British industry. (Factors such as over-manning, rigid job demarcation and various forms of unofficial output control exercised by workers were seen as causing gross inefficiencies in labour utilization.) The wage problem refers to the ever-increasing cost of labour resulting from an uncontrolled movement of earnings. This uncontrolled movement was seen by Donovan as being the product of plant level bargaining which increased earnings far in excess of those which would have resulted from nationally negotiated pay agreements.

The first distinction between the two bodies of opinion concerns the nature of the origin and causes of these problems. The unitary camp sees them as resulting from an ever-increasing and now excessive power of organized labour. The pluralistic camp, on the other hand, sees all the problems as resulting from deficiencies and contradictions which have accumulated in the post-war period and which have generated confusion and disorder in the system of industrial relations in this country. This difference of opinion seriously questions any single reform prescription, mainly because we are in the field of opinion rather than fact. On the one hand, the unitary view sees the problems as resulting from the oppressive, selfish and irresponsible activities of the trade unions, whilst on the other, the pluralists see them as resulting from the institutional lag between the nature of the needs and wants of individual workers and the development of appropriate negotiating machinery related to them.

Recent history has seen a large body of support for the unitary view. Many sectors of society, including employers and employers' associations and many members of both Labour and Conservative governments, considered trade unions to be excessively powerful pressure groups whose strength was threatening the very process of government. The use of this power was seen as having a detrimental effect on the country's economic growth and domestic and world trade through its effect on competitiveness, investment and inflation. The growth in unofficial and unconstitutional strikes was seen by many as the central causal issue related to the decline of the British economy, since such action inhibited technological change and forward planning. Legislation was seen as the appropriate control agent which would introduce a new and more acceptable balance into the system. This balance was seen as being achieved through legislative control of the behaviour of both trade unions and employers. In addition, it was seen as having a major reform influence on the nature of industrial action by workers, reducing unofficial and unconstitutional action through legislative provisions aimed at punishing the provokers and leaders of such activity.

The pluralists argue that the symptoms of the problems in industrial relations do not lead to the diagnosis of over-powerful and irresponsible trade unions as their root cause. On the contrary, they argue that through the activities of trade unions throughout this century the fundamental needs of working people have now been met (for example, wage levels, holidays and working hours) and that a new level of awareness has entered the industrial relations system. This awareness is of higher needs and wants which the workers experience as individuals. Such needs and wants can only be determined at a local level, and hence the increasing demand for localized collective bargaining. It is here, they argue, that the problems arise, since collective bargaining has been institutionalized at a national and not local level. In addition, the people at the local level are, by and large, poorly equipped as individuals to cope with the bargaining process.

It is not surprising therefore that these two sets of opinions would recommend different approaches in order to reform the present system. The unitarians advocated legislation, the pluralists a restructuring of the institutions, increased industrial democracy at the local level, and improvements in the knowledge and skill on the parts of those individuals participating in the bargaining process. The Donovan Commission, in general, rejected the use of legal sanctions as an appropriate control mechanism on the grounds that it would be over-simplistic, irrelevant, or simply unworkable, particularly in the light of the modern trend towards the more informal, localized collective bargaining. Legal sanctions were seen by the Commission as having relevance only in relation to the protection of the right of individual workers.

During the late 1960s the weight of opinion was such that the governments of the day rejected Donovan's view and the Industrial Relations Act of 1971 became law. This Act transformed the system of industrial relations in Britain from the most voluntary and least legally controlled, to one of the most restricted systems in Europe.

From the Act's short history it is possible to draw conclusions related to its effectiveness as a mechanism for control. Many believe that it had little effect as a positive inducement to more rational and efficient industrial relations practices and, in fact, that the measurements taken in the Act aimed at reform and union restraint have increased disorganization and irresponsibility. It depends here on the standpoint a commentator takes and the evidence he uses to form his judgements and opinions.

In general, the Industrial Relations Act demonstrated the inadequacy of legislation as a major reform agent, although evidence obtained from research in the pottery industry has indicated that it produced some substantial structural changes, particularly on the management side, in the field of labour management practices. Whether these structural changes are of any great long-term significance is impossible to show. Suffice it to say, that they represent a positive step in viewing the subject of industrial relations as a major issue deserving of senior management attention and substantial training.

The Donovan Committee report pin-pointed the fact that the problems in industrial relations in the United Kingdom stem from the inadequacy or malfunctioning of regulatory institutions, especially at the level of the work place. The conflict is between the formal and informal systems, but the Report was quite clear in pointing out that it rejected the suggestion that it could be resolved by forcing the compliance of the informal component with the wishes and assumptions of the formal system.

Donovan therefore rejected the use of the law as a major reform agent, although seeing it as having a significant value in the area of protection of employment rights for individual workers. In fact, Donovan's own evidence indicates a major problem for any mechanism aimed at reform in that most workers appeared to be happy with the existing position, and that the majority did not see the prevailing situation as being predominantly disorderly. This evidence suggests that any reform attempt, legal or voluntary, is doomed to failure unless the majority of workers are convinced that reform is necessary. It is apparent, therefore, that any commentary should be aware that even the aim of reform is itself suspect, let alone the mechanisms for achieving it. If disorder in work place relations is not seen as a problem by the majority on the shop floor, what chance has reformation got, particularly on a voluntary basis?

The unitary mechanism, the Industrial Relations Act, was basically drawn up on the belief that two issues, above all, produced disputes, wages drift and bargaining, namely, informal fragmented bargaining arrangements and procedures which were ineffective or non-existent.

The Pluralist Viewpoint as an Alternative

The pluralist arguments are fundamentally based on the major characteristics of the post-war developments of British industrial relations. Since the Second World War we have seen the progressive growth of the strength of trade unionism, particularly apparent in the development of bigger and stronger individual trade unions. Secondly, there has been a more acute expansion of workers' wants and expectations. Thirdly, there has been a swing of importance from national collective bargaining to plant level bargaining. This third characteristic evolves from the second, for it is really only at an individual plant level that real security of employment and fringe benefits can be negotiated. Finally, there has been an erosion of traditional areas of managerial prerogative, such issues as work practices, discipline and recruitment coming within the scope of bargaining.

These developments have resulted in an inbalanced system. On the one hand, industrial relations is formalized on a national basis, with collective bargaining being institutionalized at this level; and on the other, the demand from shop floor level is for very localized individual plant bargaining. This second informal system has become the more consequential form of bargaining for most workers, since it is more appropriate to the wider development of collective bargaining into issues resulting from the expansion of workers' wants and needs. The problem is that these two systems are, in general, unco-ordinated and often in conflict. Thus discrepancies and anomalies arise in both procedural and substantive matters which have increasingly created a real threat to work place relations. This lack of order has resulted in a serious crisis of authority in work place relations; many managements having given in far too easily on important issues, thereby creating dangerous and embarrassing precedents. There has also been an undermining of the authority of the full-time union official by local workers' representatives.

It is in the light of all these points that the pluralists argue for reform on a voluntary basis. For such a reform to take place it is argued that management and unions must recognize that informal, localized bargaining represents a loss of authority for them both. Secondly, both must recognize that the regulation of work and pay is by a joint undertaking, and thirdly, that management needs to re-examine the scope of its prerogatives.

Is this common united approach a practical proposition? Does the disparity between the authority hierarchies in companies and unions allow a common approach? Is it legitimate for a shop steward to co-operate with and even assist management in the maintenance of work place agreements? Why should labour co-operate in measures and actions which either are of little day-to-day concern to them, or reduce their bargaining strength? These are important questions which seriously bring into doubt any attempt to control the apparent disorder in modern industrial relations by concentrating on the foci of authority in the system, particularly on the labour side. Hence any attempt at restructuring the system on a voluntary basis, as suggested by the pluralists, is a very questionable concept.

Donovan argues for more education and training in order to increase the enlightenment of all those participating in the industrial relations system, as education would remove the widespread ignorance which pervades British industrial relations, and create a stage for a new sense of unity amongst all the parties, which would result in a reduction in the extent of fragmented bargaining, the maximization of the precision and formality of agreements and an extension of the scope of bargaining. But who provides the training and who controls the views and bias of those carrying it out?

Perhaps we should all accept that conflict is a natural component in the employment arena, and that what is needed is not mechanisms for reform, but a greater understanding of the sources, scope, nature and handling process of it!

7.12   WHERE THE RESPONSIBILITY LIES

The question remains, at what level and where should industrial relations be handled in British companies? This is far more difficult to answer than it may seem. Our first response might be that industrial relations should be handled by everybody in the company who is a supervisor of others. But if that supervisor does not do his job properly, then discussions in the board room are not going to put matters right. In many British companies industrial relations are handled at the shop floor level by a supervisor, often a senior supervisor. The basic belief in industrial relations is that speed is essential, and that a problem must be settled fast. It will only get worse if the firm does not move quickly.

Many companies believe that it is wrong for the board to become involved with too many specific or minor decisions, for example, whether the cycle racks are getting rusty and need repainting. The first line for settlement is shop floor supervision, where there must be clear authority up to a certain level. Supervisors' instructions must be to settle if it is within their terms of reference, or to refer it upwards fast if it is not. The board is there to ensure that the machinery for handling problems exists, is known to exist, and works. Apart from that, the board should concern itself with general policy.

Industrial relations are a board responsibility, because they are one of the major failures of British industry – certainly many large national industries have shown a reluctance to consider industrial relations at all, and, of course, this has tended to push the subject away from the board room down to line management where there is not the authority. For this reason the pattern of industrial relations policy should be laid down by the chief executives, that is, the person in charge of industrial relations should be a member of the board.

In British industry someone very senior and very experienced in the field has to take overall responsibility for industrial relations. He should spend half his time on matters concerning industrial relations in the broadest sense, such as personnel, management development, salary structures, incentive plans and wages policies, and it is in these areas that we begin to realize that we are talking not only of industrial relations, but about human relations. It is for this reason that many firms negotiate within the framework of the conventional structure, but attempt to negotiate as informally as possible. In other words, they create an atmosphere of informality at meetings and conferences, even though they are working within conventional parameters and guidelines. These firms believe it is important to create good personal relationships with union officials, providing a feeling of dignity and authority, recognizing that the union officials have a job to do, and that they have a responsibility to their members, who are also the firm's employees, to whom they also have a responsibility, and thus both parties have an ongoing commitment. So far this conventional approach within an informal atmosphere has worked for many firms.

Many firms have more non-union members than union members, though they are not adverse to trade unions. It is often the case that the majority of employees have not requested union representation. In those situations firms need to monitor and develop their communications systems through briefing groups and consultative committees where important items of a human relations nature can be discussed prior to any final decision being taken by management or the main board of the company. In these situations people are often elected to these consultative committees, and have to be encouraged to contribute and discuss freely. Another development where there are many more non-union than union members is the establishment of management groups who are, in effect, junior boards. They meet every month or so, and deal with all management problems including industrial relations. Here specialization is not mandatory and thus everyone contributes. The difficulty, of course, is if there is no one person with the intimate knowledge of industrial relations that is so often required in today's complex industrial situation.

Thus every company has its own style and character, which clearly shapes the structure and pattern of industrial relations in British industry. It may also point to the fact that there is really no ideal system that can be applied in any context because people at all levels are different, with different needs and jobs, and different demands.

Take for example the big high street banks. Here, the linchpin in the system of industrial relations is the branch manager. In banking the system stems from its branch managers, and we must remember that in this industry everybody is a banker, so the style and success of that style depends on the competence of each manager. It is to him that the staff go in the first place if they have any particular problem. The branches are linked into districts and then regions, coming finally together at Head Office in the City. Some of the local directors sit on the main board, so there is a link between the Head Office and the branch manager and his staff in any local high street, but at the centre, none the less, there is a large staff department run by a general manager. It provides members with a specialist staff committee which reports directly to the board. As a specialist committee, its sole function is to discuss industrial relations questions.

Style varies from one company to another in British industry, but all companies agree that industrial relations are primarily a line function to be carried out, under guidance, on general policy from the board.

In a company such as ICI they reserve to the centre only those things that they regard as being essential to the centre; the rest they delegate. This is because they are a large composite company, operating in all sorts of businesses. They also operate in a large number of countries. Thus, a complication can arise in that they reserve certain personnel questions to the centre. (The most obvious are senior and board appointments.) They also reserve the policy on general salary scales, and the negotiation of wage scales, even though they have advanced some way with a staff status system, and are less directly concerned at the centre with salary scales than before. ICI, though, believe their central decisions are interpreted in relation to individuals, or groups of individuals, and they lead very much to the divisions of the operation.

To understand the ICI approach one has to understand something of its structure. Under the main board in London there are nine delegate boards heading the operating divisions. Each of these divisions has a board member with particular responsibility for personnel matters, answering directly to the chairman. So you already see a system of varied local interpretation. All the local influences which affect operating board decisions will, needless to say, have to be taken into account and dealt with by the local operating board. The problem is, how does this square up with the broad company policy on given questions?

The point is that the centre of ICI must be sensitive to the pressures, to the environment, and to the actual situation which exists in each of their divisions. But this is not the only way in which the people at the centre take account of what possible or actual developments there might be in the field. In London they have a central personnel department. The staff of the department spend time 'in the field', and some time at the centre, which adds up in the end to a high level of professional expertise. It is this department which helps the board with its prime function of sifting and sorting various opinions to provide a balanced view of the operating scene. So you have a situation in which the centre has a certain definite responsibility to advise the operating boards, yet at the same time is well aware of the experience vested in those self-same boards. This underlines the point that there is no easy answer to this question, but in the example of ICI there is a vast spread of experience at all levels, up and down and across the country, that has to be pulled together and has to be taken into account when the main board is making a judgement, taking a view, or forming a policy. This in turn has to be interpreted in the light of the special requirements of each operating division.

Thus for ICI they ponder on the proper function of a board of directors, and also whether or not ICI's personnel relationships are good, bad or somewhere in between, and whether the board is making wise policy decisions in relation to personnel. Of course if they are wise, it is easier for personnel relationships to be good; but equally obviously in reverse, if any of the divisional management is not really competent in this field, then the board cannot correct it. Again, if the general policy is right, it cannot be wholly effective if the local management does not believe it to be right, and that is why ICI consult them before any defined policy is brought into being.

Advice, consultation, feedback, prove to be the key words in all discussions of those who handle industrial relations.

Industrial relations is not a unique field of behaviour; it operates under the same basic factors that guide all behaviour. The context may be different, but the principles are the same. To further our understanding of the events that take place in that context we must rely on what we have learned about behaviour in other contexts. It is true that much of what we have learned about participation has been discovered in the laboratory under conditions that all too frequently have borne little resemblance to the world of industrial relations. Yet in spite of such limitations a body of knowledge has evolved that will permit at least some informed speculations about why people behave as they do in the labour-management scene.

It is said that organizations do not have feelings, emotions and impulses; they do not think and make decisions. Decisions are made by individuals, and when these decisions are treated according to formal rules, they become policy for the organization. Decisions derive from the desires of the individual, from his information about the issue, from the consequences he anticipates, from the pressures he feels, and from the attitudes he has adopted with respect to relevant topics. The interaction of individual decisions and organization policy is far from simple, hence the interest in participation. If the person attempts to mould the organization to his way of thinking, he may encounter resistance from others. When he is strongly motivated he is tempted to mobilize friends and sympathizers into a faction which will press for the policy he prefers.

To those in control of the organization a challenge by either an individual or a clique is perceived as a threat. The hazard may be primarily the loss of power and income by those in control, but it will be described publicly as a danger to the entire company.

Without a move to participation, conflict between the individual and the company is almost assured by our modern economic system with its high specialization of labour, narrowly restricted job assignments which often are not suited to the workers' attitudes and interests, and with work rules that restrict the employees' choice as to speed of work, rest periods, and other aspects. Conflict without a measure of participation is a virtually inevitable consequence of modern systems of control.

Despite this pessimistic view, most individuals adapt to organizational life. If taken into the confidence of the company, most individuals abandon some of their personal goals, such as self-expression, and accept the goal of success for the organization as a substitute. The organization becomes an instrument, a means to their own satisfactions. They will thus support the organization and unconsciously accept the official viewpoint as their own.

Although participation is one of the most useful concepts that we have in understanding human action in any field of behaviour, it is also one of the most complicated. One reason why it is difficult to discuss is that it is an abstraction. In spite of its abstract nature, however, participation is anchored in two more tangible sub-concepts: needs and goals. We know that an individual is motivated when he or she acts with purpose and with reference to some object, even a person in his or her environment. This point has been developed earlier in the book and we can safely assume that for every goal there is some kind of need. Industrial behaviour is motivated by needs and goals, and, as we have stated, Maslow has developed the theory of people needing love, esteem and self-actualization, which are a part of 'belongingness' (participation). Thus the entrepreneur engaged in building his or her company is demonstrating a goal or need. He or she is channelling a substantial effort into the industrial organization. No less energy can be demonstrated by the rank-and-file factory worker or office worker.

The nature of management and the interaction of executives and workers, however, depend to a marked extent on what theory of participation is held by those who control the enterprise.

7.13 COMMUNICATING WITH THE PEOPLE WHO WORK IN BRITISH INDUSTRY

Most firms accept the need for as much information as possible to be given to both trade unions and workers in general. But there are doubts as to whether this information is needed or even understood. Many firms believe that there are problems of a commercial kind which make it impossible to be as frank as they would like. However, the emphasis for the future seems to be that unions and their members must have more information, even if they do not know what to do with it. We again see the creditability gap that has grown up between the managed and management, and thus we have the proposals of the possibility of workers being placed on the boards of British companies as one way of overcoming this.

How does British industry regard the proposal that firms should provide more information to trade unions and their members? If by more information it is meant the same amount of information as given to shareholders there is no problem; the unions can obtain this anyway by buying one share in the company. If companies have to give more information than is given to their shareholders, then the situation might become difficult. The more successful the company the weaker will be its bargaining position as a result of arming unions with details of its success. There is, furthermore, a security problem. How do firms prevent information leaking from the negotiating table to the desks of their competitors? However, many firms do not see this proposal being taken to such lengths. What most firms believe is that what is important is good communications, that is, the improvement of the flow of information between management and employees in both directions.

Many British companies, including Dunlop and ICI, believe that providing more information which is relevant, and which is genuinely helpful in arriving at a successful solution or outcome to wage negotiations, for example, has to be encouraged, but it is not accepted that companies are required to issue every worker with a mass of financial and other information which is first not wanted, second, possibly not understood, and third, at times potentially very damaging. For example, the circulation of accounts is subject to the general requirements of the Companies Acts, and there are auditors to make sure that these requirements are followed. On the other hand, if a firm is closing a

factory 'people are entitled to know why it is closing, what steps have been taken to avoid it, and they should really be able to prove the reason for a particular position being adopted by a company on the closure'. (G. Bull (1972) *Industrial Relations, the Boardroom Viewpoint*, Bodley Head.) In this particular example, management would have to justify its action to its employees, otherwise the unions receive what they think is a very high handed action.

At ICI, where over 80 per cent of the staff are shareholders, they get the same information as the shareholders, and at the same time. Here the company publishes a simplified version of its profit and loss account and balance sheet for employees. The directors address the central council twice a year on the state of the company, including profit figures and the general trend. This practice does appear to be a good example for the best of industry.

The Thomson Organization publishes a tabloid digest of the full company report for all its employees, which is not always easy for some to understand. (Perhaps some employees would rather not hear the bad news.) The Thomson Organization believes that those areas of commerce where information is kept secret are overdoing the secrecy. They believe there is perhaps an excuse for some information being held back, but the Thomson Organization believe in the direct approach. Management sees all the chapels in the organization and has informed talks. At these talks two conditions are always required: they must be kept to a strict time limit, and wages and conditions are not discussed. Information about the company is discussed, and it is a most effective form of industrial communication. Esso also publishes a great deal of information for its employees, and holds a series of discussions at which managers and the work force present the results to the whole of the company, and have full and frank discussions of the problems facing the industry.

We have seen that for a number of companies there are no objections whatsoever to

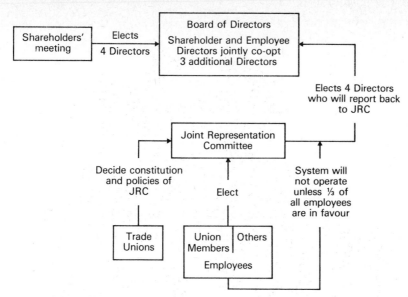

Figure 7.3 *Industrial democracy in the UK. The proposals of the majority report of the Bullock Committee, 1977, for companies employing 2000–9999 people*

the accounts being in the hands of everybody in the company. What most trade union officials would say is that they want information which is going to assist them in their collective bargaining function, so that when there are issues which arise concerning, for example, wages, they want to know how much is available for wage increases; what is the likely effect of price trends on the surplus available to the company; if there are problems of impending redundancy; if there are likely to be orders for the firm's products; what other units or factories are available where these products could be produced. The information is always required for specific purposes, because trade unions are essentially practical organizations. Most trade union officials concede that unions are not interested in information if it does not help them with their objective, but there is no reason why management should not try to encourage trade union officials to take more interest in company information.

However, it has to be conceded that change cannot be brought about overnight. On the other hand, unions are not only interested in the finance of individual firms. They can, and do, take a much broader view of the economy. If you read trade union documents, they are generally broader in outlook and perspective. Look at the *Economical Review* published by the TUC. It looks at the state of the economy generally, the level of employment, and the relationship between prices, productivity and incomes.

There is still a gap between management and worker, and to fill this gap with the unions at the centre taking a broader view it is possible that one way to close it is to have worker representatives, either from the union or the work force, on a company board, as proposed by the Bullock Committee in 1977. (See Figs 7.3 and 7.4.) It has been called co-determination. The trend has started.

In the public sector trade unionists are members of the board. At British Rail, for example, there is a member from the General and Municipal Workers. British Rail, therefore, does not see any problem with trade union directors. The general point is that it is not a bad idea having someone on your board 'who understands how people live'. But there are a substantial number of private company boards who do not have a single member who has ever personally known anybody existing on a low income. Most large company boards are almost entirely composed of people of fairly high income level who

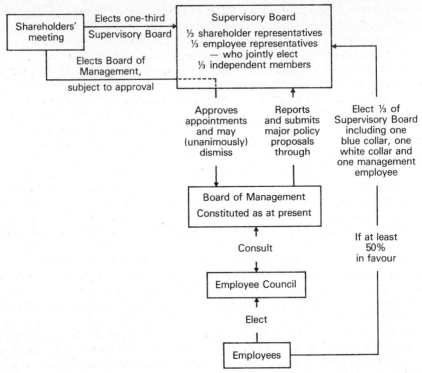

Figure 7.4 *Industrial democracy in the UK. The proposals of the minority report of the Bullock Committee, 1977, for companies employing 2000 or more people*

come from backgrounds of high income levels. Many problems you get on the shop floor cannot be understood unless you have experienced them. For example, an engineer working month in and month out on a Capstan Lathe on the same product will find his work very repetitive. It makes the person doing it very conscious of what operating on a routine, repetitive, dull, miserable job really means. Many industrialists are aware of the need for this re-education about the nature of problems they cannot imagine unless there is somebody there to tell them, or who is capable of telling them, or unless they have experienced it for themselves.

Having said this, the problem still remains about the proper function of a director. Whether he comes from a union from within the industry, or from another industry, he has to resolve the dilemma about what his job really is. Is it to go back and report to the union? Many think not. He is there to advise the board, not to act as a link with the trade unions. We come back to what we have said in previous chapters: management must manage, and management must lead, and it should be there because it is equipped to lead. It cannot have meetings that are a series of compromises, which are intended to meet all sorts of divergent objectives; the business would be bankrupt.

Are we then likely to see the growth of worker directors? Most industrialists agree that it makes a lot of sense to have representatives of the labour force at a board meeting, but it is less effective with a trade union. Many agree that it is easier to work and have more success when it is seen in the context of a company union, and given this distinction there would be an advantage in dealing with the labour force. You can see the problem of two men sitting at a board table in Kent, for example, arguing about what was negotiated in Edinburgh. While it might be of interest in terms of their general trade union experience, it would hardly be relevant to the particular problems that are faced in a given company at a given time, so company unions are a prerequisite. Many British trade unions have looked to Germany as an example. Some industrialists are sceptical, believing the whole thing is false. There are two boards, one of which has a 'window dressing' of workers on it, and is merely supervisory, the membership being one-third worker representatives; then you have an executive board, comparable to the normal board in this country. As regards, for example, the iron and steel industries, they have arrived at the position where the number of worker representatives on the supervisory board equals the employer's representatives with an independent chairman. They also, in effect, have a worker representative on the executive board. Some industrialists in this country believe that this is a big step towards communism.

If workers on the board is not viable in Great Britain, what about a managing director on the shop floor? That is the approach adopted by some British companies. It is thought that a typical board grossly underestimates the significance of human relations, and we have discussed this in this chapter. The relatively small efforts on the part of directors can make a stupendous difference in this field, but we are afraid, as the CBI and TUC are afraid, that the average board does not even make this small effort. For example, would it not be possible for a director to take a day off a month in order to do something at shop floor level? For example, a director could act as a driver's mate on one of the firm's lorries. He could spend a complete day with all the drivers of the depot. That would give the drivers the opportunity to talk to him in their own environment, and although the director may not deal with anything specific, they would all have the chance to talk to that director about general problems. Then the director could talk to them about things going on in the company. Another director could do this in the factory. This kind of relationship, perhaps artificially generated, and although not entirely significant to management, could produce a general feeling that the firm cares.

Is it a realistic situation? Would the drivers talk openly? Many who study personnel believe that most of the drivers would talk openly, and for the most part the approach could be constructive, but it would have to be recognized that this situation is not a means for employees to by-pass normal grievance procedures or line management channels. In those firms that have tried it they have been fortunately sensitive enough to realize that this could occur, and discussion therefore is kept away from direct line issues.

Is this kind, attractive approach a risk? Would it not undermine the usual channels of authority? These are the standard reactions of people who feel they may not have the 'common touch'. A director working with a driver would not talk about current issues on the shop floor, but they could talk about the whole business philosophy of the company, and it need not undermine discipline. Top managers who isolate themselves, and who refuse to talk to the worker on the shop floor are undermining discipline in that neglect. The point is that even if it is not easy for many class-conscious managers to talk freely to the people whom they manage, nevertheless by working alongside a worker they are saying one important thing: that that person's job in the company is important and contributes to the whole. It gives him a sense that he belongs, and that the director does not consider himself too dignified to work with him. However, success of this type of approach depends on the personality of the person involved, but it is the quality that should be sought when a company appoints executives.

It would be interesting to see the effect of this approach elsewhere. Tensions in the British Leyland complex might well diminish if Sir Michael Edwardes could arrange to do the odd day's stint on his shop floor!

Workers on the board, managers on the shop floor, more information – is it more information or is it more explanation that is needed?

7.14 SUMMARY

The aim of this chapter has been to illustrate the UK industrial relations system, and to examine some of the issues in the relations between employees and issues. The chapter starts by exploring the unusual ideas of investment in people, and that the nation's most precious asset is the skill, knowledge, loyalty and enthusiasm of the people employed by any organization. We argue, therefore, that organizations deal with individuals accordingly. Joint consultation is one such attempt to remove obduracy, and encourage a sense of participation; another is the reform of attitude in industrial relations. The objective of industrial relations is to resolve quickly and without coercion on either side conflicts arising from differing interests. To achieve this participation, we argue, it is important for the trade union movement to develop leadership at the shop floor level. You will find this and other problems facing the trade union movement examined in this and other chapters. Specifically, however, the question is one of the utility value of work, which is predominantly the way in which the employees' work is evaluated by the employer.

It is suggested that it is in this area of trying to secure an advancement in the quality of life for people at work that trade unions can come into conflict with employers, because the social organization, or the kind of work which would most improve the quality of life and reduce fear and tension for the employee, is not necessarily the type of organization which would best meet the productivity, profit goals and efficiency of the enterprise.

Your attention is drawn to the role of the trade unions in securing social improvements through negotiation, and to the responsibility of the TUC as the centre of the trade union movement, and its importance to the movement as an initiator of education programmes. We conclude that more education is required if the relationship between employee and employer is to improve.

It is explained that not all industrial relations are organized between employers and trade unions. Some companies, such as ICI and Ford, have individual agreements with the trade unions and often these agreements operate separately from those operating elsewhere in the industry; the example of the EEF is provided.

We examine in some detail the process of negotiation, that is, the process of arriving at an agreed solution to a shared problem without recourse to threat. You will find the common form of negotiation explained for you in the six steps of the formal structure.

The chapter moves to an examination of the law, industrial relations and the work place, as they relate to the legal status and rights of trade unions. We develop the point that the law is now firmly a part of industrial relations in Britain, even though both the TUC and the CBI subscribe to the view that industrial relations are better dealt with by the two parties face to face. Chapter 7 seeks to draw attention to some of the implications of the law that you will need to keep in mind. We further explore the issue that the system of industrial relations in Britain is as complex a system as any found in Europe.

Finally, the chapter returns to the theme of responsibility. The difficult questions of at what level and where industrial relations should be handled are posed. They are far more difficult to answer than it may seem.

Table 7.2 lists industrial and social legislation from 1963 to 1980.

7.15 A CASE STUDY IN MANAGEMENT–EMPLOYEE RELATIONS

Introduction

The following study is a description of an industrial dispute at a medium-sized engineering company, and is included to illustrate the kind of misunderstandings that arise out of a change of role without full consultation with all the parties concerned who are affected. It illustrates management's difficulty in dealing with both formal and informal groups and lines of communication in an industrial work situation. The study reflects on issues raised in Chapters 4, 5 and 7.

The objectives are:

1. To discover what breakdowns have occurred in the communication process between management and worker representatives in the particular field cited.
2. To reinforce some of the issues raised in this chapter regarding negotiation and consultation.
3. To evaluate the differing reactions of individuals to the breakdown of channels of communication.

Student Activity

This exercise is essentially a group learning situation. It will therefore be difficult for the reader working alone to derive maximum benefit from it. Nevertheless he can still obtain significant reinforcement of concepts and ideas by thinking through the issues posed.

Specific tasks are:

1. In group discussion, examine the issues which ultimately resulted in the sacking of Ted Noakes.
2. Can you justify the way in which Sid York approached responsibility as a foreman in the organization structure of the company?
3. What frame of reference do you think Don Farmer and Sid York hold? Discuss the evidence for your judgement here. (We appreciate that the case provides limited information but this should not prevent a meaningful discussion.)
4. In what other ways might the problems raised here be resolved? Give an outline of the alternative lines of action with the reasons for this appropriateness.

Carr Engineering Limited: The Situation

The Carr Engineering Company employs 700 staff and labour in a medium-sized heavy engineering works. Until six months ago there was a 'no smoking' rule rigorously carried out both in the offices and the workshops, but then, because he felt too much time was being wasted by office staff smoking in the lavatories, the office manager allowed smoking in the offices at the morning and afternoon tea breaks.

The 'no smoking' rule was still applied in the workshops, but there, too, much time was wasted by men smoking in the lavatories, and according to complaints from some foremen, men were also smoking on the job.

The management representatives raised the matter at the monthly meeting of the JCC with the general manager in the Chair. This incidentally was the first time in the committee's life of over three years that the subject had been raised.

At the committee meeting Ted Noakes, the senior workers' representative, agreed that there probably was a certain waste of time caused by men leaving the job to smoke, and that was wrong, but he added: 'It is a silly rule that just asks to be broken, because there is no reason why the men should not smoke on the job – except of course in places where a fire could start – and, as a matter of fact, the men don't like it that the office people get smoking on the job, and one of these days most of the men will just start smoking and the rule will have to go.'

The general manager's reply was: 'We are not at present discussing whether the rule is a good one or a bad one – it is, however, a condition of employment here that the rule has to be obeyed, and I must remind you that disciplinary action will be taken against any man either smoking on the job or absenting himself from the job for an abnormal period. I shall, however, sound the insurance company out as to their reaction to smoking being permitted on the shop floor.'

The subject was dropped at this stage, but before the works broke up for the annual holiday a few days later a GM circular was sent to all department heads drawing attention to the 'no smoking' rule discussion at the JCC, and before the works resumed after the holidays fresh 'no smoking' notices were posted.

Work resumed at 8 a.m., and at 8.30 Ted Noakes, while still at his machine, was seen to light up and smoke a cigarette. Immediately Sid York, the machine shop foreman, seeing this went up to Noakes and said, 'So you want to make trouble? Well, you can have it; you're sacked.'

Noakes refused to take the foreman's note to the works manager advising him of the dismissal and instead left the works, where at 8.55 a.m. he was met by Don Farmer, the works manager, arriving for his normal 9 a.m. start.

Farmer, also a member of the JCC and on reasonably good terms with Noakes, assumed that there must be some domestic reason for Noakes leaving the works, and since it was raining he said, 'Hello Ted, is there anything wrong at home? Can I run you there?'

Noakes blew up at this and, after abusing Farmer, the company and York, said, 'I've been sacked. I was hardly back on the job when I absentmindedly lit a cigarette, and York pounced on me, and now I am going home and then I will go up to raise hell about it with the union.'

7.16   A CASE STUDY IN PERSONNEL MANAGEMENT, TRAINING AND INDUSTRIAL RELATIONS

Introduction

This case study introduces the reader to three possible problem areas. The first concerns management-labour bargaining arrangements; the second recruitment practices; and the third relates to training. The study is included to illustrate the interdisciplinary nature of many business organization problems. It should also serve to reinforce many points discussed in Chapters 6 and 7, and also calls upon the reader to reflect on the issues raised in Chapter 1.

The objectives are:

1. To identify the essential features of the bargaining model described in the study.
2. To examine the deficiencies of the model in the light of the readings in Chapter 7.
3. To examine the concept of the closed shop and its appropriateness to the given situation.
4. To evaluate the introduction of a productivity agreement.
5. To analyse the approach to selection and training and to highlight deficiencies in the light of readings in Chapter 6.

Student Tasks

The study is best performed as a group discussion activity. The major points raised during the discussion should be recorded. For maximum effectiveness ensure that the group has a leader or chairman.

1. Sketch the bargaining model used to settle wage and salary levels in Ruddiman Electronics.
2. Identify the weaknesses in the model being used. Suggest alternative models which are likely to be both more acceptable and more effective.
3. Discuss the nature of the goals being pursued by management and by the unions. Is there a basis for compromise?
4. Evaluate the view Fred Jones has regarding productivity agreements.
5. Discuss the organization's approach to recruitment and selection. In what ways might the present practices be deficient?
6. Discuss the idea of the introduction of a closed shop. What problems are likely to arise if a closed shop agreement was introduced? What benefits could accrue?
7. Recommend ways of reducing the high level of labour turnover amongst the women assembly workers.

Ruddiman Electronics

Ruddiman Electronics is a company engaged in the manufacture of small-scale electronic equipment. It employs a total of about 600 people on a single day shift commencing at 8.00 a.m. and terminating at 5.00 p.m., with a one-hour lunch break from 12.00–1.00 p.m. Overtime is not usually worked either at the end of a normal working day, or at weekends. About 100 of the total number employed are white-collar workers, line managers and supervisors. Of the remainder, about one-quarter are women assembly workers, working on the assembly-line work station principle. The rest are skilled machine operators, setters, technicians, work study engineers, internal transport workers, etc., with a few research and development employees. The weekly output target is 10 000 units.

The firm is non-federated and pay rates are, if anything, a little behind those paid generally in the area for broadly similar categories of work.

There is a high degree of union membership (about 80 per cent) amongst the male shopfloor workers, and about the same proportion of the office staff are also unionized. Some of the lower and middle managers are also union members. The vast majority of union members are members of either the Amalgamated Union of Engineering Workers (AUEW) or Technical and Supervisory Staffs (TASS); a few white-collar workers are members of the Association of Scientific, Technical and Managerial Staffs (ASTMS). The company has granted recognition rights to the AUEW and to TASS, but not to ASTMS. ASTMS is currently demanding recognition and AUEW and TASS are pushing for a closed shop agreement. Both AUEW and TASS are attempting to strengthen their position by membership drives.

Fred Jones, the works manager, has, for the last three months or so, been complaining to Arthur Webster, the training officer, about the poor quality of the work being turned out by the women assembly workers. He says that the quantity of reworking is increasing almost weekly, resulting in lower production, lower productivity and disgruntled workers. Jones estimates that total production over the last three months is down by about 10 per cent.

Jones is also convinced that the rate of labour turnover amongst the women assembly workers is too high at an annual rate of almost 80 per cent but, at the same time, he recognizes that the work is tedious and repetitive. He questions the 'sitting next to Nellie' method of training, but Webster reiterates that it has always proved satisfactory in the past and, in any case, there is a ready pool of female labour available in the area. When asked about selection procedures for female labour, Webster said these were 'simple' and comprised just a face-to-face interview between the job applicant and a member of the personnel officer's staff. On the basis of this interview and the interviewer's recommendation, the applicant was accepted or rejected. Only occasionally was the immediate section supervisor called in. Asked if any job analysis was carried out, Webster replied in the negative.

This month (June) all employees, including staff, are due for a wages/salary review. The shop stewards of the two main unions are well organized on a plant basis, and the firm negotiates freely with them. Early in May the stewards presented a claim to management for a substantial increase in basic rates, and an additional week's holiday. When asked to state what was meant by substantial the stewards' spokesman declined to quantify the demand. The company indicated that, until the size of the claim was known, it could make no offer, and the meeting came to an end. A week later, the stewards asked management to meet them again. Their spokesman indicated that they were seeking an increase of 'at least 15 per cent on basic rates'. Negotiations are continuing, and the trade union side has indicated its interest in a possible productivity deal.

On hearing about the union's proposal for a productivity agreement, Eric Kirby, the production manager, declares his interest and comes down firmly in its favour. Consequently, he pressurizes Fred Jones, whom he knows to be sceptical of such an agreement, but Jones refuses to budge. Jones who, along with Janet Graham (the personnel manager) and the managing director, is a member of the management negotiating team, believes that improvements in other areas, such as those he discussed with Webster, are more important. At the same time, he does not entirely rule out the possibility of an incentive element in the make up of the pay packet of the shopfloor workers some time in the future. Jones' feelings on the matter are supported by his line managers.

Janet Graham has overall responsibility for training within the company, although she tends to interfere very little in the way that Arthur Webster carries out his job as training officer. Webster is a great believer in joint consultation and he has done much to ensure its development and success at Ruddiman Electronics. Many problems relating to methods of working, payment systems, health and safety, etc., have been discussed and solved via joint consultation. A member of ASTMS sits on the joint consultation body, but not in a union capacity. However, he is not able to take part in any negotiations which may follow as a result of decisions reached in joint consultation.

Further Reading

1. Atkinson, A. B. (1975) *The Economics of Inequality*. Oxford: Oxford University Press.
2. Batstone, E., Boraston, I. and Frenkel, S. (1978) *The Social Organisation of Strikes*. Oxford: Blackwell.
3. Clark, R. O., Fatchett, D. J. and Roberts, B. C. (1972) *Workers' Participation in Management*. London: Heinemann.
4. Coates, T. and Topham, T. (1980) *Trade Unions in Britain*. London: Spokesman.
5. Crouch, C. (1979) *The Politics of Industrial Relations*. London: Fontana.
6. Friedman, A. (1977) *Industry and Labour: Class Struggle at Work and Monopoly Capitalism*. London: Macmillan.
7. Hawkins, K. (1978) *The Management of Industrial Relations*. Harmondsworth: Penguin.
8. Hyman, R. (1977) *Strikes*. London: Fontana.
9. Keenan, D. (1979) *Principles of Employment Law*. London: Anderson Keenan.
10. Navarro, V. (1978) *Class Struggle, The State and Medicine*. Oxford: Martin Robertson.
11. Panitch, L. (1976) *Social Democracy and Industrial Militancy*. Cambridge: Cambridge University Press.
12. Rogaly, J. (1977) *Grunwick*. London: Allen Lane.
13. Wright, M. (1979) *Labour Law* (2nd edition). Plymouth: Macdonald & Evans.

8

Organizations: Decision Making, Planning and Change

GENERAL OBJECTIVES

After reading and discussing the material contained in this chapter, students should be able to analyse the decision-making activity. In addition, they should be able to relate the process of decision making to the role of business management. Students will be introduced to the causes, dimensions and consequences of organizational change.

LEARNING OBJECTIVES

The learning objective outcomes will depend on the range of activities the reader has the facility to experience in addition to reading this text, but at very least students should be able to:

1. List the key stages in the decision-making process.
2. Explain the need to set precise objectives; define information needs; and analyse and evaluate information systematically.
3. Predict probable outcomes from particular decisions taken.
4. Understand the implications of employee participation through such mechanisms as joint consultation and collective bargaining on the decision-making activity.

8.1 INTRODUCTION

By now the reader will have discovered that the business activity is complex, needing the services of capable and highly-skilled people. In the early chapters of the book it was shown that a constant object was, and is, the search for efficiency. The term efficiency has meant some relationship between the output and input of an organization, unit or department. Much effort has been devoted to improving the ratio of output to input through such measures as productivity agreements. The problem is that the search for efficiency in these terms constantly meets with problems of, in many cases, actually measuring inputs and outputs and, more importantly, ascribing a positive causal relationship between them. In addition there is the added problem of comparing the efficiencies of different operations within an organization, for example, comparing a bottling plant with an accounts department. In this case, perhaps the most significant problem is associated with the difficulty of assessing the contributions made by different units within an organization to the overall goals of the organization. In other words, we can introduce a slightly different concept, the search for effectiveness in terms of the degree of contribution towards stated objectives made by individuals, departments and the organization as a whole. In most instances the contribution is assessed in cost/benefit terms.

Such an approach relies on the identification of clear, realistic and measurable objectives for the organization. It also assumes that all individuals are either working towards them, or being directed towards them through effective leadership. It is in these terms that we can examine the issue of business decision making. In this sense we shall examine the process by which individuals employed within organizations make decisions which affect the contribution to organizational effectiveness.

8.2   THE DECISION PROCESS

The reader is advised momentarily to forget that he or she is reading a book about organizations and to devote a few moments to a short exercise in self-analysis.

1.   Identify several decision points you made in your own time on the very day you read this page. For example, what decisions did you take this morning regarding such issues as what to have for breakfast, what time to leave the house, what clothes to wear, etc.?
2.   Write down all the issues which you consider were relevant to the decisions made. For example, in the case of breakfast, factors would include what food there was; what time was available; what preparation time the food required; whether its preparation could be done while you did something else; and what your general appetite was like.
3.   Identify the stages you went through in actually reaching your final actions.
4.   Develop a simple model to illustrate the process. Keep this model by your side while we now analyse the decision-making activity.

The first conclusion your simple self-analysis exercise might have drawn is that the decision-making activity is basically a choice activity. To make a decision is to make a choice between alternative courses of action – whether to have cereal and toast, rather than bacon and eggs, or to wear a suit, rather than jeans and a T-shirt. The second conclusion may be that the choice depends upon an assessment of the merits and demerits of each alternative. This is where the list of issues you identified should be valuable. Look down the list and identify issues which were associated with the process of assessing the merits and demerits of the alternatives open to you. You will quickly realize that your decisions depended on your assessment of the outcome of the choice you made, in other words, it is likely you made decisions which were calculated to produce the best results in the prevailing circumstances. This assessment was limited by the information available to you. For example in the case of breakfast, if you were not aware of the full range of foods available, your choice would be limited to that which you know is certain to be there.

It is at this stage we begin to realize that the assessment of the choices available to us is limited by the available information we have relating to each choice. Even in the case of the very simple examples we have used so far it is clear that basic domestic and personal decisions depend upon a whole range of information relating to the alternative courses of action open to us. Try the same exercise in relation to, say, the choice of a holiday. If you have the opportunity of doing this with a group of colleagues, so much the better. In carrying out this exercise try a more structured approach, something on the lines of the following:

1. Identify the function(s) you wish a holiday to fulfil.
2. Identify the essential features you require in a holiday, for example, weather, cultural factors, geographical issues, accommodation, travel, cost, etc.
3. Assess your current situation, for example, your financial state, time available, holiday entitlement, etc.
4. Define your objectives clearly. State quite clearly the essential characteristics you require a holiday to fulfil.
5. Identify the ways in which you can meet the objectives, that is the alternative courses of action open to you.
6. List your information needs.
7. Determine a basic system by which you would go about assessing and evaluating the alternatives.

This exercise will have shown clearly the complexity of a process many of us take more or less for granted. The important realization is the fact that we can identify the same key stages in this more complex process as in the case of the breakfast menu decision, namely that there is a choice activity; the identification and evaluation of the alternatives available for us to choose from; and the crucial dependency on accurate and appropriate information. The exercise has also introduced two more and very crucial key stages: the need to clarify and state objectives, and the need to ensure that information is both accurate and appropriate.

If we now take the holiday example a stage further we realize that the total process does not finish at point 7, as at this point we have still not taken the holiday, but merely decided on what we intend to do. Let us follow it through:

8. Make all the arrangements for the holiday, that is, list all the types of action you would take (this might include identifying alternatives should something go wrong).
9. Take the holiday.
10. Return from the holiday and reflect on what happened.

We are now beginning to see, perhaps, the full cycle of events, and can add two further key stages in the process, namely, actually making the decision to select a first choice and, finally, the need to evaluate what actually happened.

From this example you should be able to develop a simple model which identifies the key stages in the decision-making process.

The Key Stages in the Decision-making Process

The model you have probably come up with is likely to be very similar to ours:

1. Recognizing and defining decision issues: the setting and defining of objectives.
2. Information collection: gathering of appropriate data, ensuring data are accurate and relevant.

3. Assessing all the issues associated with the objectives, i.e. in the case of problems, trying to determine their causes.
4. Generation of optional solutions.
5. Selection of the most appropriate solution, i.e. the best in the prevailing circumstances.
6. Implementation of the decision.
7. Evaluation of actual results.

Let us look at these stages more fully.

Setting and Defining Objectives

The setting and defining of objectives is a crucial process but, as we have already seen in the first three chapters, it is a most difficult process. It depends essentially on asking the right basic questions. For example, in the case of problem analysis, the essential feature is to make sure that the problem really is a problem, and not just a symptom of something else. Making decisions to cure symptoms is a fairly unproductive exercise: it's a bit like the medical analogy of someone taking pain relief tablets when what is required is an operation.

In the business situation many decisions are made over and over again to solve problems which are very similar and which keep on arising. This should be the first indication to management that they have not clearly understood the problem, and therefore not researched it fully and so inadequately defined the decision objectives. Frequency of problem recurrence suggests one of two things; either the matter is a basic repetitive issue, or it is a problem which previous decisions have failed to solve.

The Gestalt School (Drucker, Wertheimer, Durbin and Thomson) based their approach to the decision-making activity on the basic premise that a solution is generated in the process of reformulation of the problem. On the basis of this premise an approach to decision making would be to examine all possible solutions, and taking each one in turn and testing it for functionality and practicality. In this way the problem is redefined in terms of the proposed solution or, in other words, respecified in terms of each solution. The solution which most nearly answered the problems raised in the definition, on the basis of rational analysis, would be the decision to make. The weakness with this approach is that truly rational problem solving situations are extremely rare.

In relation to the issue of problem definition Durbin suggests four conditions for the successful process of decision making:

1. A fund of previous experience which would facilitate insights into the nature of the issues being faced.
2. A genuine positive motivation to want to face up to the issue/problem.
3. A thorough grasp of the concepts implied in the way the problem is stated. This grasp can be achieved by a process of problem restatement, questioning what each statement and term means, and what techniques are to be employed.
4. Exploration, including physical movement, trial and error, creativity (brainstorming), working out and discussing alternatives, etc.

Bloom and Broder (*Problem Solving Processes of College Students* (1950)) suggested a method of classifying problems by difficulty, format (i.e., by method of presentation), subject, and by optimum methods of solution. This classification can in many ways assist in the process of clear problem/objective definition. Try it out with whatever modifications you feel appropriate to the holiday issue we have already examined.

Whatever the weaknesses in approach, the business organization employs people in posts which are fundamentally decision-making roles. The reality of the situation is that they have to find an approach to problem identification and definition which is both workable and effective. Again we are back to the search for rationality and effectiveness. The reader will find many authors who have written convincing critiques of the rationality approach. Nevertheless, at this point the most helpful to the student of business, in our opinion, is the one based on rationale problem analysis and definition.

In the search for the root of the problem – the attempt to prevent the fruitless process of treating symptoms – we need a technique which is likely to lead to accurate problem definition. We have not come across a simpler, more effective system than the *trigger method*. This is the system:

1. Define the problem/issue/objective in the first instance. This will involve searching for problems, as it is the responsibility of management to anticipate issues even before they arise.
2. Ask the question 'What triggered the situation we have defined?' If we can obtain an answer, redefine the problem.
3. Repeat the process and again redefine the problem.
4. Repeat the process again and again until it is impossible to obtain an answer to the question. At this point it is most likely that we shall be defining the *root* of the problem.

Try the trigger method in any problem you would like to define. Try it as a group. Try a real problem you have been facing at work or college.

As a general rule remember objectives are about ends not means; goals and not activities; and that most of the real problems organizations face are not just simple situations with a single clear cause and a well-defined effect. Often the problem we start with turns out to be a whole cluster of separate sub-problems, each of which has to be worked out separately.

8.3 EXERCISES FOR GROUP DISCUSSION

Students reading this book should at this point form a study group and discuss the following as statements of objectives. The groups should assess these statements in terms of their usefulness as decision objectives.

1. Company Production Manager

'I am now asking all my work force to work 8 per cent harder.'

2. Group Chief Executive

'I shall be judging the performance of the various factories in the group by their ability to meet financial targets in terms of £ spent.'

3. Personnel Manager

'The General Manager is due to retire in two years' time. We should advertise now for his replacement. I would like an opportunity to discuss with the Board the job description and specification with a view to placing an advertisement within the next two months. Our aim should be to recruit a successor in sufficient time to allow a full year's changeover, thereby minimizing the possible detrimental effects on the company's effectiveness as measured in terms of profitability.'

You will certainly have reached different conclusions about the value of each as a definition of objectives. The important message that should have been generated by your discussions is that objectives in relation to business decision making should ideally stress the need for action; specify the criteria for selection of the best course of action; define the responsibility for achieving results; and state the standards against which the results can be measured.

8.4   INFORMATION COLLECTION

We have already seen that information is the life blood of the decision-making activity. Information provides us with the very basic ingredient necessary to be able to assess and evaluate the courses of action available to us. What do we know about information?

The first point is that information is not data. Data are sources of facts, figures, ideas and theories, that is, all recorded sources of material. Information is data which have been selected as being relevant to a specific issue. Thus data about the history and life of Oliver Cromwell would not be regarded as information in relation to the problem of whether or not to recruit the new General Manager one year before the existing General Manager retires. In this example I have demonstrated a very clear difference between data and information. In reality the distinction is nothing like so clear. Masses of data flow continuously around and through a business organization. The problem and skill are in identifying that which is relevant, useful, and in some cases, vital, information and that which is superfluous. It is an even greater problem when managers use the superfluous believing it to be information!

The second point is that information kills variety. What this means is that if we can imagine a decision situation in relation to which we have no information at all, the variety of choices of action available to us is almost limitless – we can try anything. A small piece of information limits the variety of choices to an area of action which has more relevance to the problem in hand. The more information we obtain the more we limit the field of choice, we kill off the superfluous variety.

The third point is that information must be accurate. Gossip can be information but it can be dangerously inaccurate. We must attempt to differentiate between fact and opinion, theory and law, objectivity and subjectivity, and so on. We must also be aware of such issues as differences in perception and in value bases, for example, in political, moral, religious and cultural values. This area is so complex it is worthy of a separate book in its own right, and students are recommended to read the collection of writings in *Decisions, Organisations and Society* (1971) Castles, Murray and Potter (eds.), Open University, to obtain some insights into these issues.

The final point is that information must be sufficiently relevant and plentiful to be able to identify the whole system within which the problem/issue is situated. For example, in the very basic example of the breakfast decision it is obvious that we cannot

understand the whole process by looking at the food/hunger system alone. The information needs must take into account all the sub-systems relating to the total early morning
routine from the time of actually waking to the time of leaving the house. Similarly, in
the context of the more complex issues within business organizations, we need sufficient
information for us to be able to assess the limits of the systems' boundaries in any particular situation. In this way information can be used to assess inputs and outputs of the
system and each of its sub-systems. The form of these inputs and outputs is not always
tangible and quantifiable, but includes social forces, psychological factors, economic
and political influences and market forces. The system in question may therefore be
technical, biological or social.

This need to have sufficient information to view the decision issue in its systems context is demonstrated diagrammatically in Fig. 8.1.

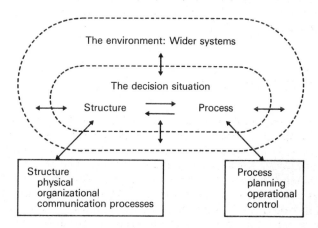

Figure 8.1   *The decision-making process shown in a structural and process sense*

Fig. 8.1 illustrates the need to view the decision situation both as a structure and as a
process. Structurally what does the decision relate to? Who is making it? In what organizational setting (refer to Chapter 2)? And what are the communications channels? In
the process dimension, to what function does the decision relate – the planning function, the operational function, or the control function?

The next issue is where does the information come from and how do we assess it?
This is an enormously important and very complex issue, with wide ramifications. In a
sense the whole of a business course is primarily concerned with this issue. We are concerned with such information areas as: market, product, research and development,
people, financial, legal, and environmental. We are also concerned with how to store
data – files, ledgers, books, computer tapes and discs, microfilm, etc. – then how to index
the data for easy identification, access and use as and when required. Information processing is a major area of concern to today's managers and is developing into a major
growth industry in the sense of providing information processing aids. The crucial skill
is identifying what information is needed and where to get it. Eisenstadt (*Problem
Solving*, Open University, D303, Unit 24) has shown that many of the insights referred
to by Durbin of the Gestalt School can now be obtained by computers, for example,
pattern recognition, data relevance, etc.

Try the following exercises in identifying information needs for yourself; again, we
would suggest that you will achieve the best results as a group exercise in each case.

1. Imagine that you are the owner of a small company which has been doing quite well, sufficiently well to encourage you to contemplate further developments. Your problem is to know whether or not to branch out into a new product area.

    The Task: Identify and list the type of information you will need both from inside and outside the company in order for you to reach a decision.

2. What questions do the following statements raise? (i) Prices jumped by another 1.8 per cent last month. (ii) Senior managers are five times as likely to die in post as shop floor workers. (iii) Labour turnover in the pottery industry is on average 25 per cent greater amongst females than males.

The discussion of the questions will probably lead you to conclude that in all cases there are many unanswered issues. What is needed is a systematic and logical approach to information collection. We would recommend the following checklist approach:

1. Who or what is involved? (Object/task/person.)
2. What is wrong? (An assessment of the size/scope/severity of the problem.)
3. When does/did the problem occur? When did it first occur?
4. Where does it occur?
5. How does it occur?
6. Why does it occur?

When obtaining information which helps to answer these questions remember the four essential qualifications which information must fulfil: quantity, quality, reliability and accuracy.

8.5 ASSESSING ALL THE ISSUES ASSOCIATED WITH THE OBJECTIVES

All students of business should be aware of the trap nearly all business decision makers fall into at some time during their careers, that of jumping to a conclusion too quickly. For example, in a particular decision-making situation where a specific problem is being tackled, always double check the problem definition you have decided upon by asking a very simple question: If what I think is the cause of the problem really is the actual cause, how does it explain all the information in the problem analysis?

This problem relates very much to the issue of setting decision objectives or problem definition. It is in the very act of jumping to conclusions too quickly that we end up solving or attempting to solve symptoms rather than getting to the root of problems.

The second important consideration is change. Nothing stands still, and the rate of change is increasing. Therefore there is a constant need to reassess what we are doing or attempting to do, in order to ensure that we are not devoting our energies to an already redundant situation. The important issue is to be constantly aware of the possibility of the existence of a variety of causes in relation to any given situation and that any decision taken should take account of them all.

8.6 GENERATION OF OPTIONAL SOLUTIONS

The problem with the system of education and training that most of us go through is that it trains us well for the process of analytical thinking, but at the same time it destroys the

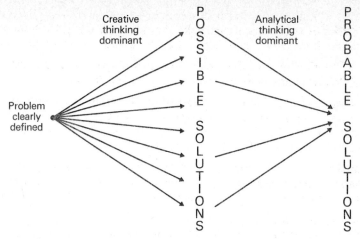

Figure 8.2 *Comparison of creative and analytical thinking*

creativity we need to solve problems, develop new ideas, or simply respond to changed circumstances. Let us look at the difference between the two, which is shown diagrammatically in Fig. 8.2.

Creative Thinking

Creative thinking is divergent, that is, it is concerned with the generation of lots of ideas, even random ones. It is a freedom in thinking unshackled by what has gone on before. It is concerned with volume and not quality of ideas. It is concerned with producing the wild ideas that would be lost if we immediately carried out the form of evaluation many of us have been trained to apply. It is concerned with shaking off the conditioning of socialization in a hierarchical system, for example, the psychological barriers most of us feel, such as the fear of looking a fool, or suggesting something that a colleague may consider silly. In many ways we should think of creative thinking as being a bit like dreaming, for in dreams the mind roams freely from issue to issue with strange and wild developments. In creative thinking, therefore, we are concerned with breaking through the barriers of conditioning, and it depends on:

1. Mental freewheeling.
2. Group work. The cross-fertilization of ideas which occurs when group members develop the ideas of each other.
3. Not evaluating too quickly. Avoiding the temptation of saying, 'That's silly,' or 'That won't do'.
4. Challenging accepted ideas and practices.

Analytical Thinking

Analytical thinking is the very opposite of creative thinking. It is convergent, that is, it is concerned with determining which ideas are workable and which are not. It is concerned with measurement and evaluation; in other words, with assessing why ideas might fail as solutions to a problem.

Analytical thinking depends on:

1. Accuracy of information,
2. Appropriateness of information,
3. Logical, systematic analysis.
4. Calculation, evaluation and judgement.

8.7   SELECTION OF THE MOST APPROPRIATE SOLUTION

This is essentially an analytical process. The first task is to examine all the ideas to see if they are sufficiently similar to be combined into a composite idea. Once this has been done the task is to examine the ideas generated against the vital tests of possibility, workability, probability and applicability. In some ways the ideas of Drucker of the Gestalt School are the most helpful here; that is, to redefine the problem in a variety of ways and compare each definition with the possible solutions that have been generated during the creative thinking stage, and select the ideas which, on this basis, appear to be the most probable.

The task facing business decision makers is then to subject these more probable ideas to a more stringent analysis. What we are trying to do is to assess why the probable ideas might, if applied, fail to provide the solution or outcome aimed for. Each idea should be fully analysed against, for example, cost, technical implications, legal considerations, political factors, resource considerations, and environment factors.

8.8   EXECUTING THE DECISION

The next stage is concerned with executing the decision made, that is, seeing that it is implemented. It is at this point many readers will realize that the process of decision making is inseparable from the process of management. The process of management is concerned with seeing that the objectives of the formal organization are met; in other words, getting things done by and through others.

Many people have written about the process of management and most agree that it can be described in the following way.

The Process of Management (Fig. 8.3)

Creativity

Creativity is the ability to develop new ideas, to sponsor innovation, to identify and cope with change, and in general the ability to shake off the shackles of conditioning which so often leads to the failure of many organizations. The need for creativity is

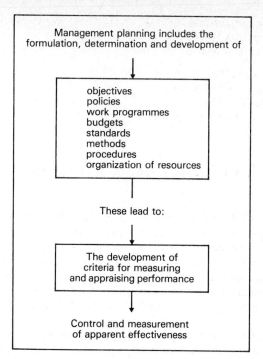

Figure 8.3 *The process of management*

perhaps best illustrated by the very process of evolution itself. Those species which were unable to change, adapt and develop were the ones which became extinct. Organizations can behave in a similar way if they pursue out-of-date objectives or practices.

Planning

Just as a ship needs a direction and destination, so work organizations need plans in order to have a co-ordinated effort put towards the achievement of objectives. As planning deals with the future, there is always, as a consequence, uncertainty. Plans are a means to an end in that they indicate the direction in which the organization intends to go, remembering that in part the future is of its own making.

The process of planning is clearly linked with innovation and change. It is concerned with:

1. the anticipation and identification of problems,
2. a thorough analysis of problems,
3. establishing and defining both short- and long-term targets,
4. identifying and organizing the resources needed to accomplish the targets, and
5. developing contingency plans should the first choice route fail in any way.

It is through the planning activity that management is able to stand back and view the organization as a whole, and the direction it is taking. It helps to ensure the co-ordination of all the people and activities of which the work organization is comprised, rather than the whole process being haphazard. Perhaps most importantly it provides the organization with a basis for *control*. Control is exercised by comparing the actual results and activities against those which were planned in advance. It is in the process of analysing the variances between planned and actual results that we can understand the nature of the various forces that are constantly in interplay in organizations. As a result, the planning activity permits a rational approach to the co-ordination of all resources and efforts. Finally, planning must provide a basis for flexibility. Nothing is certain, nothing stands still and whatever plans are made they need to be able to adjust to change.

It is important not to confuse planning with dreaming. Dreaming is associated with the divergent creative thinking process. Planning, on the other hand, is associated with the convergent analytical thinking process. Planning is the first stage in the execution of decisions that have been taken, and therefore should be a realistic process, reflecting the strengths and weaknesses of the existing organization.

Objectives are, in a sense, also plans in that they represent what we are setting out to achieve, but they are not plans until we have evaluated the possibility and the method of their being achieved.

Organizing

The management task of organization is concerned with the process of assigning work to prescribed tasks and sets of tasks. There are various theoretical and custom and practice methods of doing this as we have seen in Chapters 2 and 3. Essentially, it is concerned with having a clearly defined strategy and approach to the allocation of resources, including the human resource.

In the search for effectiveness many people believe that organizing depends on:

1. Having a detailed knowledge of the skills, abilities and aptitudes of the individuals employed by the organization. This is where the personnel function of management plays one of its important roles.
2. Having the right physical resources to do the work. By right we mean resources designed and developed to supply the function needed. This is not as obvious as it might at first sight seem because of the change process. So often circumstances overtake the organization, making some processes, equipment and buildings inappropriate to changed requirements. It is here that the research and development activity, the technical department, including production, the marketing activity and the financial operations all converge in an attempt to ensure an investment and development programme designed to provide the right physical resources to do the work.
3. Effective communications channels. Communication is perhaps the single biggest problem in the search for effectiveness. It is remarkably difficult to design a communications network which ensures that all individuals receive the information they need in order to perform their duties. In addition, the problem is further complicated by the difficulties associated with personal skills of communication, with interpersonal skills and with the use of communication aids. Perhaps one of the most significant characteristics of this century has been the growth of what has been described as the communications industry.
4. Ensuring that people are allocated to work roles which maximize the contribution they can make using their experience, skills and knowledge. (See Chapter 4, in particular.) The human resource is the most complex of all the resources used by the organization. It is in people management that many organizations find the greatest difficulty.

5.   The delegation of authority and responsibility. The authority and responsibility for achieving the organization's objectives need to be shared amongst many job roles in the organization. In this way it is possible to ensure that the work load of any individual is comfortably within his scope, whilst at the same time building job interest into subordinate roles.

Motivation

The implementation of any decision rests very largely on the willingness of people to take their part in the activities required. We must constantly remember that in the majority of organizations it is the people occupying management roles who determine the formal objectives and also the definition of the term effectiveness. As we have seen in Chapter 1, this is a very limited view. Nevertheless, it is the view most readers will experience in the organizations in which they are employed. It is therefore clear that such an approach relies on two fundamental issues: first, the ability of management to communicate clearly the meaning and implications of decisions made to all the other people employed by the organization; and secondly, the extent to which management can gain the support of employees in implementing the decisions.

The term motivation relates primarily to the latter. We are concerned here with understanding the process by which people occupying certain job roles within an organizational hierarchy can inspire the willing co-operation of people occupying subordinate job roles. Perhaps John Humble over-simplified the process when he suggested that most employees will respond positively if the organization clearly defines what is required of each individual, regular feedback is given to employees telling them how they are getting on, and guidance and direction are given when required.

This approach may be simple, but it does summarize much of the findings of research into human behaviour at work. It perhaps misses the need for greater involvement in organizational affairs, which many, but not all, employees would both like and positively respond to, and the need to relate the job tasks to the skills and abilities possessed by each individual. These two points remind us of the problems which result from the classical approach to organizational design (See Chapter 2.)

Control

The final stage in the decision-making process is also the final element of our definition of the management activity. Here we are talking about control, that is, the evaluation of the outcomes which have resulted from the implementation of the decisions. It is at this stage that we see an attempt at measuring the effectiveness of individuals and departments in terms of the contribution made towards the achievement of stated objectives.

In simple terms the evaluation is a comparison between intended and actual outcomes. It is the very basis of such techniques as budgetary control. A budget is planned projection of expenditure. This expenditure is derived from the planned activities of the organization which have been designed to meet defined objectives. With the progression of time we reach dates which correspond with checkpoints built into the plans. For example, the budget might say that by week 20 the expenditure in relation to a certain activity should have been £X, but in fact was £Y. What we need to do here is to investigate what caused the difference by tracing all the other organizational activities to week 20. Some of the variance might be accountable for in terms of labour or material costs changing at a different rate from that anticipated. On the other hand, the variance might have resulted from high wastage, or labour disputes, or simply inaccurate calculation.

Whatever the reasons, we can, over a period of time, begin to build up data banks which allow the decision-making process to be more predictable in terms of outcomes. Again, there are several important facets always to bear in mind. First, any attempt at assessing effectiveness will be limited to the decision framework with which we are concerned. In other words, the decision framework will predict and prescribe in many ways the evaluation process undertaken. Therefore, since decision issues and processes vary, so the criteria used for the evaluation of effectiveness will also vary. Some criteria will be common to a number of decision issues, and some will be unique to a particular situation or process.

The essential characteristic of this approach to evaluation is that it is a *goal–result* analysis. The basic weakness of the approach is that it doesn't, to any significant extent, concentrate on goal evaluation in the first instance. As we have seen in Chapter 1, goal evaluation is a highly complex topic, and a significant factor is how many people share and associate with the stated goals. If the goal is shared by only a minority, many questions are raised concerning the measurement of effectiveness.

8.9   COMPLEX DECISIONS

In the case of simple decisions it is possible to state the aim clearly, identify the choices of action open, collect most of, if not all, the information needed relatively easily, and predict the outcome with a high degree of certainty. These characteristics will fit many domestic decisions, as well as many organizational ones. If we concentrate on the organizational level, we should be able to identify in most job roles decisions where these characteristics are clearly evident, for example, the recurring decisions taken by a machine operative as he performs the work cycle over and over again, or the decision taken by an accounts office clerk regarding filing, the transfer of information, or postal systems, and so on.

But many decision situations do not correspond with these characteristics at all. In fact, there exists a spectrum of distribution of complex decision situations where some may be an exact opposite of all the characteristics we have described for simple decisions.

Characteristics of Complex Decisions

1.   Conflicting aims,
2.   Many possible choices (decision alternatives),
3.   Information needs and sources difficult to identify,
4.   Information supply inadequate and difficult to assess,
5.   Information range wide, requiring considerable knowledge and information-handling ability,
6.   A certain element of risk in relation to the outcome,
7.   In the most complex situations a predominantly uncertain outcome.

It is because of these characteristics of complex decisions that C. E. Lindblom (*The Policy-Making Process* (1968), Prentice-Hall) is critical of the rational approach to the decision activity described in this chapter. He points out that in extreme examples decision makers are not presented with defined problems, but have to identify and formulate the problems as *they* see them. For example, if we consider Northern Ireland, is the problem one of maintaining law and order, or of religious intolerance, political sovereignty, low income and high unemployment, incipient revolution, or what? Similarly, was the rioting evident in England in 1981 simply a basic problem of riot control, or were the riots symptomatic of other, deeper-based problems which really have to be solved?

It is clear that in setting out to define these highly complex situations we may end up by defining a series of problems many of which are directly competing and contradict each other.

Secondly, not all complex problems are analogous to ill-health, that is, problems to be cured, but are more in the nature of developing and realizing opportunities. The process only becomes a problem to be cured when we set in motion the development of a technology or a system by which the opportunity can be realized.

Thirdly, there is the problem of information handling. Modern decision situations are now so complex that the data available as information are colossal and technically complex. Lindblom argues that the volume and technical complexity are so great that no decision maker could consider it in the rational way suggested here. This may very well be true, but again we would argue that the practising manager needs a system, inadequate though it may be, to prevent the decision-making activity becoming nothing more than a haphazard process. Therefore, we would argue that the rational approach should be adopted whilst remembering the significant limitations identified by writers like Lindblom.

Risk and Uncertainty

What is the difference between risk and uncertainty? Risk refers to the state of affairs where the decision maker can predict a range of possible outcomes, but cannot guarantee which outcome will actually occur. He may be able to assess that certain outcomes are more likely than others, and can calculate this as a probability. This can be illustrated in a very simple example.

You have a valuable antique porcelain figure which you decide to sell. The decision you have to make is whether to sell to a private dealer or put it up for auction. You seek advice from the most reputable sources at your disposal. From the information you obtain you are absolutely certain that no matter which route you choose the figure is bound to sell. What you do ascertain is that the price you can expect to get could vary considerably. You calculate that the price a dealer will give is £800. On the other hand, you have been advised by an expert that at auction it could make £1500, but there is a possibility of as little as £500. Your expert suggests that there is an 80 per cent chance of the £1500 and 20 per cent chance of only the £500 at auction.

To help in making the decision we can use simple probability analysis, as shown in Fig. 8.4. On the basis of the analysis of this very simple example it is likely that you will decide to take the risk and sell the figure at auction.

In the case of uncertainty we have little or no idea about the possible outcomes, and

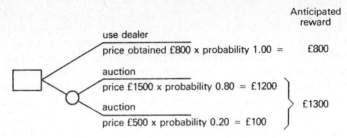

Figure 8.4 *Probability analysis for decision making*

cannot assign a probability to the occurrence of an event. This lack of predictability may result from a variety of reasons, such as lack of information or the novelty of the situation, that is, a similar decision may not have been made before. In such situations we tend to make the decision 'blind', and the best we can do is to manipulate the inputs of a system in the anticipation of an acceptable outcome. Uncertainty ranges between total ignorance and risk (but does not include risk itself).

8.10 PROGRAMMABLE VERSUS NON-PROGRAMMABLE DECISIONS

The terms programmable and non-programmable are derived from the development of computer systems and terminology, and have largely been developed as an alternative description to simple and complex decisions. In this sense programmable decisions correspond to simple decisions, and non-programmable decisions to complex decisions. In this sense we are identifying the decision-making activities which could wholly or largely be programmed and performed in many instances by a computer. For this to be beneficial, certain characteristics need to be satisfied. They are:

1. relationship to repetitive, routine and definable problems,
2. existence of definite and prescribable procedures,
3. specific, identifiable and accessible information,
4. readily available information.

The value of machine-aided decision making is that we can create more time and energy to apply the organization's manpower resources to the complex or non-programmable decisions, whose characteristics are:

1. Unique and unstructured problems and issues,
2. Precise nature of the problem is both elusive and complex,
3. Information needs are difficult to identify,
4. Information sources are obscure,
5. Information is not readily available,
6. Decision outcomes involve risk or uncertainty.

The distinctions between programmable and non-programmable decisions are important for a number of reasons. First of all in the area of staff training, particularly management staff, it is valuable in looking at how time and resources are utilized. So many people take comfort from looking busy dealing with volumes of paperwork but concentrating on routine decision issues. The objective should be to delegate the routine, to a machine if possible, thus freeing more time to manage the more complex issues. Secondly, it is important in terms of job role design. In designing job roles the nature of the decision-making process should be an important consideration. In this respect thought is given to the communications system and the information needs of the component parts of the system. As we have seen in Chapter 2, considerable attention is being given to the value of understanding and designing organizations on the basis of the pattern of information needs and information flow required by the communication and decision-making processes. Thirdly, the distinctions are important in analysing the efficiency of the various component systems making up an organization. Method study and systems analysis are the more commonplace examples of techniques that have been developed both to analyse what is happening and, more importantly, to develop and institute more simple methods and systems and to identify the most effective role for the people employed in the various job positions.

8.11 GROUP DECISION MAKING

The important issue to realize is that decision making is not an activity pursued only at the management level. Many decisions are made in committees consisting of members drawn from all groups making up the organization. In the public sector, of course, this committee system is widened to include the whole of society. In most organizations today there are a range of decision-making issues where shared decision making is now the norm rather than the exception. To use Fox's categories, we have the personnel decisions which include such issues as wage and salary rate determinations, conditions of working, such as hours, promotion, transfer, and this categorization would also include wider considerations such as health and safety, and welfare issues. The second of Fox's categories concerns the economic decisions, which have two branches, the first of which might be loosely described as the technical area, and the second the business area. It is now fairly common practice for the rank-and-file employee to be represented in decisions concerning methods, organizational arrangements, production decisions and job design. All these issues come within the technical branch. There are also examples, although perhaps less common, of workers' participation in decisions which influence wider aspects of business operations, such as organizational objectives, market policies, finance, and so on.

The extent to which rank-and-file employees actually share in the full process of decision making varies considerably. In some cases employee representatives or spokesmen (usually a union representative such as a shop steward) are consulted before management make a decision. In such cases management is not bound by the views expressed by the employees, but in very few instances would they be totally disregarded. In other cases management make a decision but consult with the workers about the predicted outcomes. In this case workers are involved in decision making about ways of accommodating the outcomes of other decisions. Such consultation may result in aspects of the original decision being altered. Redundancy is a very clear example of such a situation. In a minority of cases workers have a full voting representative on the board of management. In such cases workers have direct involvement in all decisions made by the organization.

In most organizations today the processes by which employees are involved in the decision-making activities of an organization have been formalized. In general there are two basic classifications: joint consultation and collective bargaining.

Joint Consultation

It was in 1917 that the Whitley Committee proposed the setting up of works committees to establish co-operation between employees and employers. The objective of these committees was an improvement in the effectiveness and efficiency of the organization, by providing employees with a platform to express their views regarding operational activities that affected them. Since 1917 joint consultative machinery has existed in various forms. The concept of joint consultation has enjoyed both periods of strong support from government and industry, and periods of decline through a combination of economic circumstances and fundamental disbelief in its value.

The important aspect to note is that joint consultative committees are *not* joint decision-making committees. They provide a platform by which representatives of management can meet with representatives of the work force. Such meetings allow management an opportunity of explaining to the work force what is going on, whilst at the same time representatives of the work force can raise grievances and make suggestions. Management does not bargain with the employee representatives, nor are any joint decisions made. On the other hand, management will usually listen more carefully to the views expressed by the employee representatives and will often give considerable weight to their views in the decision-making process.

The process of joint consultation makes several implicit assumptions. The first is that employers and employees actually share common interests. There would be little point in management explaining its plans to the work force if it thought the work force had no interest in them. Such a belief also suggests that management believes workers will, by and large, share in the same values as themselves, for example, that workers will share in any attempts to increase productivity. The third assumption is that management can retain the right to make the organizational decisions, even against considerable opposition from the employee representatives.

Unless both sides enter into a genuine attempt to make joint consultation effective, it can quickly degenerate into a meaningless activity. In any event, the scope of joint consultation is usually restricted to those issues which are not considered to be within the remit of collective bargaining. Since the scope of collective bargaining is ever-widening, the role of joint consultation tends to be on the decline.

In the early post-Second World War period there was a clear distinction between joint consultation and collective bargaining. Joint consultation was a mechanism which it was hoped would strengthen relationships between management and workers by concentrating on those organizational issues where there was no obvious degree of conflict. The aim was for both parties to meet regularly to discuss common interests, perhaps in a problem-solving manner. Collective bargaining, on the other hand, was developed to cope with those issues that divided the parties, predominant amongst which was pay bargaining. As we have seen since, many more issues are now the concern of the labour force, and as a consequence the role for joint consultation has diminished. It has also diminished for another reason. This is the fact that collective bargaining is a genuine decision-making activity in which employee representatives participate with management in a totally different climate from that of joint consultation.

Collective Bargaining

Collective bargaining is a general term used to embrace the negotiation activity used to settle issues relating to employment. Negotiations take place between representatives of management and the labour force, usually through the trade unions. Such negotiations take place at two levels: the national level (when industry-wide agreements are reached), and at local level (when local variations to the national agreement are determined). Two types of issues are negotiated: substantive issues, where the decision relates to specific employment issues, such as pay rates, hours of work, holiday entitlements, and so on, and procedural issues, where the decision focuses on the methods or procedures to be used in relation to specific issues such as grievance procedures, disciplinary procedures, the frequency of pay bargaining, and so on.

There are two essential differences which distinguish collective bargaining from joint consultation. The first is the basic initiative for the development of the two instruments of participation. Joint consultation stems primarily from a management initiative with the twofold aim of promoting the fullest possible use of employees' experiences and ideas in the efficient running of the organization, and the elimination of unnecessary conflict by giving management and workers the opportunity to understand each other's views and objectives. Collective bargaining, on the other hand, was developed under pressure from the trade unions. The process of bargaining entails a joint responsibility for the decision-making process, whereas in consultation responsibility ultimately rests with management. This second difference basically means that collective bargaining gives employee representatives a great deal more influence than joint consultation.

In many ways the distinction between the two is a good deal more blurred than has been indicated here. First of all, the pace of change is now so great that negotiation and consultation tend to become part of a continuing single process. Secondly, there is the basic psychological problem that employees cannot really be expected to participate in furthering the organization's objectives through joint consultation if there is no guarantee that they can have a share of any benefits that result. Therefore, there is a continuing need for a mechanism for the work force to be able to negotiate as and when the need arises.

Collective bargaining need not be a formula for continual warfare between management and unions. There is considerable evidence to show that in large part the process results in peaceful compromises being reached where the agreements made are both accepted and honoured by both parties. On the other hand, the bargaining process has not always developed with 'open, high-trust, problem solving relationships' (Fox).

There is almost always an atmosphere of distrust which prevents the open, frank and objective approach to decision making which has been the predominant focus of this chapter.

8.12 ACCOUNTABILITY

All organizational decision makers occupy a position of stewardship. This means that they make decisions on behalf of others to whom they are liable to explain their actions. It is this requirement of having to explain one's actions to others which is the essence of accountability. Thus trade union representatives are accountable to their membership, and boards of directors are accountable to the company's shareholders. Similarly, a job holder at one level is accountable to the next higher level in an organizational hierarchy. Accountability cannot be delegated.

8.13 ORGANIZATIONAL CHANGE

We are living in an age of rapid change. Technological and economic developments have occurred at such a pace that almost nothing seems to stand still and nothing is sacrosanct. New technologies and materials have meant new methods and products. Some traditional job roles have become redundant, others have changed their character, and long-held values and beliefs have been challenged. The industrial revolution was brought about through technological advancement. Man created machinery to accomplish work abilities which were hitherto impossible. The machinery required vast social re-organization for its potential to be realized. This social re-organization involved geographical relocation of people into concentrated centres of population. These centres of population grew round the location of the various industries and manufacturing processes. The manufacturing processes required three fundamental ingredients: new technological machinery and equipment, resources, and people. The combination of these three resulted in the economic and technological growth and development we have witnessed since the industrial revolution.

This very brief outline is given for two reasons: first, to indicate and remind the reader of how technological development has both affected the lives of people and the economy of nations, and secondly, to point out the triad of essential factors – people, technology and resources – which has been necessary for the achievement of the wealth and social developments that have resulted. Since the onset of the industrial revolution we have seen the development of large organizations, the creation of new ways of working and living, new philosophies and beliefs, new expectations and, of course, new problems. The outcome has been a highly complex industrial society with complex systems and sub-systems. Widespread norms and expectations have developed relating to such issues as the right to work, levels of payment, social and health protection, and so on. We have developed attitudes which in many ways have been socially structured to meet the needs of the technological society that has developed. Work as we know it today is a modern phenomenon, and yet we regard the right to work as something almost sacred. We have come to regard unemployment as quite unacceptable – a social stigma. We have, in fact, forgotten that work today is a modern artefact, designed and developed to meet a specific need.

We are now witnessing a new revolution brought about by development in micro-electronic technology, and the silicon chip in particular. Micro-electronic technology was developed some time ago but its impact was not immediately significant to the lives of most people. The technology made marvellous advances but it was, until recently, very expensive and unlikely to be used by many organizations. That was until the silicon chip was developed. This single development transformed the whole employment scene. Advanced control devices can now be developed for a fraction of the cost of a few years ago. Micro-electronic technology is now everywhere – in the factory, the office, the home, even the toy shop. It is important that we understand what this development is really doing to the structure of society, and work organizations in particular.

First, the triad of factors (people, technology and resources) has, in many cases, now been reduced to a dyad. The factor that has been removed is people, who were needed in the triad as an adjunct to technology as skilled machine operatives and process controllers, typists and technicians, clerks and basic labourers. Silicon chip technology has allowed equipment to be developed to control machinery. The age of the robot has been born. Motor-cars can now be manufactured by fully automated processes (and is being done in parts of Fiat and British Leyland), office procedures have been revolutionized – information storage no longer needs bulky filing systems, and so on – in fact, very few occupations have been or will be unaffected by the development of this new technology.

We are just beginning to see some of the social repercussions of this new technology. Its contribution to widespread unemployment, particularly among the young, is perhaps the clearest and most worrying development. These repercussions have significant implications for business decision-making. How fast to incorporate the new technology into organizational processes is perhaps the most important question. The answer will depend on such factors as the availability of finance, the decisions of competitors on a world-wide basis (no country can afford to lag behind significantly because of outside competition), redundancy and retraining implications, and the state of development of the particular technology. The decisions necessary must be taken by all parties – government, employers and trade unions. We must question many established customs and practices. We must challenge employment practices, such as the length of a working career, the length of a working week, the school leaving age, and so on. We must get to grips with the social implications of increased leisure time. Should we still retire people at 65 and have young people unemployed in large numbers? Should we continue to work 30–40 hours per week whilst millions are unemployed?

The new technology will not mean that eventually no work will be available. In some cases it is creating new jobs, particularly in the micro-technological industry itself. What it is doing is reducing and changing the nature of the work available. Since the overall population is not reducing we are left with less work per head available for people. If we wish to avoid the anomaly of some people working and large numbers not we must find a new way of sharing work. Significant decisions are needed in education. Long established curriculum beliefs urgently need challenging if we are to avoid educating young people for already redundant job roles. Similarly, our organizations will need to face manpower retraining problems on a new scale. Some people will readily accept the new job roles, others will resist and resent them. Some will not have the capabilities to perform the new tasks.

No job role is protected from these changes. The job roles of management need to change just as much as the office clerks', the machine operators' or the storekeepers'. We must recognize the potential for organizational development in new areas such as the leisure industry, health, catering, social services, environmental services, and so on.

It is not unnatural that there is a significant degree of resistance expressed by large numbers of people. Many important and far reaching developments are taking place which are beyond their comprehension and influence. People are losing their jobs or are being relocated. Others are being asked to engage in substantial retraining activities which initially fill them with apprehension. In some cases people are finding that skills which have taken almost a lifetime to acquire are becoming valueless. There is apparent confusion from management:'They don't appear to know what they are doing.' Politicians put everything down to the depressed state of the economy instead of facing up to the magnitude of the real situation. The problem is a world-wide one to be faced by healthy economies as well as depressed ones.

The fundamental problem is that we are living through the very early days of a revolution potentially greater than anything we have witnessed in the past. We are still trying to determine the probable implications of the revolution; in other words we really don't know the nature of the problems we are trying to solve. What is certain is that we need to encourage the participation of all parties, before significant and irrevocable decisions are made. Even if decisions cannot be changed in principle there should be participation regarding their implementation.

8.14 SUMMARY

We make decisions every day of our lives. Most are so simple and routine we hardly stop to think about them. It is only when decision issues are more complicated or important that we become concerned. For example, the decision to buy a house or a car is a major issue for most of us, and we usually go to great lengths in trying to achieve the best results. But it is from the simple decision making situation that we can learn how to approach the more complex.

We have viewed decision making as the process of making a choice between alternative courses of action in relation to the achievement of specific results. We have found that the process can be broken down into seven logical stages: (i) recognizing and defining decision issues and the specification of objectives; (ii) information collection, the gathering of accurate and relevant data; (iii) assessment of the issues associated with the objectives set; (iv) the generation of optional ideas and solutions to problems; (v) the selection of the most appropriate solutions; (vi) implementation of the decisions made; and (vii) evaluation of the results attained. Each of these stages is analysed in detail, and practical suggestions are made in relation to helping the reader to improve his decision-making skills.

It is important to realize that no system or technique can make decisions for us. The system or approach suggested in this chapter is nothing more than an aid which helps us identify why we are in decision-making situations, what goals we hope to achieve, what information we need, and what alternative courses of action are available. In the end we still have to make the choice ourselves. The belief is that we shall make a better, more informed choice if a logical systematic approach is adopted.

The management function in relation to the implementation of organizational decisions was examined. The function of management was identified as consisting of five elements: creativity, planning, organizing, motivating and controlling. Each of these was examined in order to understand the role of management as essentially a decision-making function.

It is important that management can differentiate between simple and complex decisions so that delegation of authority and responsibility can be implemented effectively. The characteristics of complex decisions were identified as situations of conflicting aims, with many possible choice alternatives, where the information needs and sources are difficult to identify, and the information supply inadequate and difficult to assess. The information range was identified as being wide, requiring considerable knowledge and information-handling ability. Complex decisions involve risks and sometimes uncertainty in relation to their outcome. The differentiation between simple and complex situations was further developed into programmable and non-programmable decisions.

We then reminded ourselves that the decision-making functions in formal work organizations are not an activity pursued only at management level. The involvement of employees in decision making was examined with particular emphasis being placed on the processes of joint consultation and collective bargaining. In all situations the importance of accountability for the decisions taken was stressed.

Finally the chapter concluded by examining the issue of change. Decisions made to introduce silicon chip technology are replacing the human element in work processes at an alarming rate. This is creating complex social and organizational decision situations which have no obvious solution.

8.15   BANNISTER POTTERY LTD: A CASE STUDY

This is a case study in management decision making as demonstrated through manpower management. The objectives are:

1. To demonstrate the effect of opinions held by decision makers on decisions taken, and the ramifications of a failure to challenge beliefs.

2. To relate the role of organized pressure groups to organizational decision making, and to demonstrate the importance of bargaining power in the nature of the decisions taken.
3. To illustrate one of the causes of wages drift.
4. To illustrate the need to differentiate between data and information.

The case has been deliberately constructed to provide a considerable quantity of data, and give a shortage of some necessary information.

Student Tasks

1. Discuss the case and the extent to which it characterizes any management/union relationships which you recognize. Define the problems as you see them. Identify and define the decision goals you would pursue if you were the management of the company.
2. Discuss the view that management has actively encouraged militancy and collective blackmail by the way it has reacted to trade union demands.
3. Identify ways in which management might now react to the developments amongst its staff-graded employees. What decision alternatives are available?
4. List the information needs of management in relation to decision making in this situation. Where would management get its information? How can its accuracy be ensured?
5. Examine ways in which management could regain the initiative in decision making in respect of both blue-collar and white-collar workers.
6. Examine ways in which the piecework payment system could be more controlled.
7. Examine the issues from the worker/trade union angle. If you were the representative of, say, the casters, what stance do you think you should take and why?

You may make any reasonable assumptions you wish regarding additional information.

The Company

This company is imaginary, but is based on the activities of a real organization in North Staffordshire. The names and details have been changed, but the problems presented are based on actual problems which the company faced, and is still facing to some extent.

The company is housed on three main sites. Two sites (factories *A* and *B*) are close together, in a fairly central city location. One of the two sites concentrates on the manufacture of large industrial products, the other on domestic products. The headquarters complex is also housed here. The third factory (factory *C*) is located in a rural location some 10 miles away. Each factory has a similar structure (see Fig. 8.5).

The headquarters houses the chairman, managing director and all functional directors. In addition the whole of the administrative organization is housed here. (See Fig. 8.6.)

The organization of marketing, production control, warehousing and distribution, and accounts is shown in Figs 8.7, 8.8 and 8.9.

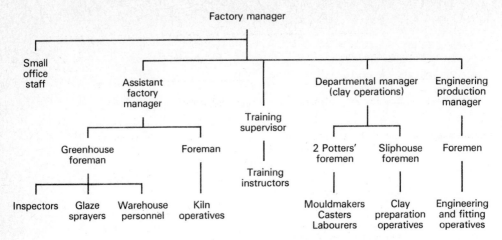

Figure 8.5 *Factory organization*

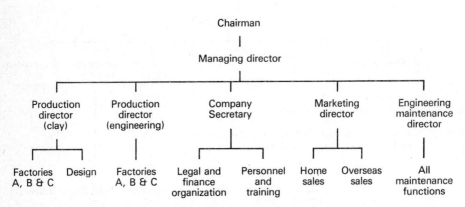

Figure 8.6 *Board and administration organization of Bannister Potteries Ltd*

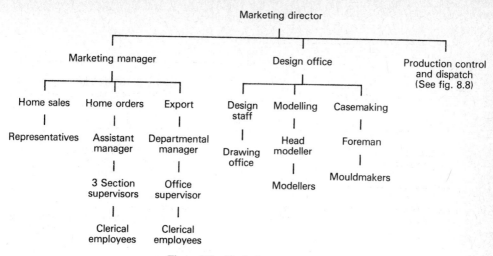

Figure 8.7 *Marketing organization*

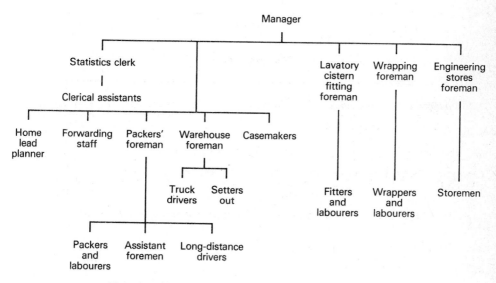

Figure 8.8 *Production control, warehousing and distribution*

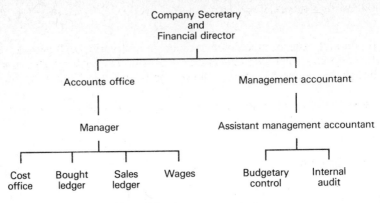

Figure 8.9 *Accounts organization*

The Manufacturing Process (Clay)

The major manufacturing process is concerned with products made from clay and called vitreous china. The clay is brought to the factories by road and rail and is of two basic types, ball clay and china clay. Raw clay, dug from the ground, varies in quality and has many imperfections. The first part of the process, therefore, is concerned with minimizing the differences in quality batches, and the removal of unwanted material. A strictly-controlled mixing process is undertaken. A 'recipe' of different clays are blunged together in large metal containers. When this process has achieved the consistency required, the clay is liquidized by the addition of water. This liquid clay (slip) is fed through pipes to the main manufacturing departments.

The first and perhaps most skilful process is casting. Here skilled craftsmen fill specially prepared moulds with the slip. The filling process has to be performed most carefully to prevent air bubbles forming which could be disastrous to later processes. The moulds are made of porous plaster of Paris. The water is soaked from the clay by the moulds and, after sufficient time, the clay becomes solid, but not hard. The casters know just the right time to remove the product from the mould, which is a very skilled and tricky activity; the body of the product can very easily be damaged. Attempts have been made to automate the process, but so far these have failed.

When the article is out of the mould it is placed on wooden trestles to dry. When completely dry the clay can be further prepared by sanding away any imperfections. Each article is then inspected most carefully. The casters are paid for each good article they make. This means that only those which are passed by the inspectors are counted for pay purposes. The area of storage and inspection is called the greenhouse.

Once the articles are dried out and have been passed by the inspectors they are sprayed with either white or colour glaze and passed through a kiln which heats them to a very high temperature. This melts the glaze and bakes the clay. The product is again inspected before being fitted with the finishing parts and then passed for storage and sale. Each of the foremen in the clay production operation has some 60–70 piecework-paid operatives reporting to him. In the engineering section, which manufactures fitments such as taps, cistern fittings and small fittings, each foreman has around 15 hourly-paid operatives reporting to him.

The Manufacturing Process (Engineering)

This involves metal casting, machining and chromium plating. All parts are manufactured by the company, including nuts and bolts. Most component parts are made from brass, although for economic reasons there has been a tendency to introduce steel recently.

All products, both pottery and metal, are designed by specialized company staff.

The Manpower Structure

Salaried Employees

In the early 1970s the company employed the services of a well-known management consultancy to evaluate and improve the organization and its systems. The company was evaluated on the basis of the Management by Objectives technique.

Using MbO, the consultants established the extent to which the company defined its objectives and the extent to which the organization was structured to achieve them. This analysis started with the boardroom and worked down through the whole organization structure. As a result of this evaluation significant recommendations for change were instituted. The company was advised to introduce corporate planning. The organization structure was modified to have clearer functional definition and defined communications networks. Areas of responsibility, usually expressed in achievement terms, were more clearly defined. Each manager was issued with a management guide (a form of sophisticated job description) which specified key result areas in financial and performance terms, that is, production targets.

Other changes were introduced including a job evaluation scheme for all salaried employees. This scheme resulted in a new grading system with clearly defined pay scales appropriate to each grade. The grading system provided a more structured career pattern and a generalized basis for pay review. (Previously all the staff employees were paid on individually negotiated salaries.) Conditions of service were linked to the grades.

In general, the staff employment characteristics are stable. (See Tables 8.1, 8.2 and 8.3.) There are very high levels of employment stability exhibited by extremely low levels of labour turnover. Most supervisors are appointed from the shop floor but this is becoming increasingly problematical for two reasons: first, the loss of income which follows promotion, and second, the increasing use of technology in certain aspects of the production process. Ultimately, it is the company's intention to try to increase the use of automated techniques. Considerable research is being undertaken to try to mechanize the casting process. If this research is successful several other problems will be generated. The first is the retraining needs of most of the supervisory and middle management staff to cope with the technological component. (Many of the supervisory staff may not have the capacity to accommodate such training.) The second is probable union reaction. The powerful bargaining position of the casters is due primarily to the high skill of the task; any attempt at deskilling will be strongly resisted.

The only significant manpower problem, as measured by such issues as labour turnover, absence and lateness figures, is exhibited by the clerical staff. There is considerable resentment regarding pay levels. There is also the growing feeling of dissatisfaction with the company and its treatment of salaried staff. They feel that their lack of unionization has been exploited and their loyalty betrayed.

Table 8.1 *Summary of staff employed (salaried employees)*

	22 April 1981			1 February 1982		
	Male	Female	Total	Male	Female	Total
Managers list	31	—	31	32	—	32
Representatives	17	—	17	17	—	17
Accounts	14	16	30	14	15	29
Home orders	19	20	39	20	16	36
Export department	9	6	15	7	6	13
Estimating	2	3	5	3	3	6
Publicity and customer service	1	4	5	1	4	5
Buying	3	2	5	3	3	6
Design office	6	2	8	6	2	8
Production control	2	2	4	2	2	4
Packaging and forwarding { Factory A	2	—	2	4	—	4
Factory C	9	3	12	8	3	11
London office	1	1	2	1	1	2
Maintenance	8	—	8	7	—	7
Modellers	4	—	4	3	—	3
Factory supervision	25	3	28	24	3	27
Commissionaires	4	—	4	4	—	4
Employment officer	1	—	1	1	—	1
Postal	1	1	2	1	1	2
Secretaries	—	4	4	—	4	4
Engineering production	7	1	8	8	1	9
Laboratory and pilot plant	2	5	7	2	5	7
Fireclay	11	—	11	10	—	10
Safety officer	1	—	1	1	—	1
Internal audit department	—	—	—	—	2	2
Management trainees	2	—	2	4	—	4
	182	73	255	183	71	254

Table 8.2 *Distribution of employees by age groups*

15–17 years		18–20 years		21–30 years		31–40 years		41–50 years		50 years +	
Male	Female	Male	Female	Male	Female	Male	Female	Male	Female	Male	Female
15	13	42	25	185	22	239	25	250	25	381	35

Table 8.3 *Length of service of employees*

	Under 1 year		1–5 years		6–15 years		16 years+		Total	
	Male	Female	Male	Female	Male	Female	Male	Female	Male	Female
Staff	19	21	58	33	42	17	62	2	181	73
Factory A	26	—	101	18	122	6	60	2	309	26
Factory B	11	1	62	1	69	1	143	9	285	12
Factory C	23	1	41	2	65	8	97	6	226	17
Other departments at headquarters	8	3	26	2	17	5	60	4	111	14
Total	87	26	288	56	315	37	422	23	1112	142

Hourly/Piecework Employees

The total number of people employed in this capacity is 1000, representing approximately 79 per cent of the total of all employees. Of these, 720 are directly employed in occupations relating to the clay production operations. Thirty-two per cent of all operatives are now aged 51 years or over. Less than 4 per cent are under 21 years. Thirty-eight per cent of employees have more than 15 years' service with the company, and 6 per cent less than one year's service. Labour turnover among the highly skilled employees is as low as 4 per cent, and even in the low-skilled and labouring areas it is only 10 per cent. An analysis of the labour force is shown in Table 8.4.

Table 8.4 *Analysis of labour by departments, hourly/piecework employees*

	Factory A		Factory B		Factory C		Headquarters		Totals	
	Male	Female	Male	Female	Male	Female	Male	Female	Male	Female
Slip preparation	9	—	6	—	2	—	3	—	20	—
Casters	64	—	80	—	60	—	1	—	205	—
Mouldmakers	9	—	10	—	8	—	4	—	31	—
Mill	—	—	—	—	7	—	—	—	7	—
Lead house and glaze preparation	—	—	—	—	2	—	—	—	2	—
Glost warehouse	44	6	30	9	30	9	—	—	104	24
Glost warehouse/ laboratory	—	—	3	—	2	—	—	—	5	—
Packers	12	—	5	—	6	—	—	—	23	—
Packers labourers	4	—	2	—	5	—	—	—	11	—
Casemakers	6	—	2	—	2	—	—	—	10	—
Accessories and stores assistants	6	—	4	—	4	2	—	—	14	2
Engineering	18	—	17	—	18	7	13	—	66	7
Boilermen	—	—	—	—	4	—	—	—	4	—
Maintenance	11	—	15	—	15	—	15	—	56	—
Weighbridge	2	—	1	—	1	—	1	—	5	—
General labourers	28	1	22	—	11	—	3	—	64	1
Fireclay makers	—	—	—	—	—	—	12	—	12	—
Ware carriers	—	—	6	—	1	—	5	—	12	—
Fireclay repairers	—	—	—	—	—	—	1	—	1	—
Glaze repairers	2	—	—	—	—	—	2	—	4	—
Glaze brushers	—	—	—	—	—	—	—	12	—	12
Glaze sprayers	16	—	14	—	6	—	6	—	42	—
Stampers/badgers	—	2	—	3	—	—	—	2	—	7
Kiln setters	—	—	—	—	—	—	5	—	5	—
Kiln attendants	13	—	9	—	7	—	3	—	32	—
Off-loaders	3	—	2	—	2	—	—	—	7	—
Warehouse	—	—	—	—	—	—	5	—	5	—
Polishers and grinders	3	—	4	—	2	—	2	—	11	—
Mould carriers	2	—	5	—	2	—	3	—	12	—
Glaze preparation	5	—	2	—	2	—	2	—	11	—
Ware inspectors	12	—	11	—	7	—	2	—	32	—
Masons	—	—	—	—	—	—	19	—	19	—
Placers	10	—	8	—	6	—	—	—	24	—
Canteen	—	1	—	—	1	—	—	—	1	1
Cistern fitters	17	17	10	—	6	—	—	—	33	17
Transport drivers	11	—	11	—	5	—	—	—	27	—
Night patrolmen	2	—	2	—	2	—	1	—	7	—
Lodgeman	—	—	1	—	—	—	1	—	2	—
Cutter/grinders	—	—	—	—	—	—	2	—	2	—
Garage mechanics	—	—	3	—	—	—	—	—	3	—
Totals	309	27	285	12	226	18	111	14	931	71

The Problems

In order to gain a full appreciation of the present problems, it is necessary first to have a retrospect of the primary issues which appear to influence the current situation. The first is the major characteristic of the production process. It requires high levels of craft skill. The work is heavy and dominated by male employees. The skills necessary are of a localized nature and possessed only by a small number of people. Automation has as yet had limited impact. The employees concerned are highly unionized. The second issue concerns management's apparent traditional attitude regarding its labour force.

Management/union relationships over the past 50 years have been influenced and changed by many factors. The most notable change has been in the relationships between management and the shop floor. The predominant factor in bringing about this change has been the unionization of the skilled and non-skilled workers. It is easy to see with hindsight that the management of this company has been the major cause of the shopfloor worker strengthening his own position by joining with his fellow workers into organized bodies in order to provide negotiating strength and protection. There was until recently a general failure to recognize the potential bargaining position of the skilled labour force. The heavy reliance on piecework payment systems has produced a wages drift which has now become almost uncontrollable by management. The bargaining power of the skilled labour force has continually forced up the price paid for each article made. In addition, management has little control over the output from each operative. Therefore, each man controls the size of his own pay packet to a large extent. In a sense the present position has come about due to the stance historically taken by management which was fairly conventional and held the following views about its shopfloor workers: the average worker has an inherent dislike of work and will avoid it if he can; because of this he must be coerced, controlled and threatened with punishment to get him to give adequate effort to the job in hand; and the average worker has little ambition and values security above all. He, therefore, prefers to avoid responsibility and to be directed if possible.

In the early days of the company, management would justify its opinion and attitudes by referring to the way its workers appeared to behave. There appeared to be considerable evidence to support them, including demands for high pay, aggression and unionization. With hindsight the company is beginning to question its old opinions. Could it be that in the past the threat of unemployment and the lack of personal family protection conditioned the workers to behave as management wanted them to behave?

As time progressed, increasing numbers of the shopfloor blue-collar workers joined unions until a position of power was reached where employers were forced to meet agreements made on a national basis between the union executive and the Employers' Federation. This provided an opportunity for the key workers to hit back at their employers through local negotiation in excess of the minimum nationally-agreed rates.

As has been stated, this particular company manufactures products which still require a considerable degree of manual craft skill. These skilled workers, who form approximately 35 per cent of the 1000 wage earning employees (250 salaried employees), have traditionally been paid on a piecework basis, and were among the first to unionize. Their particular skills have never been plentiful and they have, therefore, had a strong bargaining position with management for a long time. The basis of their wage bargaining was a negotiating body known as a Pricing Committee, made up of representatives of the skilled workers and representatives of management. The sole purpose of this negotiating body is the determination of piecework rates for each product in the product range.

During this same period, it is interesting to examine management relationships with its staff employees. They were regarded by the management as being totally different people. In fact the attitude held by management could be summarized as follows: the staff were people who found a degree of personal satisfaction from their work, which in general they performed voluntarily with the minimum of control; and they were people with ambition, loyalty and imagination who, in general, sought responsibility.

The staff employees were given more secure employment and much superior conditions of employment. In return, management demanded and expected a high level of loyalty. These white-collar employees felt that they were given a fair deal by their employers, and felt no need to organize their labour for collective bargaining purposes; in fact, they felt that they achieved a fairer deal on an individual basis.

Blue-collar Workers

Unionization of the blue-collar worker is now 100 per cent, although no formal closed-shop agreement is in force. Wage levels have overtaken the differential between blue-collar and white-collar employees. In fact, the key craft skilled have now attained weekly pay levels of £200–220 per week. In some individual instances much higher weekly wages are attained, since the level of earnings depends on the outputs attained by each worker. Since the company employs a flexi-time system with no upper limit, the output is dependent on the input of each individual.

Any attempt at replacing this piecework system has been successfully prevented by the negotiating strength of the key workers.

The other shopfloor workers have benefited from the bargaining strength of these key workers; their average wage is £120–130 per week gross.

White-collar Workers

Pay and conditions of employment differentials have gradually been totally eroded. Consensus of opinion is that management has sold their loyalty and goodwill 'down the river'. The average rate of pay for a senior clerk is £4000–4500 per annum, and an office supervisor earns, on average, £5500 per annum. Shop floor supervisors are also depressed and upset. For example, the pay of the foremen supervising the key workers ranges from £6000–8000 per annum, and the departmental managers earn £8000–9000 per annum.

There is now a strong move towards unionization shown in rapidly growing membership of ASTMS (the Association of Scientific, Technical and Managerial Staff). The general opinion among the staff is that the only way of getting a fair deal from management is by using collective blackmail, and constantly using the shop floor situation as factual proof that this is the case. They feel that their loyalty has been betrayed by management and that the blue-collar workers have shown them the way forward through their strong unionization.

Labour turnover among all categories of staff employees has gradually increased, and replacements have generally been of a poorer quality than those who left.

Further Reading

1. Bennis, W. G., Benne, K., Chin, R. & Corey, K. (1976) *The Planning of Change*. New York: Holt, Rinehart & Winston.
2. Branton, N. (1971) *Introduction to the Theory and Practice of Management*. London: Chatto & Windus.
3. Castles, Murray & Potter (1960) *Decisions, Organisations and Society*. Milton Keynes: Open University Press.
4. Drucker, P. F. (1969) *The Practice of Management*. London: Pan.
5. Fox, A. (1974) *Man Mismanagement*. London: Hutchinson.
6. Grusky, O. & Miller, G. A. (eds) (1981) *The Sociology of Organisation*. New York: The Free Press.
7. Humble, J. (1968) *Improving Business Results*. Maidenhead: McGraw-Hill.
8. Light, H. R. (1976) *The Nature of Management*. London: Pitman.
9. Lindblom, C. E. (1968) *The Policy Making Process*. Hemel Hempstead: Prentice-Hall.
10. Morrisey, G. L. (1970) *Management by Objectives and Results*. London: Addison-Wesley.
11. Simon, H. A. (1960) *The New Science of Management Decision*. London: Harper & Row.
12. Jedamus, P. (1976) *Statistical Analysis for Business Decisions*. Maidenhead: McGraw-Hill.
13. Thomson, R. (1959) *The Psychology of Thinking*. Harmondsworth: Penguin.

Index